ISRAEL: HIS PEOPLE, HIS LAND, HIS STORY

Israel

His People, His Land, His Story

Ten Authors Reflect on Biblical and Historical Themes
with Contributions on Terrorism
and Peacemaking

Edited by
FRED WRIGHT

LOVE NEVER FAILS

THANKFUL BOOKS

Compilation copyright © Love Never Fails 2005

First published 2005

The respective authors of each chapter have asserted the right to be
identified as the author of their work in accordance with the
Copyright, Designs and Patents Act 1998. Responsibility for the
views expressed belongs to the respective individual authors and
not to Love Never Fails collectively.

Published by Thankful Books
70 Milton Road, Eastbourne, East Sussex BN21 1SS, England.

ISBN 13: 978 1 905084 03 6
ISBN 10:   1 905084 03 X

Unless otherwise indicated, biblical quotations are
from the New International Version © 1973, 1978, 1984
by the International Bible Society.

Book design and production for the publisher by
Bookprint Creative Services, P.O. Box 827, BN21 3YJ, England.
Printed in Great Britain.

CONTENTS

FOREWORD

Lady Sainsbury

Few books have the power to affect a reader's view of his or her world. This collection of essays by ten authors – Christians and Jews – although not claiming to be a definitive book, reflects on the past and future prospects for the Middle East and belongs to this category.

It is a must-read for all involved with the Middle East, whether as friends, commentators or intercessors. The writers ask how we interpret Israel in biblical terms and then put the modern state into its legal and historical context. With contributions from historians inside and outside the Land, they look at different Christian interventions as part of that history and the indigenous growth of messianic fellowships since 1967. If these are Jews as well as followers of Jesus, then their biblical significance has to be considered by the Christian Church, however small their proportion of the population. They also consider the plight of the Palestinian refugees, with their call on Christian compassion, giving the book a balanced viewpoint frequently lacking in writing on this subject.

This is not just another eschatological book; it has a prophetic element alongside the consideration of the threat of terrorism in the region and approaches to conflict resolution.

As a regular visitor to the Middle East, I warmly recommend this book to all with an interest in this region; written primarily for the church, it opens up new areas and questions for understanding and prayer. It serves as both an introduction for the newcomer and a corrective for the more experienced traveller, challenging assumptions and offering a fresh perspective on Israel.

Susan Sainsbury

EDITOR'S PREFACE

It has been both gratifying and challenging preparing the following collection of essays sponsored by Love Never Fails, a forum of Christian ministries of diverse backgrounds and callings involved with the Jewish people, both in Israel and the diaspora.

The book arose from a need to give clear biblical and historical understanding of the Jewish people and the Land of Israel, their election and calling, their place in the world today and in the end times.

The contributors, Jewish and Christian, are from a variety of backgrounds and disciplines, and include some well-known authors and scholars, as well as emerging writers. The topics included cover a wide spectrum in both subject and opinion. The opinions expressed, therefore, do not necessarily represent the views of every ministry included, but could be considered to be empathetic in general. The book of essays was not collected together with the intention of presenting a work following a linear theme or a single issue; rather it draws together essays on subjects that are either the author's speciality, or the topic that is burning in their heart. Each section has its own introduction and theme in a coherent sequence. Rather than use a 'house style' throughout the work, whereas a modicum of standardisation has been used, quotations and transliterations have been left in their original forms in order to keep the full flavour of the articles and express the authors' individuality and empathy.

Essays were contributed by:

Gerald Adler
Ken Burnett

Murray Dixon
Nick Gray
Gershon Nerel
David Noakes
Tim Price
Geoffrey Smith
Derek White
Fred Wright

We would like to express our appreciation to the contributors for their willingness to offer to be a part of this work, and their co-operation and flexibility, which made drawing the materials together such a pleasure.

The book is not designed or intended to provide a last word on any of the subjects under consideration, be they theological or historical. The intention, rather, is to establish an authentic biblical and historical basis that hopefully will stimulate the reader to explore further and create dialogue.

Special thanks to CFI and Fiona Lindsay for their liaison between authors and the editor.

Fred Wright
Editor, Moscow, April 2005

INTRODUCTION TO THE AUTHORS

Gerald Adler formerly Barrister-at-law, in Ontario, Canada; Advocate at the Israeli Bar, and Solicitor in England and Wales. Professor Adler lived in Israel for 30 years, where he was Adjunct Professor of Law at the Technion, Israel Institute of Technology Haifa. Dr Adler is an orthodox Jew and not a messianic supporter. His essay is the revised version of a guest lecture given to a meeting of Christian Friends of Israel.

Ken Burnett is a Messianic Jew and was founder of Prayer for Israel, one of the first ministries of its kind, which he directed for many years. He is an adviser to Shofar Foundation International and is still very involved in supporting and encouraging the messianic communities in Israel, many from their earliest days.

Murray Dixon is Associate Rector at Christ Church in Jerusalem. Originally from New Zealand, he led PFI in that country for several years and was one of the first people there to write on Israel. He wrote a book for schools and Bible study material on that subject before joining the staff of CMJ in Israel.

Nick Gray is a minister of some 20 years' standing in the Elim Pentecostal Church following commissioned service in the British Army. In addition to his pastorate he serves on the board of Focus on Israel.

Gershon Nerel has his PhD from the Hebrew University on modern Jewish believers in Yeshua. He has been on the Executive Board of the Messianic

Jewish Alliance of Israel since 1993. With his wife Sara, Dr Nerel revised the Franz Delitzsch Hebrew translation of the New Testament. They live at Yad Hashmona, a messianic village near Jerusalem.

David Noakes has had a long standing relationship with Prophetic Word Ministries in a number of roles, and is Chairman of the Board of Hatikvah Film Trust. He is respected as a Bible teacher and acknowledged for his deep understanding of the ministry of the prophets.

Tim Price is currently UK National Co-ordinator for CMJ (the Church's Ministry Amongst the Jewish People) and has initiated a programme of advocacy for Israel and the Jewish people.

Geoffrey Smith is Deputy Director of Christian Friends of Israel (UK) and Chairman of Love Never Fails (see Appendix). He was a member of the leadership team of St Mark's, Kennington, London, and reader in the dioceses of Papua New Guinea, Southwark, Exeter and Jerusalem before joining a community church in Eastbourne.

Derek White is Founder and former Chairman of Christian Friends of Israel, serving as Director for many years. He has written and taught widely on Israel and the Jewish roots of the Christian faith. He is a member of Battle Baptist Church.

Fred Wright (editor) and his wife Maria have worked extensively with the Jewish people throughout the former Soviet Union for 20 years. He is author of several books, including *Words from the Scroll of Fire, The Cross Became a Sword, Father Forgive Us* and *Within the Pale*, along with numerous academic articles on Jewish-related themes.

SECTION I

The first group of essays commences with the essential consideration of the restoration of Israel and the kingdom of God. As
Professor Lindsay of the Jerusalem School of Synoptic Studies
pointed out some years ago, the Kingdom of God is the central
motif that runs through the teaching of Yeshua (or Jesus, as He is
known in our English Bibles). It has been said that Yeshua preached
the kingdom of God, but the church preached Christ. Tim Price
carefully examines the restoration of Israel within the context of
the kingdom of God, which is essential if one is to understand the
restoration in an authentic biblical context.

David Noakes follows with an appreciation of the eschatological
contour within the prophetic writings and in particular the subject
of 'the Day of the Lord'.

A consequence of not understanding the tensions considered in
the above essays appears in the third contribution, where Derek
White offers an overview of the tragic history of Jewish-Christian
relations and institutionalised Christian antisemitism that contributed in paving the way to the Shoah (Holocaust).

Christian antisemitism is a little understood subject and even the
term is subject to differing views. The term arose in the nineteenth
century from the pseudo-scientific movement, which attempted
racial definition by linguistics. The work is generally considered to
have commenced with the studies of Gottfried Wilhelm von
Leibnitz who, in 1704, had identified a group of cognate languages
that included Hebrew, Syriac, Ethiopic, Carthaginian and Old
Punic. These languages he suggested formed a family group to
which he gave the nomenclature 'Arabic'. These gradually became
referred to as 'semitic roots', which were considered to be grossly

inferior to the Indo-European, or Aryan, group. The problem here, of course, is that in the modern era the majority of the animus directed against the Jewish people comes from the Arab nations, who by this definition are Semites themselves. Writers such as the editor and experts writing on these subjects prefer to use the German term *Judenhaas*, in its plain meaning; namely, hatred of the Jewish people. As 'antisemitism' is the generally accepted word, the term is used throughout and written in the conventional manner of scholars in this discipline; that is, without the hyphen and upper case letter.

Antisemitism has deep spiritual roots and therefore demands a spiritual consideration. A generally accepted definition was proposed by the editor in *Father Forgive Us*, as follows.

The continued existence of the Jewish people despite thousands of years of their attempted extermination is the only concrete proof of the existence of God. When people encounter Jewish people and *ipso facto* the Jewish state they are faced with a series of challenges they dislike intensely. The challenges are at basic level: Is there a God, if there is does it follow there is an afterlife, if so is there a judgement, is there eternal life and/or eternal punishment and do I need to respond? Fallen man in his rebellion feels impotent to effect change; as he cannot destroy God, he tries to remove the evidence – the Jewish people.

THE RESTORATION OF ISRAEL AND THE KINGDOM OF GOD

Tim Price

'Israel' and 'Zion(ism)' are two words that raise passions in our world today, yet why should these words which fill the pages of Scripture have come to be regarded as pejorative by so many within the church? The prophet Isaiah said:

> The Lord will have compassion on Jacob; once again he will choose Israel and will settle them in their own land. Aliens will join them and unite with the house of Jacob. Nations will take them and bring them to their own place. And the house of Israel will possess the nations as menservants and maidservants in the Lord's land. (Is 14:1–2)

> For Zion's sake I will not keep silent, for Jerusalem's sake I will not remain quiet, till her righteousness shines out like the dawn, her salvation like a blazing torch. (Is 62:1)

In these two readings lies the redemption of these names that have become the source of such bitterness. They hold out both the hope of reconciliation between Arab and Jew, Israeli and Palestinian, and also the glorious destiny of Jerusalem within the eschatological purposes of world redemption, when, instead of being a source of division, she becomes the centre of the kingdom of God. Isaiah writing of this time said:

> In that day there will be a highway from Egypt to Assyria . . . The Egyptians and Assyrians will worship together. In that day Israel will be the third, along with Egypt and Assyria, a blessing on the earth. The Lord Almighty will bless

them, saying, 'Blessed be Egypt my people, Assyria my handiwork, and Israel my inheritance.' (Is 19:23–25)

This glorious vision of reconciliation has clearly yet to be fulfilled. The whole of biblical revelation finds its focus in this one nation Israel. Our theological understanding is shaped by the story of Israel and centres on the person of Jesus, the Jewish Messiah, who embodies and represents Israel. Around Him, the people of God, both Jew and Gentile, find their identity, mission and goal. Israel is the name that Jesus uses to describe the Land and the nation of which He is both chief citizen and King. It is the name that remained throughout the whole canon of Scripture.

Yet as I grew up, another name for the Land was in common usage. Bibles and Bible reference books would refer, for example, to Palestine in the time of Jesus and this name, despite being post-biblical, is the generic name by which the Land has largely been known by the Christian world since Roman times. The name Palestine as a description for Israel is not found in Scripture. It only came into usage in 134 CE after the Romans finally crushed the second and last Jewish revolt against its rule. They renamed Israel Syria-Palaestina, after the Philistines, Israel's most implacable enemy, as a deliberate affront to Jews. There began the great Jewish exile from the Land and the battle for the soul of the Land.

Today the names of Israel and Palestine have become powerful symbols around which the church has become polarised, as Israelis and Palestinians each seek to assert national sovereignty and to claim the moral, historical, physical and indeed spiritual right to the Land. The issue of the restoration of Israel has become the focus of appalling disunity within the body of Christ.

5th International Sabeel Conference 2004

At the 5th International Sabeel Conference held in Jerusalem in April 2004, the theme of the conference was 'Zionism, Christian Zionism and the Challenge to the Church'. The Archbishop of Canterbury, Dr Rowan Williams, in his keynote paper 'Holy Land and Holy People' wrote this:

The subject of this conference is one that goes deeper than simply the critique of a deeply eccentric form of Christian theology, and it should take us further than yet another analysis of the cyclical patterns of violence and injustice in the conflicts of the region. It should also be an opportunity for us to clarify something of what as Christians we can say about Israel, as one dimension of a 'liberation theology' that will carry good news to all in the Holy Land and more widely.

The two extreme positions with which we are wearily familiar will fail to carry such good news. At one end of the spectrum, there is the view that argues for unconditional support of any decision made by the Israeli government (whose claims for maximal territory and security are based on grounds whose relation to both Hebrew and Christian Scripture is tenuous to say the least). At the other is the view that there is essentially nothing to be said about the Jewish people and the State of Israel from the standpoint of Christian theology, a view which runs up against the complexities of much Christian Scripture, not least Paul's great and tormented meditation in Romans 9–11.

In other words, Archbishop Rowan concludes: 'I am not at all sure that we best respond to distorted theologies by denying that there could be a good theology of Israel.'

A tale of two theologies

None of us who witnesses the ongoing crisis between Israel and the Palestinians comes to it from a neutral stance. The church's attitude both for or against Israel is shaped by two theologies whose roots go back to the early church. Before the Council of Nicaea (325 CE) the church substantially believed in the restoration of Israel. They believed that God would restore the kingdom to Israel in response to the disciples' question: 'Lord, are you at this time going to restore the kingdom to Israel?' and Jesus' enigmatic reply: 'It is not for you to know the times or dates the Father has set by his own authority' (Acts 1:6–7), a verse which itself has been interpreted down partisan lines to defend or detract from a literal or physical restoration of Israel.

Certainly up to 100 CE, the time at which Jewish believers formed the majority within the church, the prevailing view was that the restoration of Israel would be both literal and physical, and that the Messiah would reign bodily, with the church, as King over a restored Israel. They would play a centre-stage role in evangelising the nations. This view was held subsequently by the Puritans, who themselves believed that the greatest world evangelisation would take place only when Israel was restored and in her own Land. Much of Jewish thought until 100 CE mirrored that of the church, which believed in a literal restoration of the kingdom to Israel, of a human Messiah who would reign as King in Jerusalem and of a literal reign of 1,000 years. It was classic historic pre-millennialism from which dispensationalism would eventually emerge in the nineteenth century under the Millerites and J. N. Darby and which today has been popularised in the writings of Hal Lindsey (*The Late Great Planet Earth*) and Tim La Haye (*Left Behind* series).

However, for much of the last 2,000 years, and certainly since the Council of Nicaea, the historic church has itself been dominated by a theology shaped by the early church fathers. They sought to put 'clear blue water' between the emerging rabbinic Judaism and Christianity, and so asserted the supremacy of church over synagogue. As we shall see later, the marginalisation and the gradual withering of the Jewish wing of the church following the two Jewish revolts against Rome in 70 and 134 CE, led ultimately to the dominance of the Gentile expression of Christianity at the expense of its Jewish origins.

The increasing enmity between church and synagogue fuelled the belief that the church had replaced or superseded Israel within the purposes of God, and indeed was now herself the 'new Israel'. This significantly contributed to the view that the church, as the inheritors of the kingdom of God and thus the new people of God, would extensively grow and expand until all the nations were 'Christianised'. The church would then hand over the kingdom to Christ as His inheritance, and they would then reign with Christ over the nations. This view was substantially post-millennial in outlook, with Christ coming again only at the end of the 'Church Age', or at the end of an indefinitely timed millennium in which the church rules with the unseen Christ, until Christ comes in person to usher in the new heaven and new earth.

This view by the church has significantly shaped the church's attitude to Jewish people, breeding an arrogance towards them in which they are but the ghosts at the Christian banquet, consigned to be damned and cursed for ever, and denying them any future role within the purposes of God or even as an independent nation. Any ongoing theological role for them is restricted to that within a Gentile-dominated church, in which any Jewish expression has been marginalised or excluded. It has been the dominant theology that has led to Christian antisemitism and paradoxically to the very Zionism about which it is often so voluble and vitriolic today.

Today the church is polarised around two theological positions whose origins go back to the early church. On the one hand we have dispensationalism, which has its roots in classic pre-millennialism, and on the other hand covenant or replacement theology, whose roots lie in the traditional teaching that the church has now superseded Israel.

The Christian world largely mirrors that divide, with one end advocating the restoration of Israel to its full biblical borders, and the other coming to the rescue of a beleaguered part of the church, oppressed by a nation that it regards as having no ongoing spiritual significance and indeed scarcely any legal or moral right to exist at all. For one, the Land is covenanted to Israel, the Jewish people, for ever; for the other, the Land only has significance as it relates to all the people of God, rather than to an ethnic group whose historic claim has been forfeited by divine decision and as the outcome of their long departure from that Land. This powerful polarisation can be expressed by two leading proponents at opposite ends of the divide. Naim Ateek, Canon of St George's Cathedral, Jerusalem, and a leading figure within Sabeel, for example, in the 2003 winter edition of *Cornerstone* says in his article 'The Dark Side of Religion': 'Without any shadow of doubt, Christian Zionism is one, if not the most dangerous, biblical distortion that is challenging us today.' By contrast the late Derek Prince, in probably his final message 'A Call to Britain', gives a warning of judgement to the church if it persists in its belief that the church has replaced Israel. He says: 'The truth of the matter is, we determine our destiny on how we respond to what God is doing for Israel.' He goes on to quote from Isaiah 60: 'The nation and the kingdom that will not serve you, re-gathered Israel, will perish. Those nations will be utterly ruined.'

The vision

How have we got into this position and is there any way in which those differences can be reconciled?

Perhaps an appropriate place to begin is to look at the bigger picture of God's great purpose for world redemption, the bringing of the nations under the lordship of Christ through the whole people of God, Jew and Gentile. That is the vision of Psalm 2 when the Lord promises to give to the Anointed One, literally the Messiah (Hebrew) or the Christ (Greek), the nations as His inheritance.

The overarching message of Scripture is not about either Israel or indeed the church; it is about the restoration of our world to God's rule. It concerns the establishment of the kingdom of God in which the kingdoms of this world become the kingdom of God and of His Christ. It is epitomised in that image from Daniel 2 of the huge statue representing the empires of this world being brought to nothing by the stone from heaven, which eventually grows to fill the whole earth – a similar picture to the gradual in-breaking of the kingdom of God, which like a grain of mustard 'though it is the smallest of all your seeds, yet when it grows it is the largest of garden plants' (Mt 13:32).

The establishment of God's kingdom then is played out in the theatre of nations and through the instruments that God has brought into being to fulfil His purposes, namely Israel and the church. The final outcome of that work is seen in pictures given both in Hebrews and in Revelation. The writer of Hebrews, recording the faith of Abraham, says of him that 'he was looking forward to the city with foundations, whose architect and builder is God' (Heb 11:10). John, in Revelation, describes that city as the New Jerusalem on whose gates are inscribed the twelve tribes of Israel, and on whose wall's foundations are inscribed the names of the twelve apostles of the Lamb (Rev 21:12). In this profound picture of the new heaven and earth we see the ultimate goal of God's redemptive purpose in which God comes to dwell with humanity. It marks the reconciliation of earth and heaven, of nature and spirit, of Israel and the church. It marks the goal of redemption when God indeed dwells on earth with man.

Jesus said: 'I tell you the truth, at the renewal of all things, when the Son of Man sits on his glorious throne, you who have followed me will also sit on twelve thrones, judging the twelve tribes of Israel' (Mt 19:28). This passage is significant because it encapsulates the core issue that divides the church today – the restoration of Israel. In two separate commentaries on this passage, the authors reach very different conclusions about the relationship between the twelve tribes, Israel, and the twelve apostles, the church. R. T. France concludes that the twelve apostles supersede the twelve tribes and rule over them as the new Israel, whereas Edward Schweizer sees the apostles as being installed as regents over Israel, which itself will be restored, during the last days, to its full complement of twelve tribes. The climax or goal is reached when, as 1 Corinthians 15:24 states: 'Then the end will come, when he [Christ] hands over the kingdom to God the Father after he has destroyed all dominion, authority and power.' God's purpose in establishing His kingdom under the rule of Christ is to bring the nations of the earth back under His sovereignty and once He has established God's undisputed title, so His 'servant' role is completed as He hands back the kingdom to God the Father.

As I have made clear from Revelation, on the new earth that parity of relationship between Israel and the church is restored, as symbolised by the gates of the tribes of Israel and the walls of the apostles of the church in the new Jerusalem where dwells the presence of God. This wonderful picture of reconciliation, renewal and transformation is depicted by John so well:

> I did not see a temple in the city, because the Lord God Almighty and the Lamb are its temple. The city does not need the sun or the moon to shine on it, for the glory of God gives it light, and the Lamb is its lamp. The nations will walk by its light, and the kings of the earth will bring their splendour into it . . . the glory and honour of the nations will be brought into it. (Rev 21:22–26)

The descent of the new Jerusalem to the renewed earth marks the culmination of God's completed work where God Himself comes to dwell with mankind. It answers that question of Solomon after the dedication of the Temple: 'But will God really dwell on earth?' (1 Kings 8:27).

God's plan of redemption is far bigger and greater than we can imagine, and is global in concept, encompassing all the nations of the world. It concerns the ultimate restoration of our world to its right and lawful rule under God. Although God is sovereign over the whole cosmos, the kingdom of God has to be seen first in the mending then the renewal of creation, and concerns the expulsion of sin and the bringing of the world under God's direct rule and authority.

Both Israel and the church are God's chosen instruments for bringing in the kingdom, and are therefore the agents and executives of His government under Christ.

Israel, the church and the kingdom

The overwhelming emphasis in the teaching of Jesus is on the kingdom of God or the kingdom of heaven, for both mean the same thing. The thrust of Jesus' ministry was always to teach and display what the reign or rule of God means in practice. The signs and demonstrations of power, whether through the stilling of the storm, the feeding of the five thousand, the diverse array of healings, the deliverance from the demonic, the raising from the dead, His ethical and moral teaching, the parables of the kingdom were all to describe the nature of the kingdom and to show the meaning of life under the rule of God. So often when we think about the kingdom of God, we think of it in territorial terms, yet time and again in Scripture the emphasis is first and foremost on the person of the King. The kingdom is present when the King is present. Kingdom events happen when the King comes and the presence of the King is seen and observed. At present the kingdom is displayed through the indwelling presence of the King in the life of the believer, but one day that kingdom will expand to fill the whole earth with the knowledge of God as the waters cover the sea.

Kingdom teaching set against the backdrop of Israel

Jesus' kingdom teaching is always set against the backdrop and context of Israel, because Jesus saw His mission as exclusively to Israel. Israel is the dominant motif throughout the whole of Scripture, both Old and New Testaments, and the kingdom of God relates to the outworking of both the mission and the task of Israel. It is noteworthy that there are only two references to the church throughout the gospel accounts, and in both cases they can be seen as relating to the community of Israel. Yet today the emphasis is on the church rather than on the kingdom of God, and Israel is seen as an embarrassment, a relic of God's earlier purposes and of a nation whose services are no longer required. What a travesty of the truth!

Kristell Sandell, writing in *Christ's Lordship and Religious Pluralism,* says: 'It remains a fact worth pondering that Jesus preached the Kingdom while the Church preached Jesus. And thus we are faced with a danger. We may so preach Jesus that we lose the vision of the Kingdom, the mended and restored creation.'

One plan

The church needs to rediscover its mission of being an agent and an instrument of God's kingdom whose purpose is to bring this world under the rule of its King and to share in that rule. As the body of Christ, we are not only called as co-heirs with Christ, we are also called to co-reign with Him. We need to understand that both the election and choice of Israel and the church are not Plan A and Plan B, but are complementary to one another in the outworking of God's one and only plan. This plan began with its announcement in the Garden of Eden, known as the proto-gospel, where God promises to rescue and restore mankind and indeed the whole creation, and concludes with its culmination in the new heaven and the new earth. The whole of biblical revelation then concerns the outworking and fulfilling of this great plan of redemption. Paul commentating on God's original curse on creation and anticipating its glorious liberation says:

> The creation waits in eager expectation for the sons of God to be revealed. For the creation was subjected to frustration, not by its own choice, but by the will of the one who subjected it, in hope that the creation itself will be liberated from its bondage to decay and brought into the glorious freedom of the children of God. (Rom 8:19–21).

The ultimate goal of world redemption is then the lifting of the original curse over creation and its ultimate liberation within the kingdom of God. The prophet Isaiah indicates what that will mean in terms of the nations of the world when he says of the Servant: 'On this mountain [Zion], he will destroy the shroud that enfolds all peoples, the sheet that covers all nations' (Is 25:7). Just as Paul says there is a shroud or veil preventing Israel from recognising its own Messiah (2 Cor 3:14–15), so there is a veil over all the nations, and this veil is only lifted as God brings to completion His goal of world redemption and liberation of the creation under the sons of God.

Paul gives the reason as to why this veil hangs over all the peoples when he says: 'The god of this age has blinded the minds of unbelievers, so that they cannot see the light of the gospel of the glory of Christ, who is the image of God' (2 Cor 4:4). For nearly 2,000 years there has been a veil covering the Jewish people caused by their unbelief, but Paul says that one day that veil will be lifted and all Israel will be saved (Rom 11:26). Perhaps this is a foretaste of God's final strategy for bringing the nations under His lordship. And just as the veil over Israel is even now being lifted, so this will happen among all the nations.

This brings us to the priority of mission, for just as the priority for individual salvation and incorporation into the kingdom of God is 'first for the Jew, then for the Gentile' (Rom 1:16) so too, of nations, Israel first then the nations. Christ will receive all the nations as His inheritance and the very glory of those nations is taken into the new heaven and new earth! However, for the time being, the focus of God's work lies elsewhere.

The ecclesia (church) – kingdom people

For the present, God is drawing out a community of people, kingdom people, who live and walk by faith, and who are making His kingdom purposes their primary consideration, transcending their Jewishness or Gentileness. They are called to reign with Christ in His kingdom, first under His unseen rule and then later as it becomes visible and manifest. Walter Riggans has commented that when Jesus urges His followers to 'seek first the kingdom of God' this is tantamount to saying, 'seek first the outworking of God's redemptive plan.' When we pray, 'Your kingdom come, on earth as it is in heaven,' we are praying principally for two things: first, for the manifestation of God's kingly presence now among the community of believers gathered in Christ's name, but secondly we are anticipating the glorious day to come, when His kingship is acknowledged by the whole world, as the kings, the rulers of this world, throw their crowns at His feet.

A principal feature of the kingdom of God (or kingdom of heaven) is the manifestation of God's redemptive power at work in the affairs of humanity. At present this is partial – 'now but not yet'. The kingdom is embryonic, but one day we will see it in its full maturity. For the present we see small outbreaks of His kingdom, but one day we will witness it in its totality as John records:

> And they [the elders], sang a new song: 'You are worthy to take the scroll and to open its seals, because you were slain, and with your blood you purchased men for God from every tribe and language and people and nation. You have made them to be a kingdom and priests to serve our God, and they will reign on the earth.' (Rev 5:9–10)

As the Life Application Bible puts it: 'The song of God's people praises Christ's work. He was slain and through that act purchased men by his blood sacrifice and so gathered a kingdom of priests who are appointed to reign on earth.' Jesus has already died and paid the penalty for sin. He is now gathering us into His kingdom from every ethnic group, language, people and nation, and making us priests. In the future we will reign with Him when He fully establishes His kingdom on earth as it is in heaven. Someone has remarked that the church, in its truest expression, is shown as colonies of heaven where the evidence of God's reign can be observed through the kingdom lifestyle of its citizens.

America was once just a series of small and disparate colonies, but today it is a whole nation, indeed a superpower. One day the colonies of heaven on earth will give way to the full expression of God's reign in the affairs of men. The kingdom will be as real and substantial on earth as it is at present in heaven when 'he will rule the world in righteousness and his people with the truth'. We are not short of examples of what this means, for times of revival are evidence of the in-breaking of God's kingdom, where whole communities are transformed by the manifest presence of God. During the Welsh Revival of 1904/5, the last major revival in Britain, public houses were closed, police and magistrates stood down, because there was no need for them. The rule of God was tangible and real!

So then the kingdom of God is literally the reign of God as King in the affairs of men. However, God has chosen two vehicles, two instruments, to bring in His kingdom: Israel and the church. Although often perceived as two separate and unrelated entities, they are intricately connected and dependent on one another. To have the church without Israel is not the church, and to have Israel without the church is not Israel. In a sense they are two sides of one coin. This is a fact largely overlooked by the church during the church era. We need to see, in a much more holistic sense, both the election or choice of Israel and the election of the church. In the Old Testament, the church or ecclesia was present but hidden. As Paul said: 'The mystery that has been kept hidden for ages and generations, but is now disclosed to the saints' (Col 1:26). The writer of Hebrews records the great Old Testament saints. Similarly in the New Testament, though the ecclesia or church is to the forefront, Israel does not cease to have relevance. There cannot then be one without the other nor, if they ever did, could one replace or supersede the other. There is mutuality in their calling and election.

Election

'Election' and 'choice' are unfortunate words because they often imply favouritism, and sadly that has been true in the way the church has regarded itself as having gained or acquired God's favour from Israel. However, in the biblical understanding of election or choice, it is not because either is special in or of itself, though time and again God describes both Israel and the church as His 'beloved'. They are special primarily in relation to the function and purpose for which they have been chosen or elected. Their 'belovedness' is related to the person who has bestowed that 'belovedness'. God makes it quite clear that His choice is not based on any intrinsic merit on the part of Israel (Deut 7:7) or indeed the church. Their value is the outcome of their election and choice by God. Indeed the Bible makes clear that the choice of Israel is not because they are the greatest or the most powerful of all the nations, but because they are the least. Paul makes a similar point to the Corinthian church, who were caught up in factionalism, when he says: 'Not many of you were wise by human standards; not many were influential; not many were of noble birth. But God chose the foolish things to shame the wise; God chose the weak things of the world to shame the strong' (1 Cor 1:26–27). Election or choice in God's book is never intended to be a source of pride, arrogance or superiority, but simply the means through which God accomplishes His purposes. It is meant to instil a sense of humility and complete dependence upon God.

When Paul quotes Malachi 1:2–3 in Romans 9:13, 'Jacob I loved, but

Esau I hated', this is not a statement of God's emotional reaction to these twin sons of Isaac, but a statement of God's intention to prefer the younger to the older for the carrying forward of His elective purpose. It could then be translated: 'Jacob I loved, but Esau I loved less.' We need to look at Israel and the church with this in mind.

The election of Israel

Why did God choose Israel and for what purpose? The first indications are given in the promise made to Abraham: 'Leave your country, your people and your father's household and go to the land I will show you. I will make you into a great nation and I will bless you; I will make your name great, and you will be a blessing. I will bless those who bless you, and whoever curses you I will curse; and all peoples on earth will be blessed through you' (Gen 12:1–3). Here we see announced God's intention to bless all the peoples on earth through Abraham. This promise is later confirmed by the covenant, which itself is later ratified through circumcision:

> 'I will make nations of you, and kings will come from you. I will establish my covenant as an everlasting covenant between me and you and your descendants after you for the generations to come, to be your God and the God of your descendants after you. The whole land of Canaan, where you are now an alien, I will give as an everlasting possession to you and your descendants after you; and I will be their God.' (Gen 17:6–8)

Of course, Abraham's decision to accomplish God's promise by having a child by Hagar has complicated the issue. The Arab nations base their claim to the Land through the line of Ishmael. Indeed in Islamic tradition it is not Isaac that is offered up on Mount Moriah, but Ishmael (Q. Sura 39:97–110).

However, that may be Islamic tradition, but it is not biblical, and in fact God makes it clear that the covenant will be through the union of Abraham and Sarah, through Isaac. Indeed it is just after Abraham offers up Isaac that God reaffirms the covenant, and says:

> 'I swear by myself, declares the Lord, that because you have done this and

have not withheld your son, your only son [Ishmael is not recognised], I will surely bless you and make your descendants as numerous as the stars in the sky and as the sand on the seashore . . . and through your offspring all nations on earth will be blessed, because you have obeyed me.' (Gen 22:15–18)

Then, as if to leave us in no doubt as to the line, God renews the covenant with Jacob at Bethel, making it very specific that the covenant relates to his family line:

And God said to him, 'I am God Almighty; be fruitful and increase in number. A nation and a community of nations will come from you, and kings will come from your body. The land I gave to Abraham and Isaac I also give to you, and I will give this land to your descendants after you.' (Gen 35:11–12)

Later, when God encounters Moses at the burning bush, He makes Himself known through linking His name to that of a particular lineage: 'I am the God of your father, the God of Abraham, the God of Isaac and the God of Jacob' (Ex 3:6).

The covenant is unconditional and everlasting

If we are left in any doubt as to whom the covenant is for, and how permanent it is, other passages make this clear: 'For the Lord your God is a merciful God; he will not abandon or destroy you or forget the covenant with your forefathers, which he confirmed to them by oath' (Deut 4:31), or Jeremiah: 'This is what the Lord says: 'Only if the heavens above can be measured and the foundations of the earth below be searched out will I reject all the descendants of Israel because of all they have done,' declares the Lord' (Jer 31:37).

Ezekiel, one of several of the post-exilic prophets, speaking of a future restoration declares:

This is what the Sovereign Lord says: It is not for your sake, O house of Israel, that I am going to do these things, but for the sake of my holy name, which you have profaned among the nations where you have gone. I will show the holiness of my great name . . . the name you have profaned among them. Then the nations will know that I am the Lord, declares the sovereign Lord, when I show myself holy through you before their eyes. (Ezek 36:22–23).

The central calling of Israel then is that she should be a blessing to the nations and the means through which God's name will be sanctified, made holy, among the nations. God's faithfulness to Israel is ultimately linked to the manifestation of His holiness to the nations. That is why, despite Christian tradition, there is ultimately no discontinuity between the two Testaments, for the New Testament bears witness that God has never and will never break covenant with Israel.

Of special significance then for Christians is the fact that in the New Testament Luke includes, in the opening words of his Gospel, the testimony of Zechariah that the covenant with Abraham was still in effect, coming now to its great fulfilment but not its completion: 'Praise be to the Lord, the God of Israel, because he has come and has redeemed his people . . . to show mercy to our fathers and to remember his holy covenant, the oath he swore to our father Abraham' (Luke 1:67–73).

For those who insist that these verses now apply to all the people of God in Christ, Paul asks: 'Did God reject his people? By no means!' (Rom 11:1). He then goes on to stress his own Israelite pedigree and so identifies himself as part of national or ethnic Israel, Israel according to the flesh. And later: 'As far as the gospel is concerned, they are enemies on your account; but as far as election is concerned, they are loved on account of the patriarchs, for God's gifts and his call are irrevocable' (Rom 11:28). Let's look then at how this calling was to be expressed.

Mosaic covenant

It is at Mount Horeb, or Sinai, that Israel's central calling is articulated, in the covenant God makes with Israel: 'Now if you obey me fully and keep my covenant, then out of all nations you will be my treasured possession. Although the whole earth is mine, you will be for me a kingdom of priests and a holy nation' (Ex 19:5–6).

This covenant is very different from that made with Abraham. It is a conditional covenant. There are clear conditions attached to it, which result in consequences if it is broken by either party. The most serious consequence was exile, but not banishment from the Land. This has happened only twice with the Babylonian exile and what has become known in Jewish tradition as 'the Great Exile', the nearly 2,000-year

exile which began in CE 70 and only ended with the re-establishment of
the State of Israel in 1948. The hymn writer J. M. Neale picks up this
theme in his Advent hymn: 'O come, O come, Emmanuel, and ransom
captive Israel that mourns in lonely exile here.' Israel had and still has a
high calling to be a priest to the nations, as the imagery within the verses
of this hymn depicts. On Yom Kippur, the Day of Atonement, the high
priest offered a bullock as a sacrifice on behalf of the nation of Israel.
During the Feast of Tabernacles the priests at the Temple in Jerusalem
offered up 70 bullocks on behalf of the nations (goyim), thus demonstrating their priestly role to the nations.

One of the titles the Lord gives to Israel is 'firstborn', showing just
how intimately His name is associated with the Jewish people, but perhaps more profoundly still that Israel is the *primus inter pares*, holding a
unique but not exclusive position among the nations. Although they may
be His firstborn, in this respect, they are not His 'only' born. God's longing is for all the nations to acknowledge His fatherhood.

A paradigm nation

Israel out of all the nations of the world belongs exclusively to God and
has a high calling over all the nations of the world. Archbishop Rowan
Williams, in 'Holy Land and Holy People', says:

> It helps to ask what covenantal promise is thought to be for in the Hebrew
> Scriptures. And the answer is given in various forms in parts of Leviticus, in
> many strands of the prophetic tradition especially Isaiah, in aspects of the
> Wisdom literature and might be summarised by saying Israel is called to be
> the paradigm nation, the example held up to all the nations of how a people
> lives in obedience to God and justice with one another. This is how a nation
> is meant to be: living by law, united by a worship that enjoins justice and rev-
> erence for all, exercising a special concern for those who have fallen outside
> the safety of the family unit (widows and orphans) and those who fall out-
> side the tribal identities of the people (the resident alien, 'the stranger within
> the gates'). What is more, as Deuteronomy insists (Deut 4:5, 6, 32–34; 17:7,
> 8), this is a people, a community, that exists solely because of God's loving
> choice; they have been called out of another nation, specifically to live as a
> community, whose task is to show God's wisdom in the world.

This is maybe the reason why we become so offended when we see Israelis mistreat Palestinians, behaving as if they have no right to be within the Land; why we are shocked that Israel has the highest abortion rate in the world. The millions of unborn aborted children greatly exceed the loss of life experienced by Israel in all its many wars. We somehow know that God has called Israel to be that paradigm nation and we want to hold it to account for its actions when it steps over what we regard as acceptable bounds.

This covenant then outlines how God expects Israel to live under His kingship; it does not abrogate His earlier covenant with Abraham. The writer of Galatians, commentating on the relationship between the two covenants, says: 'The law, introduced 430 years later, does not set aside the covenant previously established by God and thus do away with the promise' (Gal 3:17). Clearly then the Abrahamic covenant is not nullified at Sinai. It is stated that Israel is God's firstborn son (Ex 4:22; Deut 8:5), and this call came through Abraham.

The national constitution: Israel and Torah

One way of putting it is to say that it is as if God formed a people through Abraham, and then created a national constitution for that people through Moses. They are to be a holy people called to serve a holy God. In Leviticus this is articulated: 'I am the Lord your God; consecrate yourselves and be holy, because I am holy' (Lev 11:44). In order for the people to live in a holy way, God needs to provide directions to make His will known, to teach His people about Himself and His requirements, and this revelation of God's will is precisely what is conveyed by the Hebrew term 'Torah'.

The standard translation of this word is 'Law', which not only fails to do justice to the original Hebrew, but it has become positively harmful. Why? Because Christians see the word 'Law' and then conjure up images of Jewish legalism and bondage to the Law. However, although Torah does contain laws, it contains far more than just laws. Torah comes from the root word 'to fire at a target'. The best single word is 'instruction'. It conveys a sense of direction, directions on how to get to a goal, but also a sense of authority; when your leader gives a directive, then you make sure you do it. Christian theology has too readily forgotten that the Torah was God's idea! As Paul writes in Romans: 'So, then, the law is holy, and the commandment is holy, righteous and good . . . the law is spiritual.'

At this point it is important to clear up a major misunderstanding that has dogged our understanding of the relationship between grace and Law. 'Law' is not an Old Testament concept and 'grace' a New Testament one. The Abrahamic covenant is entirely of grace. There was nothing that Abraham had to do to keep covenant with God. Everything within this covenant is accomplished by God from start to finish. Abraham is even put to sleep when it is put into effect! What more definite illustration of the unilateral action of God in effecting this covenant is required? Grace precedes Law by at least 430 years, and even earlier with Noah: 'For Noah found grace in the eyes of the Lord.'

One of the most deeply ingrained Christian stereotypes is that Israel's relationship with God is based on living a life of righteousness, constantly in fear of God, whereas the New Testament (Christian) way is said to be based entirely on the gracious love of God. This perception and teaching is not only mistaken, but insulting and damaging to Jewish people, not to say a distortion of the New Testament witness about Christian lifestyle. The truth is that both Testaments present the same teaching about a covenant relationship with God. It is always based on God's prior grace and will, and it always makes demands on the people who are involved, with respect to how they must live their lives once they are in a special relationship with God.

Christ the goal of the Law and the embodiment of Israel

Christians often say that the coming of Christ marks the end to the Law, and justify their stance from Romans: 'Christ is the end of the law' (Rom 10:4).

However, the choice of the word 'end' is unfortunate, because it implies termination. The Greek word for 'end' is *telos*, which also means 'goal'. Christ is the goal, fulfilment or culmination of the Law, and the purpose of the Law is to bring us to Christ. The Christian is no longer 'under the Law' since Christ has freed us from its condemnation, but the Law still plays a role in our lives. We are now set free by the Holy Spirit to fulfil its moral demands. As Christians our lives centre on the one who kept the Law perfectly, and who fulfils it entirely in His person. In this respect Jesus embodies the Law, showing what it truly means to be Israel. Ultimately He is the only true Israelite. As Christians we are under a greater obligation than Israel of old.

Obedience to God is as central to New Testament teaching as it is to the Old Testament. However, while Israel sought to obey God by keeping the Law, the church is required to obey God through recognising the lordship of Christ in every aspect of its life. To come under the lordship of Christ is the only way we can keep the Law of God and not come under its judgement. Jesus requires of us a far higher standard: 'If you love me, you will obey what I command' (Jn 14:15). Jesus did not ignore the Torah, the Law of Moses; He obeyed it fully and increased our understanding of its true intent. As John says, the keeping of His commands enables us to know we are His children (see 1 Jn 3). Jesus as the true Son of Israel embodies the Law, and by the power of the Holy Spirit we are empowered to obey Him and so to keep the Law.

Israel's election and calling is to be that paradigm nation through whom all the nations of the world will be blessed, and whose election and calling is supremely embodied in the one who personifies Israel. The church, by contrast, is called to 'flesh out' what that means, through becoming a community of believers drawn from Israel and the nations, who by their lives reflect the Messiah of Israel, becoming, to use Paul's analogy, the body of the Messiah, with Messiah himself as its head. Messiahship is both individual, located in the person of Jesus, and corporate in so far as the church, the ecclesia, is called to model and demonstrate the kingdom values of the Messiah. To understand that, we need to look at Israel's relationship to God as King.

Royal Israel

Perhaps one of the saddest verses of the Bible is where the Lord says to Samuel: 'Listen to all that the people are saying to you; it is not you they have rejected, but they have rejected me as their king' (1 Sam 8:7). As we have seen earlier, Israel's calling was supremely to be a theocratic nation living under the rule of God. This was the very purpose for which Israel was called out from among the nations, to model what a nation under God means. However, the very rejection of God as King was the catalyst to bring about God's kingdom in our world. God granted

Israel's request for a king, and later, through a covenant with one king in particular, He pushed forward His strategy for world redemption and divine sovereignty over the nations.

King David longed to build the Lord a permanent dwelling place in Jerusalem, yet the Lord made clear that it would not be David who built the Temple, but his son, Solomon. Yet through that seeming rejection, God promises to David something far greater:

> The Lord declares to you that the Lord himself will establish a house for you. When your days are over and you rest with your fathers, I will raise up your offspring to succeed you, who will come from your own body, and I will establish his kingdom. He is the one who will build a house for my Name, and I will establish the throne of his kingdom for ever. I will be his father, and he shall be my son. (2 Sam 7:11–13)

The reigns of David and Solomon were seen as the golden age of Israel. Under David the tribes were finally united and the borders of the Land reached their furthest extent. It is no wonder that years later, when the nation yearned for a Messiah, they looked to the reign of David as their model. He united the country against enemies, established peace throughout the kingdom, exercised justice and laid the foundations for the great prosperity of the nation under his son, Solomon.

Later, through the writings of the prophets, the role of the Messiah became defined with clear expectations of what He would do, and by what line He would come. Luke, announcing the birth of Jesus, describes the descendant of David in this way: 'He will be great and will be called the Son of the Most High. The Lord God will give him the throne of his father David and he will reign over the house of Jacob for ever. His kingdom will never end' (Luke 1:32–33). This prophecy, if for no other reason, should convince us that Jesus is supremely Israel's Messiah, who has yet to establish His universal reign of peace.

Stephen Travis, in *End of Story*, says:

> And there is one Messiah for all. This is a hard thing to say. Isn't it arrogant for Christians to say to Jews, 'You are missing the heart of your faith. The Messiah for whom you're waiting has already come, and his name is Jesus'? Aren't we disqualified from saying such things by centuries of Christian anti-

semitism and persecution of the Jewish people? Didn't Hitler think he was speaking for 'Christian civilisation' when he wrote in Mein Kampf: 'By warding off the Jews I am fighting for the Lord's work'?

Yet to give up on Christian witness to Jewish people would be to saw off the branch on which we are sitting. Christian faith rests on the conviction that Jesus came to be the Messiah, and we are committed to sharing that faith with Jews whose Messiah He came to be. Deny that He is the Messiah and there is no reason for Christianity to exist. If Jesus is not the Messiah of the Jewish people, He cannot be my Saviour or the Saviour of the world.

It is significant that at the beginning and end of His life, Jesus is given the title 'King of the Jews'. In the birth narratives it is the Magi who enquire of Herod the Great: 'Where is the one who has been born king of the Jews?' (Mt 2:2). In the superscription above the cross is recorded the crime for which He is convicted: 'The King of the Jews' (Mk 15:26). There is one in heaven who is not only the Saviour of the world but who remains King of Israel, entitled to take up the earthly throne of His father David. During His earthly ministry Jesus never asserted His physical kingship over the pretenders to the throne, or to those appointed to rule over Israel by the Roman occupying power. Israel has yet to acknowledge His Messiahship over them – something Jesus Himself alludes to in His prophecy over Jerusalem when He declares: 'You will not see me again [O Jerusalem] until you say, "Blessed is he who comes in the name of the Lord" [until you greet me as Messiah]' (Mt 23:37). A prophecy of hope after judgement. It follows the prophecy of desolation and dereliction of both the people and the Land of Israel, but anticipates that glorious day to come when the very nation that once rejected its Messiah will receive Him. Earlier Jesus had warned the leadership of Israel of impending judgement in the Parable of the Tenants when He says: 'Therefore I tell you that the kingdom of God will be taken away from you and given to a people who will produce its fruit' (Mt 21:43).

Certainly this passage speaks of the transfer of that which hitherto had been Israel's prerogative to the new community forged around Israel's Messiah. That was not to the exclusion of an ongoing national expression of Israel. The kingdom may now be invested in the community of the Messiah, but Jews formed the exclusive and core nucleus of that community until the grafting in of Gentile believers.

Paul makes clear that Israel as a nation has been set aside but not removed from God's purposes. The kingdom of God may have been transferred and now be expressed in the Messiah, but God has not forsaken or rejected His covenant people. 'Did God reject his people?' asks Paul, to which he emphatically replies: 'By no means!' And again: 'God did not reject his people' (Rom 11:1–2). The stumbling of Israel was to draw in the Gentiles, who had previously been excluded from Israel, and as a consequence to make Israel envious.

The Gentile church owes a deep debt of gratitude to Israel, and she has been warned that if she becomes arrogant she will suffer a similar fate to Israel. Israel has been set aside for the benefit of the Gentiles. Paul goes on to say that if her rejection is the reconciliation of the world, what will her acceptance mean but life from the dead? If her transgression means riches for the world and her loss means riches for the Gentiles, how much greater riches will her fullness bring? The desolation of Israel has led to great blessings for the Gentiles, but Paul says that even blessings as great as these will pale into insignificance when the Jews return to centre stage. For the last nearly 2,000 years we have seen a largely Gentile body of the Messiah, with only a very faint glimmer of Jewish expression. The kingdom of God is incomplete.

The Puritans believed that the regathering and restoration of Israel would lead to the greatest evangelisation the world has ever witnessed, and would indeed usher in the fullest expression of the kingdom of God and the return of the King to reign. Perhaps when Paul speaks of 'the salvation of all Israel', he is speaking of the coming together of Israel according to the Spirit, the body of the Messiah, the ecclesia, together with a large part but not necessarily all of the nation of Israel. The prophet Zechariah reinforces the view of a national turning by Israel to her Messiah: 'I will pour out on the house of David and the inhabitants of Jerusalem a spirit of grace and supplication. They will look on me, the one they have pierced, and they will mourn for him as one mourns for an only child, and grieve bitterly for him as one grieves for a firstborn son' (Zech 12:10).

That is the ultimate goal of the gospel: to bring in the kingdom of God. Israel could not do it, as it rejected its own Messiah and so rejected its own King, around whom the kingdom would be gathered. The

Gentile church can only bring it in so far. It requires both Jew and Gentile together, united under the Messiah of Israel, to bring in the kingdom that will renew the face of the earth. National Israel may be subordinate to the body of the Messiah for the purposes of completing world redemption and to bring in the kingdom of Christ, but in the age to come, both Israel and the church come together as the walls and gates of the celestial city which descends to the renewed earth and where the God and the Lamb will reign for ever.

THE DAY OF THE LORD

David Noakes

There is today a famine of the truth of the word of God in many parts of the church, and it is a famine which is increasing in severity. It is of the greatest importance that in the difficult days that lie ahead, God's people should not find themselves either deceived by false teaching or taken unawares by events that their teachers had not told them to expect. It is a matter of urgency that we try to grasp clearly and accurately the whole of what Scripture predicts for the closing days of this age – but stripped of the speculation and sensationalism which so often surrounds it.

To establish truth, we need the illumination of the Holy Spirit; and we need to allow Scripture to interpret Scripture, allowing the word of God to be its own commentary upon itself, and letting the weight of the whole of the prophetic writings taken together build up a clear picture of the events which are being predicted. It could be likened to a jigsaw puzzle, scattered through the pages of the books of the prophets, which only the Holy Spirit can assemble correctly.

The topic of 'the Day of the Lord' is a thread that is interwoven into the Scriptures from the time of the earliest writing prophet, Obadiah, right through to the book of Revelation. Almost every prophet makes reference to it, either directly or indirectly. Sometimes, as with Isaiah in chapters 9–12, their prophetic vision leaps back and forth, from the time of the immediate future of which they are speaking, to the time of the end of this age. Sometimes, as with Joel and Zephaniah, the Day of the Lord is completely central to their writings, and the prophetic revelation arises either out of considering historical events that have already taken place –

in Joel's case a judgement on the Land of Israel by means of an invasion of locusts which had already happened in his own day (Joel 1:1–2:11) – or as with Zephaniah, out of a prophetic awareness of the imminence of the invasion and destruction of Judah by the Babylonians, which took place some 45 years later in 586 BCE (Zeph 1:4–2:3; 3:1–13).

A major theme of biblical prophecy

The Day of the Lord is a theme to which the prophets were drawn like moths to a candle flame. What is this great event that so occupied their thoughts and which keeps breaking into their writings as if they had suddenly taken off their reading glasses and instead had picked up a telescope to gaze with astonishing clarity of vision into the distant future?

It is a major theme of biblical prophecy, running like an unbroken thread through the writings of the Hebrew prophets, in which the phrase 'the Day of the Lord', with its unique significance, occurs 21 times between Isaiah 2:12 and the very last verse of the Old Testament, Malachi 4:5. Parallel to that phrase is another that has similar theological significance when used by the prophets: 'in that day', which is found 107 times in their writings and out of which 80 references are directly related to the future Day of the Lord.

The Day of the Lord is thus mentioned by the prophets more than 100 times. It is continuously interwoven into the book of Isaiah, appearing in no fewer than 17 of the first 35 chapters. Of the 17 books of the Old Testament prophets, only five fail to mention it directly by name; and of those five, Daniel in chapters 7–12 deals with the subject extensively, while both Nahum and Habakkuk also contain relevant prophecy relating to the closing days of this age. This prophetic theme continues through the New Testament, emerging, for example, in the Olivet Discourse (Mt 24:15–31; Mk 13:14–27; Lk 21:20–36), in 1 Corinthians, Philippians, 1 and 2 Thessalonians, Hebrews, 2 Peter, Jude and of course almost the whole of the book of Revelation.

How should we understand this term 'the Day of the Lord' and its counterpart 'in that day'? What do they signify? There is no special significance in the actual Hebrew or Greek words used in the two phrases. In the Hebrew Old Testament the ordinary Hebrew word for day, *yom*, is used; while in the Septuagint and the New Testament the usual Greek word, *hemera*, is found. *Yom* is translated variously in the Scriptures as 'day', 'time' or 'year'. It can express either a particular point in time, or a period of time that may extend during months or even years. When included in the phrases 'the Day of the Lord' or 'in that day', it is used prophetically to indicate a particular future period of time when God's personal and direct intervention in human history will occur in order to fulfil His purposes.

God's purposes

What are these purposes? The evidence from Amos 5:18 indicates that the popular understanding among the people at the time of his ministry in the northern kingdom of Israel (c.760 BCE) was that it would be a day when God would intervene in such a way as to exalt Israel to be chief among the nations, irrespective of Israel's unfaithfulness towards Him. This was the view being taken by the people at a time of relative peace and prosperity, which had led to great complacency (Amos 6:1–7). Amos, however, hastens to disabuse them of such an idea. The Day of the Lord will certainly be an occasion when God intervenes, but first to punish sin, which has reached a climax: 'Woe to you who long for the day of the Lord! Why do you long for the day of the Lord? That day will be darkness, not light . . . will not the day of the Lord be darkness, not light – pitch-dark, without a ray of brightness?' (Amos 5:18, 20).

All the prophetic writings confirm Amos's understanding of the Day of the Lord as a day of terror, involving the invasion of Israel and an experience of unparalleled destruction. Zephaniah, prophesying to Judah in about 630 BCE, says:

> The great day of the Lord is near – near and coming quickly. Listen! The cry on the day of the Lord will be bitter, the shouting of the warrior there. That day will be a day of wrath, a day of distress and anguish, a day of trouble and ruin, a day of darkness and gloom, a day of clouds and blackness, a day of trumpet and battle cry against the fortified cities and against the corner towers. (Zeph 1:14–16)

Both these and other passages in the prophetic writings underscore the fact that the Day of the Lord is to be a day when the terror of divine judgement is to be poured out on the unbelieving nation of Israel (see, e.g., Isaiah 2:6–21; Jeremiah 30:4–17; Joel 1:15–2:11; Malachi 4:1). Yet this by no means represents the whole of God's purposes at that time. The unbelieving nations of the world will also be brought into judgement; and in addition a surviving remnant of the nation of Israel will enter into a national conversion, forgiveness of sins, cleansing, and restoration to possession of the entirety of the Land that God promised to Abraham (see, e.g., Isaiah 4: 2–6; Jeremiah 30:18–31:40; Micah 4:1–8; Zechariah 12:10–13:2).

The tribulation period

The Day of the Lord is always found in the context of a prophetic prediction of a future disaster, involving certain signs that will portend its arrival, notably convulsions of nature and periods of darkness in the sky. The Day itself involves the direct intervention of God in the affairs of men, bringing judgement and great destruction upon Israel through military invasion by the Gentile nations, which in turn results in destruction by God of those armies at the return of the Lord Jesus and deliverance for the repentant remnant of Israel. This leads directly into the fullness of restoration of both the nation and the Land of Israel, God's judgement upon the Gentile nations, and the establishment of the millennial kingdom of the Messiah upon the earth.

What we are describing is thus that period of prophetic prediction in human history known in the New Testament as the Tribulation or the Great Tribulation. It may be helpful to tabulate some of the other terms also used in the Old Testament to represent this period of time. It is variously referred to as:

The Time of Jacob's Trouble	Jeremiah 30:7
Israel's Day of Disaster	Deuteronomy 32:35
His wrath	Isaiah 26:20
The Overwhelming Scourge	Isaiah 28:15, 18
God's Strange Work	Isaiah 28:21
God's Alien Task	Isaiah 28:21
The Day of Vengeance	Isaiah 34:8; 35:4; 61:2
The Seventieth Week of Daniel	Daniel 9:27

The Time of Wrath	Daniel 11:36
The Time of Distress	Daniel 12:1
The Day of Pitch-darkness, without a ray of brightness	Amos 5:18
The Day of Darkness and Gloom	Joel 2:2; Zephaniah 1:15
The Day of Clouds and Blackness	Joel 2:2; Zephaniah 1:15
The Day of Judah's Disaster	Obadiah 13
The Day of Wrath	Zephaniah 1:15
The Day of Distress and Anguish	Zephaniah 1:15
The Day of Trouble and Ruin	Zephaniah 1:15
The Day of Trumpet and Battle-Cry	Zephaniah 1:15

These descriptions alone are sufficient to indicate that this period will be a time of unparalleled distress for the whole world, but pre-eminently for the house of Jacob, for whom it will be the final outworking of God's judgement upon their national sin and apostasy. This must come to pass before the restoration of the kingdom to Israel (Acts 1:6) can take place. That it will be a time of unequalled distress in Judah is confirmed by Jesus in Matthew 24:15–29 in the course of speaking to His disciples about the events leading to the end of the age.

The uniqueness of the nation of Israel

To understand rightly what the Scriptures reveal, it is of critical importance to bear in mind that what we are examining is the writings of Hebrew prophets, prophesying to Hebrews about what is primarily, in the purposes of God, an event which involves His final dealing in judgement with the nation of Israel before her national vindication and restoration. His judgements on the nations, vital though they are, take second place to His dealings with His covenant people so far as the heart of God is concerned.

It is impossible to understand the events that will mark the closing days of this age without understanding the relationship between Hebrew Israel, the physical descendants of Jacob, and the God of Abraham, Isaac and Jacob. This relationship is special, unique and irreplaceable; and no third party, including the church, can ever be a substitute within it.

A key biblical distinction is between the place of Israel and the place of the church, and failure to observe and maintain that distinction leads to misunderstanding of much of what the Bible teaches. As far as eschatology is concerned, the distinction is vital, for a right understanding of the covenant relationship between Israel and her God is crucial in comprehending the revelation of Scripture as to its outworking. That relationship is pivotal, the hub at the centre of the wheel, around which all the other events of the last days revolve. If it is not in proper position in our thinking, other matters of eschatology become as loose spokes of the wheel, with no central point of reference.

The Bible speaks of Israel as the Wife of the God of Jacob and of the church as the Bride of Christ. They are by no means the same in this age, although ultimately they will be united in the new Jerusalem. Israel is revealed progressively in Scripture as a wife married to God, who becomes adulterous, is separated, then divorced, then punished, rejected and abandoned, but finally restored into the fullness of the marriage covenant (Is 54:1–8; Is 62:4–5; Hos 2:14–23). The church, however, is presented as a betrothed virgin who is not yet joined by marriage to her husband; the wedding feast is yet to come. Unlike Israel, the adulterous wife forgiven, cleansed and restored, the church is in the future to be presented to Christ as a pure virgin (1 Cor 11:2; Eph 5:25–27). The two are presented in Scripture as being different and distinct from one another, and it is important to realise that God deals with them as such.

The consistent testimony of the many passages of Scripture that relate to God's future dealings with the nation of Israel – which will include both the formerly divided kingdoms of Israel and Judah (see, e.g., Is 11:12–14; Jer 31:27, 31; Ez 37:15–23) – leaves no room for doubt that the faithfulness of the God and Father of our Lord Jesus Christ will fulfil every promise and every prediction made concerning the Hebrew people, with whom He remains in a covenant relationship. As He says in Malachi 3:6: 'I the Lord do not change. So you, O descendants of Jacob, are not destroyed.'

Judgement and salvation

The Scriptures predict exactly what we see today in the nation-state of Israel: a nation being restored to her Land in a state of unbelief. The prophetic word of God is being visibly fulfilled in our own day, which is a cause for rejoicing since it heralds the imminent return of Messiah. It is nevertheless at the same time a cause of foreboding, for the Scriptures also make it plain that before Messiah comes, this restoration to the Land must be the inevitable prologue to a final terrible outpouring of satanic antisemitic hatred. This will bring about the completion of God's judgements upon His covenant nation in her own Land in the Day of the Lord, which Jeremiah 30:7 describes as 'the time of Jacob's trouble': 'Alas! for that day is great, so that none is like it: it is even the time of Jacob's trouble; but he shall be saved out of it' (KJV).

An examination of the passages of Scripture dealing with the topic of the Day of the Lord leads to the realisation that, as we have already said, the period of time being described in the Old Testament writings is the same as that which the New Testament identifies as the great tribulation (Rev 7:14). At every place in Scripture where the phrase 'the Day of the Lord' is to be found, it is in a context which relates it to the tribulation period.

Although the period of the tribulation is first and foremost the time of Jacob's trouble, it will include also God's judgement on the Gentile nations and will result in the salvation and restoration of the surviving remnant of the nation of Israel. In addition, as it runs its course, it will bring about a worldwide harvest of salvation among the Gentiles (Rev 7:9–17).

To put some more flesh on these bones and to substantiate what has been said, we need to examine certain key passages of Scripture that make detailed reference to the Day of the Lord. Since, however, the theme runs like a continuous thread through the prophetic writings, from Isaiah to Revelation, we cannot attempt to cover every place where it is mentioned.

Let us begin with the book of Joel, after Obadiah the first of the writing prophets to deal with the subject of the Day of the Lord. He prophesied to the southern kingdom of Judah, probably in the reign of King Joash, about 835 BCE. Certainly he must predate Amos, who prophesied to the northern kingdom of Israel in the following century during the reign of Jeroboam II (Amos 1:1), because Amos quotes Joel twice: Joel 3:16 is quoted in Amos 1:2, and Joel 3:18 in Amos 9:13.

Military invasion of the Land of Israel

In chapter 1:2–14, Joel describes an actual historical invasion of the Land by locusts in four successive waves (v. 4), bringing total destruction of the crops. From an examination of Jeremiah 15:3 and Ezekiel 14:21, it is apparent that, prophetically, four stages of a disaster indicate its completeness. It brings lamentation among the people and a call to the priests for national repentance (vv. 13–14). From the springboard of this account of an actual invasion by locusts in Joel's own day, he moves immediately into the prophetic future, using the analogy of the invasion by locusts to describe an invasion of the Land of Israel which will take place at the end of this age, in the Day of the Lord. This will be similar to the plague of locusts in that it will bring a complete devastation to the Land. The account begins in verse 15, where the theme of the Day of the Lord is introduced and is stated to involve destruction in the Land of Israel. This continues to verse 11 of chapter 2.

Although there was at least some limited measure of fulfilment of this prophecy in both the Assyrian and the Babylonian invasions of 722 BCE and 586 BCE respectively, this passage has its real and ultimate fulfilment in an even more catastrophic event yet to come. This invasion will be the worst in Israel's entire history (2:2b). It will involve a vast army (2:2, 11), which will bring destruction by fire upon the whole Land (1:19–20; 2:3). The devastation will be complete (1:16–20). Although it will be a hostile army that will invade Israel and bring the disaster, this is nevertheless the hand of God at work in the final judgement to fall upon Israel. It is 'destruction from the Almighty' (1:15) and the army is described as the Lord's army in 2:11.

More than three centuries later, following the return of the remnant of Judah from the Babylonian exile, the prophet Zechariah received a more detailed account of that same invasion, which even in the post-exilic period was still revealed as a future event. In Zechariah 12, the Lord states in verses 2 and 3: 'I am going to make Jerusalem a cup that sends all the surrounding peoples reeling. Judah will be besieged as well as Jerusalem. On that day, when all the nations of the earth are gathered against her, I will make Jerusalem an immovable rock for all the nations.' In Zechariah 14:2 the word of God further states: 'I will gather all the nations to Jerusalem to fight against it; the city will be captured, the houses ransacked, and the women raped. Half of the city will go into exile, but the rest of the people will not be taken from the city.' It is generally understood that this situation will be the culmination of the campaign of Armageddon (Rev 16:12–16).

Turning to the book of Zephaniah, whose central theme is also that of the Day of the Lord (1:14), we find that the whole of chapter 3 is speaking to the unrepentant city of Jerusalem concerning God's future judgement, and beyond that to the subsequent restoration of a saved remnant of her people. Again, we are told that God's judgement will be executed at the hands of Gentile nations, who will in turn themselves be judged by the Lord. Zephaniah 3:7–8 reads:

'I said to the city, "Surely you will fear me and accept correction!" Then her dwelling would not be cut off, nor all my punishments come upon her. But they were still eager to act corruptly in all they did. Therefore, wait for me,' declares the Lord, 'for the day I will stand up to testify. I have decided to assemble the nations, to gather the kingdoms and to pour out my wrath on them – all my fierce anger. The whole world will be consumed by the fire of my jealous anger.'

To digress briefly at this point, the translation here may be somewhat misleading. The final sentence, translating the Hebrew word *erets*, which is translated only rarely as 'world', but more usually as either 'earth' or 'land', says that the whole world will be consumed, while the KJV renders it 'All the earth shall be devoured.' Both translations appear to assume that God has here turned His attention to speaking solely of His judgement on the Gentile nations of the world. However, God never states that He is jealous over the nations of the world, but states frequently that He is jealous over His people Israel and over the city of Jerusalem; and in the context of the whole passage, it may be that the final sentence of 3:8 should read: 'The whole land will be consumed by the fire of my jealous anger.' This statement can be understood either to be literal, or as a metaphorical expression of the overflowing of the Lord's heated indignation against the corruption about which He has already protested with solemn warnings.

The likelihood of this possibility appears to be reinforced by an examination of the language used by Zephaniah in chapter 1. In verses 2 and 3, which clearly refer to widespread destruction on the whole inhabited earth in the day of the Lord's judgement, the word translated 'earth' is *adamah*; whereas in verse 18, in the context of a passage which begins in verse 4 and in which the prophet is specifically addressing Judah, the word *erets* is chosen. This distinction in the choice of language in the original inspired texts is surely significant for our understanding and interpretation: *adamah* is used to describe the earth as a whole, *erets* when the Land of Judah is in view.

God speaks primarily to Israel, secondarily to the Gentiles

A factor of importance in our eschatological understanding of biblical prophecy concerning the closing days of this age is that although it is not at all unusual for the prophets to speak of specific Gentile nations as being the recipients of God's judgement, when they do it is almost invariably made clear by the fact that those nations are mentioned by name. Except where that is the case, we need to bear in mind that the usual task of the Hebrew prophets was to prophesy to their own people concerning the nation and the Land of Israel or Judah. If the Gentile church were to gain a firm grasp on this principle, much confusion would be removed. It is very common, for example, among Christians to find the belief that the campaign of Armageddon is bound to involve a worldwide military conflict, including a nuclear holocaust. This may of course prove to be so, but the Scriptures do not necessarily seem to warrant this particular conclusion. We must beware of falling into the trap of 'going beyond what is written' (1 Cor 4:6) in the revelation of the word of God. What is clear is that the military action of the campaign of Armageddon will take place in the Land of Israel.

The rest of the world will, of course, experience the supernatural manifestations of the wrath of God as revealed in appalling detail in the book of Revelation; and the clear implication of scriptures such as those found, for example, in Isaiah 24 and in the Olivet Discourse is that the entire world will experience the shakings and disasters that result from the overflowing of God's judgement upon the sin of all the nations (cf. Hag 2:20–22 and Heb 12:26–27). When the world's cup of iniquity is full, His final judgements will fall in the Day of the Lord.

Worldwide warning signs

We have already quoted Amos 5:18 and 20, stating that the Day of the Lord will be 'darkness, not light – pitch-dark, without a ray of brightness'. Returning to Joel 2:2 we find similarly that the day will be one of 'darkness and gloom, a day of clouds and blackness', and in 2:10 that 'the earth shakes, the sky trembles, the sun and moon are darkened, and the stars no longer shine'. This is not just symbolic darkness; there will also be a literal aspect to it. Jesus said in Luke 21:25 that 'there will be signs in the sun, moon and stars'. Even as there was physical darkness when Jesus was enduring the judgement of God against sin at Calvary (Mt 27:45), so Scripture also speaks of more than one period of physical darkness in the time of the judgements that will take place in the Day of the Lord.

The terrible invasion described in Joel 2 brings forth God's call to Israel to repentance in order to avert the disaster before the destruction is total (2:12–17). They are to call upon the name of the Lord, reminding Him that they are His covenant people and that the Land is His inheritance (v. 17; cf. Ps 79:10).

Salvation of a remnant

Following this repentance, God responds to the surviving remnant and delivers those who have called upon Him for salvation (2:32; see also Mal 3:16–4:3). The second part of Joel's prophecy moves from the invasion and destruction of Israel to the salvation and restoration of Israel. The invading army (2:20) will be destroyed by God in the desert of the Negev, and it will be so large as to be pushed at either end into the Dead Sea and the Mediterranean respectively. The Land will be restored (vv. 19, 21–27). Following this deliverance there will be an outpouring of the Holy Spirit on all the survivors of the nation of Israel (vv. 28–29).

Thus far, we see the Day of the Lord as being a time of terrible judgement on the Land and nation of Israel. Joel 2:30–31 tells us that there will be dramatic and awful warnings of the impending arrival of that Day by means of:

(a) upheavals in nature;
(b) a period of unnatural darkness.

These are warnings to all those who have ears to hear and especially to Israel, together with an assurance (v. 32) that there will be deliverance on Mount Zion and in Jerusalem for those who call upon the Lord for salvation – but they will only be the surviving elect remnant of Israel. Zechariah 13:8–9 speaks of this remnant and says:

'In the whole land,' declares the Lord, 'two-thirds will be struck down and perish; yet one-third will be left in it. This third I will bring into the fire; I will refine them like silver and test them like gold. They will call on my name and I will answer them; I will say, "They are my people," and they will say, "'The Lord is our God."'

In Romans 9:26–29, Paul quotes from Hosea 1:10, Isaiah 10:22–23 and Isaiah 1:9 to establish the fact that a remnant – but only a remnant – of Israel will be saved; and on examination of the scripture that he has quoted from Isaiah 10, we find that it is at the time of the Day of the Lord, the complete quotation beginning in verse 20 with the theologically significant phrase 'in that day'. The whole passage, Isaiah 10:20–23, reads:

In that day the remnant of Israel, the survivors of the house of Jacob, will no longer rely on him who struck them down but will truly rely on the Lord, the Holy One of Israel. A remnant will return, a remnant of Jacob will return to the Mighty God. Though your people, O Israel, be like the sand by the sea, only a remnant will return. Destruction has been decreed, overwhelming and righteous. The Lord, the Lord Almighty, will carry out the destruction decreed upon the whole land.

Jesus also confirmed that there would be a surviving remnant. In Matthew 24:15, He turns His attention to the time of the great tribulation and gives prophetic warnings relating to it. It is to be, in Judea particularly (v. 16), a time of unparalleled distress (v. 21) from which there would be no survivors except for divine intervention (v. 22), but God will intervene and bring an end to the tribulation in Judea 'for the sake of the elect' – that is, the remnant of Israel that is to be saved out of it.

The 'Little Apocalypse' of Isaiah 24–27

Another key passage of Scripture that is prophetic of the Day of the Lord is the 'Little Apocalypse' of Isaiah 24–27. Many commentators appear to think that the whole of chapter 24 is speaking about God's judgement solely on a worldwide basis, but this assumption does not seem to equate with the usual prophetic methods of expression.

We noted previously that when the Hebrew prophets are speaking about nations other than Israel and Judah, they specifically name those nations. Between chapters 13 and 23, Isaiah has prophesied judgement concerning Babylon, Assyria, Philistia, Moab, Damascus, Ethiopia, Egypt, Edom, Arabia and Tyre; in chapter 24, however, no individual nation is named. This may be, of course, because the prophet intends to include every nation without distinction, and it has been assumed by many that because in translation this chapter speaks over and over again of 'the earth', the prophecy is therefore entirely to do with events that are to occur on a worldwide basis. However, as with the book of Zephaniah, on 15 occasions out of 17 the word translated 'the earth' is again the Hebrew 'erets', which can equally well be translated as 'the land'. It is interesting to note that Dr David Stern's translation of Isaiah 24 in *The Complete Jewish Bible* relates verses 1–12 to the Land of Israel, but renders verses 13–23 as having global application.

It appears significant when considering the language of Isaiah 24 that when the prophet wishes to make reference to the earth in a worldwide sense, he uses a different Hebrew word. In this context he does not use *erets* but *adamah*, which means the ground or the soil of the dry land. *Adamah* is used in Isaiah 23:17, where Tyre is said to 'ply her trade with all the kingdoms on the face of the earth'. It is also the case that in verse 21 of chapter 24, which reads 'In that day the Lord will punish the powers in the heavens above and the kings on the earth below', Isaiah, having used the word *erets* throughout the chapter until that point, suddenly switches and uses the word *adamah* in speaking of the kings on the earth on what is obviously intended as a worldwide basis. This deliberate choice of the different words under the influence of the Holy Spirit cannot be without reason.

Of the two occasions when the word translated as 'the earth' or 'the world' is not the usual *erets*, Isaiah employs the word *adamah*, once in verse 21; while on the other occasion in verse 4, he uses the less common word for the habitable earth, *tebel*, sandwiched between two uses of *erets* in the very same verse. Why should there be these variations of usage on only two out of seventeen occasions when 'the earth' is in view?

It is easy to see in verses 21–23 that the prophetic revelation shifts its emphasis into a clear global perspective of judgement upon world rulers, both human and spiritual; hence the change of emphasis signified by the sudden use of the different word *adamah*. In verse 4, however, the sudden single use of *tebel* may be to enable the prophet to speak in the same sentence of the simultaneous total impoverishment of both the Land of Israel and the whole of the rest of the planet. The cause in both cases is the outpouring of God's judgement – the cup of iniquity – on both His own covenant people and also the global community of the Gentile nations, to bring to an end the rebellion of both against His sovereign rulership. The result of this global judgement will be the repentance and total restoration of Israel as the redeemed messianic covenant nation, taking her appointed place as chief among the nations of the world (Jer 31:7), and the judgement of the returned Messiah upon the Gentile nations on the basis of their acceptance or rejection of His covenant people in the hour of their great distress.

It seems very probable, from the actual content of this chapter also, that the prophecy does relate primarily to the Land of Israel and only secondarily to the earth as a whole. The prophecies of laying waste, devastation and plundering that it contains are entirely at one with the prophetic predictions elsewhere in the Scriptures concerning the invasion of Israel and the siege of Jerusalem. Verse 5 is extremely thought-provoking; the charge is that the Land 'is defiled by its people' who have 'disobeyed the laws, violated the statutes and broken the everlasting covenant' thereby bringing upon themselves a curse (v. 6). The only nation mentioned in Scripture as having received laws and statutes, the breaking of which brings a curse, is Israel. Neither have the Gentile nations of the world ever been party to any 'everlasting covenant' which they have broken, although the Noahic covenant is also expressed to be everlasting in Genesis 9:16. That covenant, however, is unilateral on the part of God; and taken in its context, the only tenable argument for its infraction by the earth's inhabitants would seem to lie in the sin of shedding innocent blood (vv. 4–5). In view of the increasing global violence and bloodshed in our day, as in the days of Noah, and particularly the widespread sin among the nations of the mass murder of unborn children through legalised abortion, there is perhaps at first sight something in favour of that possible argument.

However, in the context in which Isaiah is writing in chapter 24, it seems much more likely that the broken covenant which is in the prophet's view is God's covenant with Abraham, Isaac and Jacob, expressed in 1 Chronicles 16:15–18 and Psalm 105:8–11 to be an 'everlasting covenant' concerning Israel's inheritance of the Land of Canaan, ultimately to be possessed by the restored nation in its entirety from the Mediterranean Sea to the River Euphrates (Deut 11:24). What, one must ask, would amount to an infraction of this covenant by God's chosen people? Could it be that in the sight of God the willingness to surrender His Land (Joel 3:2) in return for a spurious peace amounts to such a denial of that covenant He has made with His people?

In verses 10 and 12 we find reference to a ruined, desolate city, which would fit with the condition of Jerusalem according to the prediction of Zechariah 14:2. In verse 13 comes a reference to an olive tree being beaten; the translation of this verse in the KJV is: 'When thus it shall be in the midst of the land among the people, there shall be as the shaking of an olive tree, and as the gleaning grapes when the vintage is done.' There is a similar reference to Jacob as an olive tree in Isaiah 17:6 (and see also Jeremiah 11:16 and Hosea 14:6). In Romans 11:24 the whole nation of Israel is, of course, referred to as an olive tree. No other nation is so described in Scripture.

In verses 18b–20 of Isaiah 24 the Scripture makes reference to a great earthquake. Is this to be a worldwide earthquake? In Zechariah 14:4–5 it is predicted that in the Day of the Lord there will be a great earthquake in the Land of Israel which splits the Mount of Olives in two immediately prior to the Lord's Second Coming. Revelation 11, which speaks of events in Jerusalem during the tribulation, tells us in verse 13 that there will be a severe earthquake which causes a tenth of the city of Jerusalem to collapse. However, the earthquake mentioned in Zechariah 14 is probably that which is predicted in Revelation 16:17–21. It appears that this earthquake certainly could be of worldwide proportions, since it is stated to be the greatest earthquake that has ever occurred since man has been on earth (v. 18); it causes Jerusalem (the 'great city' – see

Revelation 11:8) to be split into three parts, and also we are told that 'the cities of the nations collapsed' (v. 19).

All of this, taken together, appears as compelling evidence that Isaiah 24 is speaking of the Day of the Lord in a way that is entirely consistent with other prophetic writings, first concerning the final judgement on Judah and Jerusalem prior to the return of her Messiah in deliverance, and secondly of the outpouring of God's wrath on the Gentile world whose rebellion has filled its cup of iniquity to the full. The three following chapters, 25–27, also fit with the predictions of the other prophets, speaking not to the Gentile nations, but principally of the Lord's renewed favour to the restored and converted nation of Israel, after the period of tribulation has been ended by the return of her Messiah. Terrible though it is to contemplate, the last and most awful expression of satanically inspired antisemitism has yet to occur. However, this will constitute the very action which brings that cup of iniquity to the full, resulting in God's judgement on the Gentile world system and the deliverance of His covenant people through the return of Messiah Yeshua.

God's subsequent judgement of the nations

Returning to the book of Joel, the prophet's attention turns in chapter 3 towards the judgement of the Gentile nations of the world. This also forms part of the events of the Day of the Lord, and will happen (v. 1) at the time of God's restoration of the fortunes of Judah and Jerusalem. It will take place in the Valley of Jehoshaphat, the Kidron Valley between Jerusalem and the Mount of Olives.

Judgement on their armies

Verses 9–11 underline that the nations have come to Israel for war. The Hebrew of verse 9 means literally 'sanctify a war'. The armies of the nations, summoned by the Antichrist to a 'holy war' against Israel with the aim of wiping her out totally, and lured by the influence of the demonic powers released in the sixth bowl judgement of Revelation 16:12–16, will have assembled in the valley of Megiddo in northern Israel. They will move south against Jerusalem and take the city, after which God will intervene personally through the return of

Messiah (Zech 14:3–15; Rev 19:11–21) to overthrow the armies and to deliver Judah and Jerusalem. He will halt those armies by sending upon them madness, panic, plague and blindness (Zech 12:1–9; 14:1–3, 12–15).

Judgement on the individual Gentile survivors on that Day

Following this deliverance, and the repentance and restoration of the surviving remnant and of the Land, which we have already mentioned and which is also described in Zechariah 12:10–13:1 and 14:6–11, the returned Messiah will bring the survivors of all the nations before Him for judgement in the Valley of Jehoshaphat (Joel 3:1–8, 12–17). They will be there in huge numbers (v. 14).

The judgement of God upon the Gentiles will be on the basis of either their antisemitism or their prosemitism (v. 2). His charges against them will be those of scattering the people of Israel, dividing up the Land and enslaving the people (vv. 2–3). They will be judged on the basis of their attitudes and behaviour towards the Hebrew people, and this is re-affirmed by Jesus in Matthew 25:31–46, where He speaks of dividing the people of the nations into the categories of sheep or goats according to whether they treated His brethren well or badly. Joel 3:13 speaks of the salvation of some in the figure of getting in the harvest, and of the condemnation of others in the figure of the crushing of the grapes in the winepress (see also Isaiah 63:1–6).

Judgement of particular nations

Space will not permit the lengthy examination of God's dealings with specific individual nations, but Scripture has much to say on the subject. For example:

- Babylon and Edom (the descendants of Esau) will both become permanent desolate wastelands, dwelling-places only for demons (Jer 50:35–40; 51:37–43 [Babylon]; Jer 49:13, 15–18; Obad 15–18; Is 34:5–16 [Edom]).
- The descendants of Lot (the nations of Moab and Ammon) will be restored after judgement (Jer 48:47; 49:6).
- After judgement, both Egypt and Assyria will enter into the blessing of the Lord and a close relationship with Israel (Is 19:23–25).

- Philistia will be taken over by Israel (Obad 19; Is 11:14), and so will Lebanon (Obad 20). The judgement of both is mentioned in Joel 3:4–7.

The establishment of the millennial kingdom

The final outcome of the Day of the Lord is the establishment of the millennial kingdom. The Lord will dwell in Zion (Joel 3:17, 21). In verse 18, the prophet tells us that the fruitfulness of the Land will be restored, and there will be abundant water, ending the problem of drought. The same verse refers to the millennial river, also described in Ezekiel 47:1–12 and Zechariah 14:8, which will flow from below the threshold of the millennial temple. From Ezekiel 47:13–48:29, we learn also that at that time Israel will at last possess the entirety of the Land promised to Abraham's descendants in Genesis 15:18–19. That covenant was unconditional; the 'everlasting covenant' of which we have already spoken. God will have proved His faithfulness to keep His covenant to the very letter. His word cannot fail, because He cannot be unfaithful to what He has unconditionally undertaken to do.

What will be the signs to warn us of the impending approach of the Day of the Lord?

1. Specific to the nation of Israel will be the re-establishment of the ministry of the prophet Elijah, which will have the particular emphasis of calling the nation to repentance in the area of its collapsing family relationships (Mal 4:5).
2. We have already seen in Joel 2:31–32 the prophetic prediction that 'before the coming of the great and dreadful day of the Lord', there will be certain signs:
   (a) 'wonders in the heavens and on the earth, blood and fire and billows of smoke' (v. 30), corresponding to the effects of the first, second, fifth and sixth trumpet judgements found in Revelation 8:7–9 and Revelation 9:1–21;
   (b) 'the sun will be turned to darkness and the moon to blood' (v. 32), corresponding to the judgement released at the Lamb's opening of the sixth seal in Revelation 6:12–17.

The whole of the order of nature in the heavens and on the earth will be thrown into turmoil and upheaval as a result of the outpouring of the judgements of God, before the culmination of the Day of the Lord in the Armageddon campaign and the Second Coming of Messiah.

Isaiah 13:9–10, Amos 5:20 and Zephaniah 1:15 all speak similarly of periods of darkness coming over the earth at that time, and Jesus underlined these events during the Olivet Discourse. He says in Luke 21 that:

(a) there will be 'wars and revolutions' (v. 9);

(b) 'Nation will rise against nation, and kingdom against kingdom' (v. 10);

(c) we'll see 'great earthquakes, famines and pestilences in various places' (v. 11);

(d) there will be 'fearful events and great signs from heaven' (v. 11);

(e) 'before all this, they will lay hands on you and persecute you' (v. 12).

All these events of war, and upheavals of nature on earth and in the heavenly bodies, have been predicted by more than one of the writing prophets. Daniel 9:26, speaking of the times of the end when the Antichrist will rule, says: 'The end will come like a flood: War will continue until the end, and desolations have been decreed' (see also Psalm 46:8).

3. To these predictions, however, Jesus adds one more: the severe persecution of the church, together with the apostasy this will bring about (Mt 24:9–13).

4. This apostasy is mentioned by Paul in 2 Thessalonians 2:3, which leads us on to one final and crucial indication that the Day of the Lord is drawing near. This will be the emergence of the 'man of lawlessness', the Antichrist. Paul writes to the church at Thessalonica in 2 Thessalonians 2:1–4:

> Concerning the coming of our Lord Jesus Christ and our being gathered to him, we ask you, brothers, not to become easily unsettled or alarmed by some prophecy, report or letter supposed to have come from us, saying that the day of the Lord has already come. Don't let anyone deceive you in any way, for that day will not come until the rebellion [Greek *apostasia*] occurs and the man of lawlessness is

revealed, the man doomed to destruction. He will oppose and exalt himself over everything that is called God or is worshipped, so that he sets himself up in God's temple, proclaiming himself to be God.

What will initiate the Day of the Lord, the period of the tribulation?

The final sign, just mentioned, is that of the emergence into recognition of the man of sin, the Antichrist. The same figure appears constantly as a king in Daniel chapters 7, 8, 9 and 11. We read in 7:25: 'He will speak against the Most High and oppress his saints and try to change the set times and the laws'; in 8:25: 'He will destroy many and take his stand against the Prince of princes. Yet he will be destroyed, but not by human power'; and again in 11:36: 'The king will do as he pleases. He will exalt and magnify himself above every god and will say unheard-of things against the God of gods. He will be successful until the time of wrath is completed, for what has been determined must take place.'

This same figure is in focus in Daniel 9:24–27, the well-known passage relating to the 70 weeks of years that Daniel prophesied. There is still remaining one period of seven years to run in God's prophetic time-clock for Israel. The event that will initiate this final seven-year period is that which is specified; the Antichrist will make a seven-year covenant with the nation of Israel: 'He will confirm a covenant with many for one "seven" but in the middle of that "seven" he will put an end to sacrifice and offering (v. 27).' This latter event marks the starting point of the period of three-and-a-half years of the great tribulation, the Day of the Lord of the Hebrew prophets. The passage concludes by telling us of the Antichrist: 'And on a wing of the temple he will set up an abomination that causes desolation, until the end that is decreed is poured out on him.'

The warning of Jesus is specific: 'So when you see standing in the holy place "the abomination that causes desolation", spoken of through the prophet Daniel . . . then let those who are in Judea flee to the mountains . . . For then there will be great distress, unequalled from the beginning of the world until now – and never to be equalled again' (Mt 24:15–16, 21).

Speaking of the Antichrist, 2 Thessalonians 2:4 says: 'He sets himself up in God's temple, proclaiming himself to be God.' This event, break-ing His covenant made with Israel, will be the clear signal to the Jewish nation that their time of false security (for that is what it will have been) is over and that the final and intense period of Jacob's trouble, their last great persecution at the hands of the Gentile nations, is about to begin.

What are the purposes of the Day of the Lord?

1. To bring a great harvest of salvation from all nations into the kingdom of God (Rev 7:9–17).
2. To break the stubbornness of the nation of Israel against God (Dan 12:5–7). This will come about through the severity of the judgement upon her, followed by the national restoration of the surviving repentant remnant.
3. To deal with the sin of the Gentile nations, of which Babylon in Isaiah 13:9–13 is a representative example (and see also Isaiah 2:10–21).
4. To usher in the millennial kingdom, with Jesus on the throne in Jerusalem (Ps 2; Obad 21; Mic 4:1–5; 5:3–5, 7–9; Zeph 3:14–17; Zech 14:9–11, 16–21; Rev 11:15–18; 20:4–6). Appropriately, the book of Obadiah closes his prophecy concerning the Day of the Lord with the simple statement: 'And the kingdom will be the Lord's.'

THE ROAD TO THE HOLOCAUST

A Brief Survey of the History of Christian Antisemitism

Derek White

January 2005 marked the sixtieth anniversary of the liberation of Auschwitz and the national observation of 'Holocaust Memorial Day'. It is therefore appropriate to address the connection of historic Christian attitudes to the Jews with the horror of the Holocaust when, during the Second World War, some 6 million Jews – men, women and children – perished in the extermination camps of Nazi–occupied Europe, in what Hitler called 'the final solution of the Jewish problem'.

The pages of this dark period are stained not only with the inhuman actions of the immediate Nazi perpetrators, but with the apathy of the free world, who, by almost total failure to speak and act on behalf of the Jews of Europe, gave Hitler a free hand to pursue his diabolical plan. The free Western nations, including the USA and Britain, stand guilty in silent acquiescence. Asking the reasons for this silence, the *Jerusalem Post* commented on the prevailing belief both in London and Washington that saving millions of Jews was not a desirable war aim, combined with genuine doubts about Jewish veracity.[1]

Britain carries a full share of responsibility through the indifference of the British Foreign Office to the information received from Occupied Europe. 'Why should the Jews be spared distress and humiliation when they have earned it?' reads one Foreign Office minute. And another: 'In my opinion, a disproportionate amount of the time of the Office is wasted on dealing with these wailing Jews.' And another: 'What is disturbing is the apparent readiness of the new Colonial Secretary to take Jewish Agency "sob–stuff" at its face value.'[2]

It is not generally appreciated to what extent the ground for the

Holocaust was prepared by the Christian church, so that a major portion of guilt must be apportioned to long–standing and deep–rooted Christian attitudes to the Jewish people. The history of nearly 19 centuries of Christian antisemitism is a black stain on the record of the Christian church, although recognised by very few, and without it the Holocaust might conceivably have never taken place.

Christ-Killers?

The kernel of Christian antisemitism is historically the charge of 'deicide' or 'God-killing' – that the Jews crucified and killed Christ. Let it be said at the outset that the gospels in no way allow this charge to be brought against the Jewish people. The synoptic Gospel records (Matthew, Mark, Luke) show without any shadow of doubt that the Jewish people in general did not assent to the crucifixion, but rather that the political manoeuvrings of the religious leaders (chief priests and elders) were delayed by the popular acceptance of Jesus (Mt 21:46; Mk 11:18; 12:12; 14:2; Lk 19:47–48; 22:2).

Jesus' arrest and subsequent death was engineered by the religious leaders only with the support of an incited rabble (Mt 26:47, 59–62; 27:20), who also formed a majority of those present at the trial and who replied with the fateful words: 'His blood be on us and on our children' (Mt 27:25).

Concerning the high priest, a Jewish scholar states that, in addition to being an ignorant man and a Sadducee heretic, he was the appointee of Roman power – for not only did the Romans give the high priest power, they actually selected him and appointed him to office. Thus the high priest who handed Jesus over to the Romans, fearing that His activities would offend the Roman occupying officials, was not acting on behalf of Jewish religion, which he did not represent, but in his capacity as a Roman-appointed police chief (Jn 11:48).[3]

Peter, in his sermon on the Day of Pentecost, summed up the situation in these words: 'And now, brothers, I know that you acted in ignorance, as did your leaders', and this was confirmed by the massive response among his Jewish hearers to his preaching (Acts 3:17).

The idea that the Jews crucified Christ, murdered the Saviour, killed God, took root like a cancer in the early Christian centuries and has persisted until almost the present day, being the pretext for every form of pillage, humiliation, murder and pogrom. It soon became common belief that the whole Jewish people were guilty of the death of Christ, for all time, and that they and their children's children to the last generation were condemned by God to a life of misery and degradation. It became easy to spill Jewish blood on the pretext that the perpetrators were carrying out the will of God.

It may be noted that opinions differ as to whether or not antisemitism as such existed in the church during the first three centuries. What, however, is ominous is the emergence of a teaching clearly enunciated in St Hippolytus and Origen, that the Jews are a people punished for their deicide who can never hope to escape their misfortunes – a teaching that greatly contributed to the course of antisemitism from the fourth century onwards. Thus Origen (185–254) stated: 'We say with confidence that they will never be restored to their former condition. For they committed a crime of the most unhallowed kind, in conspiring against the Saviour of the human race . . .'[4]

We should note that the growth of Christian antisemitism is closely linked with the development of the theology of replacement.

Early Christian writings

A survey of Christian writings, as reflecting then current preaching and teaching down the centuries, is a sufficient testimony to the scope and nature of these hostile Christian attitudes, and when the power of the church is taken into account during centuries of 'Christian Europe', their influence on the beliefs and behaviour of the masses can be understood.

One of the earliest was Justin, surnamed the Martyr (100–c. 165), described as 'one of the earliest and most distinguished apologists of the Christian Church'.[5] In his *Dialogue with Trypho* the record of an actual discussion with a rabbi, he wrote:

> 'You hate and (whenever you have the power) you kill us.' Justin was the first to give voice to the theme that Jewish misfortunes are the consequence of divine punishment for the death of Christ. 'Tribulations were justly imposed upon you, for you have murdered the Just One.' Justin further insisted that

the scriptures and promises were now no longer the property of the Jews, but were now the property of the church.[6]

The nature of such early Christian preaching and writing is illustrated by the language of St John Chrysostom (CE 347–407) 'the Golden-Mouthed', one of the greatest of the church fathers, whom Cardinal Newman described as 'a sensitive heart, a temperament open to emotion and impulse; and all this elevated, refined, transformed by the touch of heaven – such was St John Chrysostom'.[7] The chief venting of his ire was six sermons delivered in his see of Antioch, where Jews were numerous and influential and where, apparently, some of his flock were frequenting synagogues and Jewish homes. 'The synagogue,' he said, 'is worse than a brothel . . . it is the den of scoundrels and the repair of wild beasts . . . the temple of demons devoted to idolatrous cults . . . the refuge of brigands and debauchees, and the cavern of devils.' 'Whatever name even more horrible could be found, will never be worse than the synagogue deserves.' 'As for me, I hate the synagogue . . . I hate the Jews for the same reason.'[8] He was the first Christian preacher to publicly accuse the Jewish people of 'deicide': 'The Jews have assassinated the Son of God! How dare you take part in their festivals? . . . You dare to associate with this nation of assassins and hangmen! . . . O Jewish people! A man crucified by your hands has been stronger than you and has destroyed you and scattered you.'[9]

He taught that they were hated of God: 'Why then did He rob you? Is it not obvious that it was because He hated you, and rejected you once for all?'[10] On the strength of Psalm 106:37 he said in CE 387 that the Jews:

sacrificed their sons and daughters to devils; they outraged nature; and over-threw from their foundations the laws of relationship. They are become worse than the wild beasts, and for no reason at all, with their own hands they murder their own offspring, to worship the avenging devils who are the foes of our life. The synagogues of the Jews are the homes of idolatry and devils. The Jews do not worship God but devils, so that all their feasts are unclean. God hates them, and indeed has always hated them. It was of set purpose that He concentrated all their worship in Jerusalem that He might more readily destroy it. It is childish in the face of their absolute rejection to imagine that God will ever allow the Jews to rebuild their Temple or return to Jerusalem. When it is clear that God hates them, it is the duty of Christians to hate them too.[11]

These three words of St John Chrysostom, 'God hates you', have echoed down the centuries in the ears of both Christians and Jews.

Jerome (345–420), universally regarded as the most learned and eloquent of the Latin church fathers, said: 'There could never be expiation for the Jews . . . God had always hated them.' He called it incumbent on all Christians to hate the Jews who, he said, 'were assassins of Christ, and worshippers of the devil'.[12]

St Augustine (354–439), a contemporary of Chrysostom, wrote: 'The Jews held him; the Jews insulted him, the Jews bound him, they crowned him with thorns, dishonoured him by spitting upon him, they scourged him, they heaped abuses upon him, they hung him upon a tree, they pierced him with a lance.'[13]

To these could be added Cyprian, Eusebius, Hippolytus, St Gregory of Nyssa, St Agobard (Archbishop of Lyons), Pope Gregory VII, as well as others, and all these set the tone for the church's attitude for centuries to come. It is not true to say that these men were not real Christians. One certainly cannot say this of the early church fathers, nor Luther, nor countless others. The fact that they were, in part, victims of contemporary attitudes in no way excuses the deep wrong of their words.

Separation from the roots

Efforts to sever the church from her Jewish roots were unrelenting in church history, and a quotation from Constantine indicates the spirit of the Roman imperial church of the fourth century and onwards: 'We ought not therefore to have anything in common with the Jews, for the Saviour has shown us another way . . . In unanimously adopting this mode [Easter Sunday], we desire, dearest brothers, to separate ourselves from the detestable company of the Jews.'[14]

Such a severance has resulted in incalculable loss to sincere Christians and an impoverishment of their faith, and it has provided a door to serious misunderstandings and distortions of the Bible and its teaching.

The Crusades

To the average Christian, the Crusades of the eleventh century constitute a romantic chapter in the story of England and Europe, with such popular heroes as Godfrey de Bouillon and Richard the Lion-Hearted. Unhappily the Crusades, carried out in the name of Christ and His church, were for the Jewish people a blood-drenched episode in their history, resulting in the slaughter of countless thousands of Jews. Wherever the Crusaders came, from the Rhine to the Holy Land, they bathed the ground with Jewish blood. Surely one of the strangest anomalies in Christian history was this setting forth of thousands of Christians to deliver the sepulchre of the Jewish Saviour with their hands stained with Jewish blood. Even the heroic knight Godfrey de Bouillon declared that he would avenge the blood of Jesus on that of the Jews.

The first Crusade began to move down the Rhine Valley in May 1096. The hordes were fired by such words as:

> We are marching a great distance to seek our sanctuary and to take vengeance on the Moslems. Lo and behold, there live among us Jews whose forefathers slew Jesus and crucified Him for no cause. Let us avenge ourselves on them first, and eliminate them from among the nations, so that the name of Israel no longer be remembered, or else let them be like ourselves and believe in the son of Mary.[15]

One chronicler, Guibert of Nogent (1053–1124), reported the Crusaders of Rouen as saying: 'We desire to combat the enemies of God in the East; but we have under our eyes the Jews, a race more inimical to God than all the others. We are doing this whole thing backwards.' Turning this logic into action, the Crusaders fell upon the Jews in Rouen and other places in Lorraine, massacring those who refused baptism.[16]

They fell upon the Jews of Germany, where by July 10,000 Jews had been slaughtered, and whole Jewish communities reduced to a memory. At Treves, women, having deliberately tied stones to themselves that they might sink, plunged from the bridge to save their honour and escape baptism. The survivors of the massacre fled to the bishop's palace as a place of refuge. They were received by the bishop Engelbert with the words: 'Wretches, your sins have come upon you; ye who have blas-phemed the Son of God and calumniated his Mother. This is the cause of your present miseries – this, if ye persist in your obduracy, will destroy you body and soul forever.' Some in despair accepted baptism as the price of life, but most refused to be 'defiled by the proud waters'. Fathers rather killed their wives and daughters, brother slew brother.[17]

Having thus plundered and killed in the Rhine Valley they entered Bohemia, where they wiped out the Jewish community of Prague. On 15 July 1099, after a siege of five weeks, the Crusaders entered Jerusalem. Maddened by their victory they rushed through the streets and into the houses and mosques killing all they met – men, women and children alike. A band of Crusaders forced an entry into the al-Aqsa mosque and slew everyone.

No one can say how many victims perished, but 70,000 Muslims were slaughtered. The Jews fled in a body to their chief synagogue, but no mercy was shown to them. The building was set on fire and they were burned alive.[18] Then, in the words of a chronicler: 'sobbing with an excess of joy and embracing one another with joy and release, the Crusaders rushed to the Church of the Holy Sepulchre where they folded their blood–stained hands in prayers of thanksgiving'.[19]

The second Crusade (1146–7) brought the same sufferings as the first. Peter the Venerable, the influential abbot of the French monastery of Cluny, wrote an angry letter to the French king Louis VII urging him to punish the Jews because 'they defile Christ and Christianity'. He con-tinued: 'I do not require you to put to death these accursed beings . . . God does not wish to annihilate them; but like Cain the fratricide, they must be made to suffer fearful torments and be preserved for greater ignominy, for an existence more bitter than death.'[20]

There was one notable exception in this tide of murder in the person of St Bernard of Clairvaux.[21] Despite his repeating those sentiments concerning the Jews current at his time, during the second Crusade he wrote many letters in defence of the Jews. R. Joseph ben Meir records in his *Chronicles*:

The Lord heard their cry, and remembered His Covenant . . . and He sent . . . the Abbot St Bernard of Clairvaux (who said): 'Come, let us go up unto Zion, to the sepulchre of their Messiah; but take ye heed that ye speak to the

Jews neither good nor bad; for whoever toucheth them is like as if he touched the apple of the eye of Jesus; for they are His flesh and His bone.'[22]

Sadly, however, St Bernard also preached sermons almost as provocative as those of St John Chrysostom: 'You see, O Jew, that I am milder than your own prophet, I have compared you to the brute beasts; but he sets you even below these', and 'O evil seed . . . whence hast thou these figs crude and coarse? . . . For war was their business, wealth their whole craving, the letter of the Law the only nurture of their bloated minds, and great herds of cattle, bloodily slaughtered, their form of worship.'[23]

The trail of Jewish suffering and ruin ran on through the second and third Crusades, and all was done 'in the name of Christ and in the sign of the cross'. When the Crusaders arrived in the Holy Land there were 300,000 Jews living there. When Benjamin of Tudela, a Spanish Jew, visited the Holy Land in CE 1169, he found only some 1,000 Jewish families still alive.

The blood libel

About the time of the second Crusade the blood libel found its origin in the English city of Norwich in CE 1144. According to a contemporary Christian document: 'The Jews of Norwich brought a child before Easter, and tortured him with all the tortures wherewith our Lord was tortured, and on Long Friday hanged him on a rod in hatred of our Lord, and afterwards buried him.'[24]

The horrifying lie, which claimed that Jews need Christian blood for their various religious rites, especially for the Passover matzot, first claimed its victims in the French city of Blois in May CE 1171, when about 40 Jews of the city were burned alive. Between the twelfth and fifteenth centuries Jews, and often whole Jewish communities, were put on trial on over 150 occasions for engaging in ritual murder. In almost every instance Jews were tortured and put to death. Historian Haim Hillel Ben-Sasson wrote: 'Generation after generation of Jews in Europe was tortured and Jewish communities were massacred or dispersed because of the libel.'

The blood libel in fact persisted into the twentieth century. In central Europe there were almost more examples of the accusation between

1880 and 1945 than in the whole of the Middle Ages.[25] An instance is recorded as recently as 1928 in New York State, and in the Polish town of Kielce in July 1948 when 42 Jews were murdered – and the blood libel was used by the Nazis for anti-Jewish propaganda.[26] Although common coinage in the Islamic world, a recent blood libel was in 1993 when Prada accused the Lubavitch of ritually sacrificing two members of the Orthodox novitiate. Some time later the accusation was rebutted in Isvestia.

The Inquisition

The period of the Inquisition in the fifteenth and sixteenth centuries brought further horrors. Most Christians remember the Inquisition for the many true Christian believers who were tortured or burned to death. What many do not know is that hundreds of thousands of Jews died equally terrible deaths at the hand of the inquisitors – 'in the name of Christ and in the sign of the cross' – and whole Jewish communities were destroyed.

So one could go on, mentioning the pogroms in Russia of the late nineteenth and early twentieth centuries, carried out to the age-old cry of 'Christ-killers', and often at Christmas or Easter.[27]

Martin Luther

For the evangelical Christian, it is a particular sorrow to recollect the words of Martin Luther towards the end of his life. In 1523 he had written:

> Popes, bishops, sophists, monks and other fools treated Jews like dogs. They were called names and had their belongings stolen. Yet they are blood-brothers and cousins of the Saviour. No other people have been singled out by God as they have; they have been entrusted with His Holy Word.

Luther, however, was disappointed that the Jews made little response to his evangelistic overtures, and in 1543 he published a pamphlet entitled 'On the Jews and their Lies' in which he wrote: 'Doubt not, beloved in Christ, that after the Devil you have no more bitter, venomous, violent enemy, than the real Jew, the Jew in earnest in his belief.'

He set out 'his honest advice' as to how Jews should be treated:

First, their synagogues or churches should be set on fire, and whatever does not burn up should be covered or spread over with dirt so that no one may ever be able to see cinder or stone of it. And this ought to be done for the honour of God and of Christianity in order that God may see that we are Christians, and that we have not wittingly tolerated or approved of such public lying, cursing and blaspheming of His Son and His Christians.

Secondly, their homes should likewise be broken down and destroyed. For they perpetrate the same things there that they do in their synagogues. For this reason they ought to be put under one roof or in a stable, like gypsies, in order that they may realise that they are not masters in our land, as they boast, but miserable captives, as they complain of us incessantly before God with bitter wailing.

Thirdly, they should be deprived of their prayer books and Talmuds in which such idolatry, lies, cursing and blasphemy are taught.

Fourthly, their Rabbis must be forbidden under threat of death to teach any more.

Fifthly, passport and travelling privileges should be absolutely forbidden to the Jews. For they have no business in the rural districts since they are not nobles, nor officials, nor merchants, nor the like. Let them stay at home.

Sixthly, they ought to be stopped usury. All their cash and valuables of silver and gold ought to be taken from them and put aside for safekeeping. For this reason, as said before, everything that they possess, they stole and robbed from us through their usury, for they have no other means of support. This money should be used in the case (and in no other) where a Jew has honestly become a Christian, so that he may get for the time being one or two or three hundred florins, as the person may require. This, in order that he may start a business to support his poor wife and children, and the old and feeble. Such evilly-acquired money is cursed, unless, with God's blessing, it is put to some good and necessary use.

Seventhly, let the young and strong Jews and Jewesses be given the flail, the axe, the hoe and spade, the distaff and spindle, and let them earn their bread by the sweat of their noses as is enjoined upon Adam's children. For it is not proper that they should want us cursed *Goyim* to work in the sweat of our brow and that they, pious crew, idle away their days at the fireside in laziness, feasting and display. And in addition to this, they boast impiously that they have become masters of the Christians at our expense. We ought to drive the rascally lazy bones out of our system.

If, however, we are afraid that they might harm us personally, or our wives, children, servants, cattle, etc. when they serve us or work for us – since it is surely to be presumed that such noble lords of the world and poisonous bitter worms are not accustomed to any work and would very unwillingly humble themselves to such a degree among the cursed *Goyim* – then let us apply the same cleverness (expulsion) as the other nations, such as France, Spain, Bohemia, etc. and settle with them for that which they have extorted usuriously from us, and after having divided it up fairly, let us drive them out of the country for all time. For, as has been said, God's rage is so great against them that they only become worse and worse through mild mercy, and not much better through severe mercy. Therefore away with them.

To sum up, dear princes and nobles who have Jews in your domains, if this advice of mine does not suit you, then find a better one so that you and we may all be free of this insufferable devilish burden – the Jews.[28]

The Holocaust

The Holocaust stands out as the most horrific expression of anti-semitism, possibly of all recorded history. This systematic attempt to destroy all European Jewry began in the last week of June 1941, and continued without respite for nearly four years.

At its height, during the autumn of 1941 and again in the summer of 1942, many thousands of Jews were killed every day, and by the time Nazi Germany had been defeated, as many as 6 million of Europe's 8 million Jews had been slaughtered. It is impossible to grasp the magnitude of this event. Perhaps one can only appreciate something of it by isolated cameos which to a degree represent the whole.

Treblinka was one of the Nazi death camps deep in the heart of the Polish countryside. It is recorded that some 800,000 (others say 1 million) were exterminated in Treblinka over a period of 13 months between July 1942 and August 1943. In one month in the summer of 1942, 300,000 Jews died. At its peak Treblinka was killing 15,000 people a day. It took only 50 Germans, 150 Ukrainians and just over 1,000 Jewish prisoners to accomplish it.

Treblinka railway station, where Jews from all over Europe disembarked, was made to look like an ordinary railway station, complete with a uniformed ticket collector, a left luggage room, the façade of a restaurant, timetables, and even a station clock (with painted hands).

Deceptions continued all the way to the camp, with false shop-fronts, a little zoo and a final street sign announcing 'TO THE GHETTO', although this was in fact the road to the gas chambers.

At the entrance to the gas chambers was a small booth in which a 'cashier', guarded by SS men and Ukrainians, demanded all money and valuables. The transfer from the 'cashier's' booth to the place of execution took six to seven minutes. The final bizarre deception arrived when the naked, frightened people came face to face with an elegant stone building, in the style of an ancient temple with wide ornamental doors and all around flowers and potted plants. Above the doors was the single word 'BATHHOUSE'.

Beyond these doors lay the gas chamber, and all around, armed guards, ferocious dogs and pitiless SS men, driving human beings forward to their death. A thousand people at a time were driven into the gas chamber. After execution, seven 'dentists' extracted teeth with gold fillings and then the bodies were thrown into enormous pits – the furnaces of Treblinka.

The whole process, from the arrival of the train to the remains being hurled into the pit, took less than two hours and most of the victims never fully realised where they were or what was happening until it was too late.

According to one account, 'the pyres of dead bodies burned by day and night. The smoke that rose from the chimneys of dozens of crematoria could be seen over the entire district. Human dust settled down on the entire area, and the death factory never ceased its work even for a single day.'

The sadism in Treblinka did not cease even in the brief hours that elapsed between arrival and death. The same account tells of one of the Nazis who lived in the camp together with his family: 'It was this man's habit to murder a few Jews before his meals, otherwise he could not sit down at table. The *Untersturmer* Meuter and *Scharfuhrer* Fast used to amuse themselves by setting dogs on Jewish children.'[29]

Treblinka was but one of many similar camps scattered throughout greater Germany and German-dominated Europe, including names such as Dachau, Buchenwald, Ravensbruck, Sobibor and Auschwitz. The atrocities committed by the German armies as they advanced throughout Russia are another horrific story. Hitler had launched his attack on the Soviet Union in June 1941. As the German army advanced, special killing squads – *Einsatzgruppen* or strike commandos – massacred the Jews in every town and village. For more than a year these killings continued, diligently accounted for in report after report, in every village of Lithuania, eastern Poland and western Russia. It is recorded that more than 90 per cent of the Jews of these areas were killed, a total of 1,400,000 people.

Adolf Eichmann himself inspected the *Einsatzgruppen* at work. At his trial in Jerusalem in 1961 he told the court how, near Minsk, he had seen the young troopers shooting into a pit already full of writhing bodies. 'I can still see', he said in his interrogation, 'a woman with child. She was shot and then the baby in her arms.'[30]

Later that year (1941) Eichmann formulated the Nazi 'Final Solution'. Heydrich explained, from a draft memo prepared by Eichmann, 'in the course of the practical implementation of the final solution, Europe will be combed from east to west'. It was intended, according to the statistics that had been prepared by Eichmann for the Waldsee Conference, that a total of 11 million Jews should 'fall away', including those of countries yet to be conquered, including Britain, Ireland, Spain and Portugal.[31]

It must be asked: how could a cultured and Protestant nation such as Germany be corporately involved in such a crime? It is sometimes urged that the initiative lay with Hitler and his immediate associates. The explanation has been offered that 'we fell under Hitler's spell' and 'we acted under orders'. Indeed Hitler and his immediate associates do carry a major responsibility for this darkest stain in Germany's history as a nation. Yet it has been shown as a result of recent studies that in fact Hitler gave relatively few explicit orders for the carrying out of his schemes, and left very wide scope to the initiative and interpretation of his subordinates. Although he sanctioned the policies and actions of his subordinates, these were not necessarily the result of his direct instructions.

In 1932 a majority of Germans knowingly voted for parties committed to the overthrow of German democracy.[32] The fact of the matter is that ordinary Germans, as well as other nationalities, were the agents of the demeaning and later wholesale murder of the Jews of Europe.

The testimonies of more than 50 eye witnesses, many of whom were committed Nazis . . . confirm that there was massive collaboration with the Nazi regime, both at home and on the war fronts, and that the terrible atrocities in the east were the work not just of elite killing squads but also of ordinary German soldiers and of local civilian populations.[33]

A recent author similarly presents the thesis that the Holocaust was as much a product of the antisemitism of the average German as it was of a Nazi blueprint for genocide.[34] The Holocaust did not come about out of the blue. The way had been prepared by centuries of anti-Jewish attitudes, mainly from 'the church', and sadly it seems that the words of Luther provided the final preparation for Hitler's hatred of the Jews to find acceptance in the heart of the German nation.

Hans Kung, a Swiss-born theologian who went through World War II as a teenager, wrote in 1974: 'The mass murder of Jews by the Nazis was the work of godless criminals, but without the almost 2,000-year history of Christian antisemitism . . . it would have been impossible.'

> The killing of the Jews in the twentieth century was the final result of a tradition of denigration and rejection of Jews and Judaism dating from early in Christian history, which also tried to strip Jesus of his Jewishness to produce a home-made God and Saviour, a Gentile hero.[35]

Hitler was appointed Chancellor of the Third Reich on 30 January 1933. In April 1933, following his decision to establish concentration camps and to boycott Jewish shops, Hitler said to Cardinal Faulhaber: 'I am only doing what the Church itself has been preaching and practising against the Jews.' He repeated this in a conversation with Bishop Berning and Msgr Steinman, Berlin's Vicar-General, on 26 April 1933, shortly before signing the Concordat between the Vatican and the Third Reich on 20 July the same year. It was when signing this crowning achievement of 13 years' work by the man who was to become Pope Pius XII that Hitler acknowledged himself a Catholic.

A few years later, in 1938, in the presence of his legal adviser, Hans Frank, Hitler said: 'In the Gospels the Jews called out to Pilate when he refused to crucify Jesus: "His blood be upon us and upon our children's children." Perhaps I have to fulfil this curse.' It is no wonder that in his book *Mein Kampf* Hitler could write: 'I believe that I am today acting in accordance with the will of the Almighty Creator: by defending myself against the Jews, I am fighting for the work of the Lord.'[36]

When Julius Streicher in 1941 recommended 'the extermination of that people whose father is the devil' he was simply echoing the sentiments of Bernard of Clairvaux in the twelfth century when he had described the Jewish people as 'a race who had not God for their father, but were of the devil, and were murderers as he was a murderer from the beginning'.[37]

Passive support for Hitler's policies towards the Jews came from many sections of the church. During the Holocaust, M. D. Weissmandel, a Polish Jew, appealed for help to the Papal Ambassador, asking him to intervene on behalf of innocent Jews, especially children. He was told: 'There is no innocent blood of Jewish children in the world. All Jewish blood is guilty. You have to die. This is the punishment that has been awaiting you because of that sin' (namely the crucifixion of Jesus).[38]

The official attitude of the Protestant Church during this period was also by and large a matter of shame. On 17 December 1941 German Protestant church leaders published a statement on the position of Protestant Jews within the church:

> The National Socialist leadership of Germany has given irrefutable documentary proof that this world war was instigated by the Jews . . . As members of the German national community, the undersigned Protestant provincial churches and church leaders stand in the front line of this historic struggle which has made enemies of the Reich and the world. Even Martin Luther, from bitter experience, advocated stringent measures against the Jews and demanded their expulsion from Germany.
>
> From the crucifixion to this day the Jews have fought against Christendom or exploited and misrepresented it for their own ends. Baptism changes nothing in the racial separateness, national status, or biological character of the Jews. The task of any German Evangelical Church is to cultivate and promote the religious life of Germans. Christians who are Jewish by race have no place and no rights in this Church. The undersigned German Protestant churches and church leaders have therefore severed all links with Jewish Christians. We are determined not to tolerate any Jewish influence on German religious life.

Even as late as 1948 the German Evangelical Conference proclaimed: 'The terrible Jewish suffering in the Holocaust was a divine visitation and a call to the Jews to cease their rejection and ongoing crucifixion of Christ.'

Thankfully in 1980 this same conference was able to declare: 'Stricken, we confess the co-responsibility and guilt of German Christendom for the Holocaust . . . We believe in the permanent election of the Jewish people of God and understand that through Jesus Christ the Church is taken into the covenant of God with His people.'

Despite such welcome changes in attitude, can it nevertheless be any surprise to us that so many Jewish people regard Christians, the church and all attempts to preach the gospel of Jesus Christ to them with the deepest suspicion? Their history is etched deeply into their minds and hearts. So many today, either personally or in their immediate families, have suffered in the Holocaust, which is understandably seen by them as the final expression by a Protestant nation of centuries of Christian anti-semitism.

Elie Weisel, Holocaust survivor and Nobel Prize Winner said in 1996:

> You must understand why I feared Christians, why I had to change side-walks when I saw a priest and why I resent it when you say that the Holocaust is a problem for both of us. I say, 'No! The victims are my problem, the killers are yours.' I say, 'You must understand that the cross for you is a symbol of love and compassion; for us Jews it is a symbol of suffering and oppression.'

Lest it be objected that we today in the West no longer repeat the crude antisemitism of our forebears, let us face up to the fact that anti-Zionism – opposition to the restoration of the Jews to their Land and to the State of Israel – is also Jew-hatred. Moreover, the widespread Christian teaching that the Jews have forfeited their position as God's covenant people and have been replaced by the church as the 'new Israel' is of the same sort.

It may be that we no longer cry 'Christ-killers'. It is now 'Israel the aggressor'. Anti-Zionism is the new expression of antisemitism which has drawn thousands of sincere Christians, as well as non-Christians, into its snare.[39]

God's call to repentance

'In that day, when history shall be written in the light of truth, the people of Israel will be known not as Christ-killers, but as the Christ-bearers;

THE ROAD TO THE HOLOCAUST

not as the God-slayers, but as the God-bringers to the world.'

The Christian church is in deep need of repentance for its past, and sometimes present, attitudes. There is a great need for Christians everywhere to say to the Jewish people, 'We are sorry – please forgive us,' and to show the reality of that repentance by practical support and by standing alongside the Jewish people. Christians need to stand alongside Israel and pray for her. Christians need to do all in their power to prevent any new tide of antisemitism from rising or spreading. Christians must also accept and understand the deep-seated suspicions with which we are so easily viewed by Jewish people, as their history is etched so unmistakably into their hearts and minds, even their history of suffering at the hands of Christians. Perhaps then we might be able to humbly ask that the Jewish people at least consider reaching out in forgiveness towards us.

God's attitude to the Jewish people is declared clearly in the Scriptures:

> But Zion said, 'The Lord has forsaken me, the Lord has forgotten me.' 'Can a mother forget the baby at her breast and have no compassion on the child she has borne? Though she may forget, I will not forget you! See, I have engraved you on the palms of my hands; your walls are ever before me.' (Is 49:14–16)

> In all their distress he too was distressed, and the angel of his presence saved them. In his love and mercy he redeemed them; he lifted them up and carried them all the days of old. (Is 63:9)

Let our heart attitude be that of the God we profess to know and worship.

Sources of information

Brown, Michael L., *Our Hands are Stained with Blood* (Destiny Image, 1992).

Flannery, Edward H., *The Anguish of the Jews* (Paulist Press, 1985).

Gilbert, Martin, *Final Journey: The Fate of the Jews in Nazi Europe* (Allen & Unwin, 1979).

Guinness, Paul Grattan, *Hear, O Israel* (Vantage Press: New York, 1983).

76   ISRAEL: HIS PEOPLE, HIS LAND, HIS STORY

Hay, Malcolm, *The Roots of Christian Antisemitism* (Freedom Library
    Press: New York, 1981).

Passow, Meyer, *Five Great Dates* (WIZO: Israel).

Prager, Dennis and Joseph Telushkin, *Why the Jews?* (Simon & Schuster:
    New York, 1985).

Rees, Laurence, *The Nazis: A Warning from History* (BBC Books:
    London, 1997).

Notes

1. *Jerusalem Post,* 24 August 1993.
2. *The Listener,* 16 September 1982.
3. Hyam Maccoby, *Judaism in the First Century* (Sheldon Press, 1989),
    p. 8.
4. Edward H. Flannery, *The Anguish of the Jews* (Paulist Press, 1985),
    p. 41.
5. *Chambers Encyclopedia,* 1901.
6. Edward H. Flannery, *op.cit.*, pp. 35, 39–40.
7. *Historical Sketches*, II, 234, quoted in Malcolm Hay, *The Roots of
    Christian Antisemitism* (Freedom Library Press, 1981), chap. 1, p. 27.
8. *Ibid*, chap. 1, pp. 27–8.
9. *Ibid*, chap. 1. p. 30.
10. *Sixth Homily Against the Jews*, quoted in Malcolm Hay, *op.cit.*,
    chap. 1, p. 31.
11. Chrysostom, *Homilae Adversus Iudaeos*. A similar selection is given
    by Edward H. Flannery, *op.cit.*, pp. 50–52, 306; Marvin R. Wilson,
    Our Father Abraham (William B. Eerdmans Publishing Company &
    Center for Judaic–Christian Studies, 1989), p 95; Denis Prager and
    Joseph Telushkin, *Why the Jews?* (Simon & Schuster, 1985), p. 94.
12. Jerome revised the Latin New Testament in 382, and between 390
    and 405, while living in Bethlehem, made a new translation of the
    Old Testament into Latin from the Hebrew (the Vulgate).
13. Augustine, *The Creed,* 3:10, cited by Edward H. Flannery, *op.cit.*,
    pp. 52–53.
14. *Life of Constantine* 3.18–19.
15. Meyer Passow, *Five Great Dates* (WIZO, Israel), p. 8.
16. Edward H. Flannery, *op.cit.*, pp. 91–2.

17. Henry Hart Milman, Dean of St Paul's, *History of the Jews* (John Murray, 1866), Vol. 3, pp. 176–8.

18. Steven Runciman, *The First Crusade* (CUP, 1980), chp. 14; Malcolm Hay, *op.cit.*, chp. 2.

19. Passow, *op.cit.*, p.10; Edward H. Flannery, *op.cit.*, p. 92.

The crusaders took Jerusalem by assault on July 15 1099, after a siege of five weeks. No age or sex was spared; infants on the breast were pierced by the same blow with their mothers, who implored for mercy; even a multitude to the number of 10,000, who had surrendered themselves prisoners and were promised quarter, were butchered in cold blood by these ferocious conquerors. The streets of Jerusalem were covered with dead bodies; and the triumphant warriors, after every enemy was subdued and slaughtered, immediately turned themselves with sentiments of humiliation towards the (church of the) Holy Sepulchre!

They threw away their arms still streaming with blood: they advanced with reclined bodies, and naked feet and hands, to that sacred monument; they sang anthems to their Saviour, who had there purchased their salvation by his death and agony; and their devotion so overcame their fury, that they dissolved in tears, and bore the appearance of every soft and tender sentiment! (Abbe Vertot; Hume). Joseph Haydn, *Dictionary of Dates* (Edward Moxon, 1853), under 'Crusades'.

20. Edward H. Flannery, *op.cit.*, p. 94; Passow, *op.cit.*, p. 11.

21. Malcolm Hay, *op.cit.*, chp. 2.

22. Henry Hart Milman, *op.cit.*, p. 181.

23. Malcolm Hay, *op.cit.*, chp. 2.

24. Dennis Prager and Joseph Telushkin, *Why the Jews?* (Simon & Schuster, 1985), p. 98.

25. *Ibid*, p. 100.

26. See Edward H. Flannery, *op.cit.*, under 'Ritual Murder Accusations'; Henry Hart Milman, *op.cit.*, pp. 224–8.

27. See Edward H. Flannery, *op.cit.*, under 'Spanish Inquisition'.

28. *Encyclopedia Judaica*, article on 'Anti–Semitism'; Edward H. Flannery, *op.cit.*, pp. 152–4.

29. Martin Gilbert, *Final Journey: The Fate of the Jews in Nazi Europe* (Allen & Unwin, 1979), chp. 9, pp. 121–2.

30. *Ibid*, chp. 4, p. 62.

31. *Ibid*, p. 64.

32. Laurence Rees, *The Nazis: A Warning from History* (BBC Books,

1997).

33. *Ibid,* jacket cover.

34. Daniel Goldhagen, *Hitler's Willing Executioners: Ordinary Germans and the Holocaust.* Review by *The Times* 12 Jan 1998, p. 12.

35. *The Times,* 3 April 1985.

36. Adolf Hitler, *Mein Kampf* (Houghton Miflin, 1943), p. 65; quoted by Edward H. Flannery, *op.cit.,* p. 210.

37. Malcolm Hay, *op.cit.,* chp. 2.

38. Eliezer Berkovits, *Faith after the Holocaust* (Ktav, 1973), p. 19, quoted by Michael L. Brown, *Our Hands are Stained with Blood* (Destiny Image, 1992), p. 218.

39. See Edward H. Flannery, *op.cit.,* pp. 267–69.

SECTION II

Many misunderstandings and prejudices underpin anti-Israelism. Some are theological, but many owe their origins either to revisionist history or to simple assumptions arising from not being in possession of the facts. Media bias and 'sloganising' have malformed public opinion to the extent that Israel, rather than being a defender of a sovereign state, is viewed as an aggressor and opportunist state that illegally occupies land and keeps another people in captivity.

Tim Price opens the section with a challenge to Christians to develop an authentic hermeneutic concerning Israel in the purposes of God. It is essential to view history through a biblical lens, therefore this article precedes a most seminal article by the distinguished Professor Gerald Adler, who offers a legal view of Israel in the Land. The work presents the case elucidating the legal right(s) of Israel to be in their homeland and illustrates the muddled thinking of those opposed to their right to dwell in, and maintain, a sovereign state.

Geoffrey Smith picks up the theme, and in a clearly presented work discusses the role and responsibility of Christians regarding the quest for peace.

The section ends with a consideration of Just Peacemaking Theory, extracted from the forthcoming book *A War of Symbols* (F. Wright).

READING AND UNDERSTANDING SCRIPTURE
Towards a Biblical Hermeneutic of Israel

Tim Price

Israel is the stage upon which the drama of world redemption is played out, and the whole of Scripture needs to be interpreted through the story of that nation, and supremely through the one who came as its Servant and King. Today the church seems almost embarrassed by this story and the Jesus of (Jewish) history has been eclipsed by the Christ of faith, and detached from the Hebraic context which enables us to understand His person and work.

The way we read, understand and interpret Scripture significantly informs our theology, which in turn shapes the way we view any ongoing significance of Israel within the purposes of God. For 2,000 years of almost exclusive dominance by Gentiles, the church has treated the Jewish people with contempt, 'stolen her biblical clothes' and established a supremacist theology which has failed to recognise the aspirations of that faith community, and has alienated Jewish people from their own Messiah. In so doing, the church has forgotten its deep indebtedness to biblical Judaism, and indeed the fact that the Christian faith does not stand apart, but as a faith that is existentially rooted to that tradition through the person of Christ.

This essay will look at a number of issues that affect the way we read, understand and interpret Scripture in the light of the coming of Christ. It begins with the centrality of Christ for whom and about whom all the Scriptures were written.

The centrality of Christ

The prologue of John's Gospel begins with these authoritative words: 'In the beginning was the Word, and the Word was with God, and the Word was God. He was with God in the beginning' (Jn 1:1–2). Any discussion on how we read and interpret Scripture must begin with the assertion that all Scripture finds its focus in the one who came as the Word made flesh, as God in human form. The whole of Scripture pivots on the person of Christ and concerns the revelation and understanding of the one who came as the Word made flesh. The clear and unambiguous purpose of the Bible, then, is to lead us to Jesus Christ. The words of the Bible exist only to serve the 'Word made flesh'.

Augustine wrote: 'We ought to use Scripture, not with such a love and delight as if it was good to rest in, but with a transient feeling rather, such as we have towards the road or carriages, or other things that are merely the means.' The written word is simply the means God uses to bring us to the living Word.

Jesus said that the study of Scripture can become an aim in itself and miss the very goal for which it was written: 'You diligently study the Scriptures because you think that by them you possess eternal life. These are the Scriptures that testify about me, yet you refuse to come to me to have life' (Jn 5:39–40). In that wonderfully poignant conversation between Jesus and the two disciples on the road to Emmaus, Luke records: 'And beginning with Moses and all the Prophets, he explained to them what was said in all the Scriptures concerning himself' (Lk 24:27). The Scriptures exist for Jesus alone. In this and other passages Jesus is not speaking about the New Testament but the Hebrew Scriptures (Old Testament), the very Scriptures that informed the disciples of Jesus and enabled them to interpret Scripture in the light of His coming. These Scriptures shaped the theology of the emerging church, and in time led to the formulation of the canon of the New Testament. It was only subsequently that the New Testament Scripture was regarded as being equally authentic to that of the Old Testament.

What are the Scriptures?

But what are the Scriptures? For the writers of what became the New Testament, 'the Scriptures were simply the Scriptures'. In Hebrew they are known by the acronym *Tanach*, standing for *Torah* (Instruction), *Neviim* (Prophecy) and *Ketuvim* (Writings). These formed the Hebrew Scriptures, the Old Testament, and were the same Scriptures that Jesus was able to confidently endorse as being divine in origin: 'But he who sent me is reliable, and what I have heard from him I tell the world' (Jn 8:26) and: 'I gave them the words you gave me and they accepted them. They knew with certainty that I came from you' (Jn 17:8).

This has great significance for all who have not known Jesus during His earthly life, for it means we can have confidence that Jesus, who received the Father's own words, has faithfully transmitted them to His disciples, and through them to us. In turn, this is very important in authenticating the apostles' message concerning Jesus to those who had not known Him. It also authenticates their own words, for as Paul says: 'We are therefore Christ's ambassadors, as though God were making his appeal through us' (2 Cor 5:20). Although Jesus quotes relatively few passages from the Hebrew Scriptures during His ministry, what emerges is His utter confidence that these Scriptures originate in God, and when He speaks of people or actual events from these Scriptures, He is in no doubt that these people existed or that these events happened.

To Jesus the most important thing about the Scriptures is their divine origin and the fact that, although a number of writers have written these Scriptures, behind each of them stands the divine author. When Jesus says 'It is written', as He does on several occasions (not least in His confrontation with Satan during His temptations in the Judean wilderness), He is in no doubt that He is uttering words from God Himself.

This perspective was brought into the writings of Paul, who similarly saw the interchangeability between what Scripture says and what God says. So, picking up the theme that what the Father conveys to the Son will now be conveyed to His followers through the mediation of the Holy Spirit, Jesus tells His disciples that the Holy Spirit will guide them into all truth (Jn 16:12). Just as the Son expresses the words of the Father, so now the Holy Spirit will only express the words of the Son to the followers of Jesus who form the 'community of the Son'. In the

Upper Room, as He tells His followers what to expect after He has ascended to heaven, He implies that certain people will be given words by the Holy Spirit that are of divine origin and which bear equal status to Scripture, to the words uttered by the Father and the Son. This was a quite extraordinary development, yet complementary to the manner in which God spoke through imperfect human instruments to produce the Hebrew Scriptures.

Peter, speaking of the process by which prophetic Scripture was produced, says this: 'Above all, you must understand that no prophecy of Scripture came about by the prophet's own interpretation. For prophecy never had its origin in the will of man, but men spoke from God, as they were carried [literally bowled] along by the Holy Spirit' (2 Pet 1:20–21). The writers, though flawed men, were nevertheless caught up in the activity of the Holy Spirit to write Scripture that we can trust is from God. The point here is that the church recognised in the activity of the Holy Spirit that God was speaking still, and so Scripture was no longer to be regarded as simply the Hebrew Scriptures, because the ascended Jesus, as the appointed agent of the Father, was still speaking through the agency of the Holy Spirit.

The difference, then, between the two Testaments lies in the executor or agent. In the Hebrew Scriptures it is God the Father who mediates His word to humans through the Holy Spirit; in the New Testament, it is the Holy Spirit speaking only what the Son says, as the writer to the Hebrews records: 'In the past God spoke to our forefathers through the prophets at many times and in various ways, but in these last days he has spoken to us by his Son, whom he appointed heir of all things, and through whom he made the universe'(Heb 1:1–2).

The essential unity and integrity of Scripture

What is clear is that both Testaments are to be equally regarded as Scripture, and because of the unity of the Trinity, each Testament will reinforce the other. There can be no contradiction between the two without creating disunity in the Godhead and a dualistic approach to Scripture. This is very significant when many within the church would wish to set the two Testaments at variance with each other. The testimony of the centrality of Christ to Scripture is as much an Old

Testament concept as it clearly is in the New Testament. This can be illustrated through Jesus' adoption of the phrase 'Son of Man' as a title for Himself, which features significantly in both Testaments, especially in Daniel and throughout the Synoptic Gospels.

A recognition of the underlying unity of revelation between the two Testaments is essential if we are to counter the Islamic charge that Islam is the final revelation of God's will – a view which is largely based on the church's own theology of progressive revelation in which the church supersedes Israel within the revelatory purposes of God. The maintenance of a holistic understanding of the common revelation of the two Testaments is essential, to challenge the Islamic assertion that the Jewish faith was the initial revelation, the Christian faith the next and Islam the final and complete revelation.

One of the chief marks of acknowledging which texts should be regarded as authentic Scripture and so be included in the canon of the New Testament, was apostolicity – that is, whether the text was written by one of the apostles or someone close to them. Whether the apostles in the Upper Room realised it or not, it becomes clear that the promise Jesus made in John 16:12, 15 was directed specifically at them, and was laying the groundwork for more Scripture to be incorporated. It is clear that later New Testament writing began to show awareness of the implications of this promise, as Peter refers to Paul's letter as Scripture (2 Pet 3:16). In Thessalonians Paul tells his readers to: 'Thank God that when you received the Word of God that you heard from us, you accepted it not as human words, but as what it really is – God's words' (1 Thess 2:13).

So to conclude this section, we need to appreciate that both Testaments are to be viewed as Scripture, that they bear a common testimony to the centrality of Jesus and that there is a unity in God's revelation. This is important when many would wish to marginalise and diminish the Old Testament and to give a greater status to the New Testament, because it asserts more definitively the centrality of Christ. Both Testaments are vital to a full understanding of the purpose and mission of Christ, of Israel and of the Church.

Colin Chapman asserts in his book *Whose Promised Land?*: 'Everything must be read through the eyes of the Apostles. It is they who, so to speak, give us the right spectacles for a genuinely Christian reading of the Old Testament.' However, David Torrance in his review of this book in *Shalom* (Issue 6: 2002) says: 'This is true, and yet the opposite is equally the case. We can only properly understand the New Testament, Jesus and the Apostles, through the eyes of the Old Testament.'

Hebraic contour of Scripture

Part of the problem for Jewish people in recognising Jesus as their Messiah is the lack of a Hebraic contour within the Christian faith which might enable them to overcome their negative appraisal of the person of Jesus. This is the result of many years of hostility and oppression by the Church, which has not only annexed their Scriptures and allegorised much of them away, but which often required forcible conversion into the Christian faith. The Church in its arrogance has thus invalidated a major tool, the New Testament, which would enable the Jewish people to interpret for themselves their own Scriptures. It has made 'Christ' a name of such hatred and offence to Jewish people that they fail to recognise in Him their own Messiah.

The church has much to answer for, not only historically, but even now in its invalidation of any Jewish claim to Israel through the very covenants which were uniquely made with them. It is often compounded by a theology of replacement of Israel by the church, in which Christians continue to assert arrogantly that all that was once invested in Israel is now invested in the church – a view that is hardly likely to endear them to the Jewish community, or to make this community want to take a fresh perspective on the person of Jesus and the New Testament. The fact that they are doing so is an act of God's grace and faithfulness. Sadly, the reasons for this often cannot be attributed to the church, which for the most part seems hostile to sharing the gospel with Jewish people.

Scripture needs to be viewed in the light of both comings of Christ

The hermeneutic by which the Scriptures should be evaluated is complementary to the view expressed by David Torrance. They certainly must be seen in relation to the person and mission of Jesus, but must also be read and studied in the light of both comings of Christ. Without this hermeneutic, as we shall see shortly, many of the Hebrew Scriptures that speak of the regathering and restoration of Israel can be dismissed, if we interpret them either through the first coming alone or through the distorted lens of much Christian theology. It is perhaps because the church has fused both comings to such an extent that she now has no place for a literal interpretation of many of the prophetic Scriptures of the Old Testament, which only really make sense if they are applied literally to future events in history.

One of the main criticisms of Christian Zionism, especially the more extreme end, is its highly developed eschatology, which in the words of Dr Rowan Williams, the Archbishop of Canterbury, advocates an 'apocalyptic myth whose relation to Hebrew and Christian Scripture is tenuous' ('Holy Land and Holy People – International Sabeel Conference 2004'). The fact is that there is within Scripture the possibility of developing such an understanding, and more especially so if you move from the dominant position of the church in the way it reads Scripture. What the church has failed to do adequately is to wrestle with these texts. It is content simply to dismiss them or to give to them a spiritual or allegorical interpretation.

It can be said with some certainty that the Hebrew prophets wrote in the context of real history, yet their words have certainly been applied to events that happened at Christ's first coming. For example: 'The virgin will be with child and will give birth to a son, and will call him Immanuel' (Is 7:14) no doubt refers to the circumstances about which Isaiah was more immediately concerned, yet they are seen as being fulfilled supremely in the birth of Christ. Why then have other prophecies been disregarded as having a double or even triple application when applied to the circumstances surrounding the Second Coming of Christ? This is where it may be very helpful to engage with Jewish theologians in interpreting within their own tradition these prophetic passages from their Scriptures.

The question of whether the State of Israel, as currently expressed, is within the purposes of God is also a factor that affects the Jewish community worldwide. The fact that it is supported by many such communities, both from a religious and from a humanitarian perspective, is significant. Even for those who, from an Orthodox religious viewpoint, cannot accept the legitimacy of the present State of Israel, it should not be taken that they have no aspirations concerning the Land.

It is precisely because 'land' still remains significant and precious that they take the view that only the Messiah can reconstitute the State. Whatever way you approach it, the Land remains significant – a view which runs contrary to the dominant position of the church concerning the Jewish people and the Land.

As I have argued in my earlier chapter in this book, 'The Restoration of Israel and the Kingdom of God', God's faithfulness to Israel is not to the exclusion of justice to the Palestinians or indeed to any other ethnic groups within this troubled Land. Eventually we will see how both God's justice and His faithfulness come together in the outworking of His purposes for Israel and the nations.

However, for the present we need to consider further the way in which we view Scripture. Sadly the legacy of Greek dualistic thought has eclipsed the Hebraic and more holistic understanding of Scripture.

The central integrity of Scripture

It has been said that the one blank page between the Old and New Testaments has been the cause of many of the problems between Christians and Jews because it introduces a break in what should be viewed as a seamless whole in Scripture. As David Torrance writes in *Shalom*:

> The Word of God witnessed to in the Old and New Testaments, is one and must be interpreted as a whole. They together are the Word of God. A great deal of harm can be done by imagining that we can understand the New Testament simply as a progression from the Old, or on its own (as many Christians seem to want to do today). If we do, we tend to understand it in a Gentilised way and when, in the light of it, we turn to the Old Testament, we misunderstand it.

This separation is most unhelpful, as instead of seeing Scripture as an integral whole, we see it in two distinct parts, a Jewish part and a Christian part, whereas in fact both were written by and for a largely Jewish readership.

The simplest caricature that has developed is that the Old Testament is for Jews, the old people of God, and the New Testament for

Christians, the new people of God. This has led, in turn, to the various strands of the Judeo-Christian tradition and revelation being set at variance one with the other – Law/grace, spirit/nature, Israel/church. Instead of there being continuity and complementarity between the Testaments, they are set in opposition to and contradiction with one another. Our view of Scripture becomes distorted with a Plan A/Plan B mentality. Israel is cast as the failed people of God and the church the triumphant and victorious community of God. In so doing, it profoundly overlooks the interconnectedness between Israel and the church. The Old Covenant is seen simply as the precursor to the New Covenant. Old Israel is, if you like, seen merely as the instrument through which the New Israel, the church, emerges like the capsule from the discarded rocket from which it has been launched. The sad history of Jewish/Christian relationships demonstrates the travesty of such a restricted view of God's salvation purposes.

John Walvoord writes in his book *Major Prophecies Unfulfilled*:

> Though the entire Bible bears witness to a gracious, loving God, there is a sharp contrast between the basic revelation of the Old Testament compared to the New. This is captured in the simple statement of John 1:17: 'For the law was given through Moses, grace and truth came through Jesus Christ.' The Old Testament is not entirely law, nor is the New Testament entirely grace, but there is a broad contrast between the two.

While there is an element of truth in this statement, it is erroneous to say that with the coming of Christ, the Law no longer matters or indeed is defunct, either because grace supersedes the Law or because Christ has rendered it obsolete. Jesus Himself categorically denies this when He says that He has not come to abolish the Law but to fulfil it (Mt 5:17). Jesus personifies both Law and grace. His unseen presence is as much part of the Old Testament as His seen presence is in the New. Grace and Law are two sides of the same coin. If you really want to 'nit-pick', you could argue that grace precedes the Law by over 400 years or longer, especially if you include Noah or even Adam! Adam and Eve lived under the grace of God both before and after the Fall.

Grace, then, was as much an aspect of God's character in the Old Testament as it clearly is in the New. Similarly Christ does not abolish the Law, even though He brings a new clarity to certain parts as, for example, the separation of Jew from Gentile. Paul makes it clear that in respect of the law relating to separation, the law has been abolished through the person of Christ, who now brings together these two divided communities through His one flesh (Eph 2:14f.). However, other aspects of the Law still function. The word 'Law' here is drawn from the word 'Torah' (or instruction) and clearly this is a good thing (see Psalm 119). Indeed much of what Jesus commanded was oral law. He commended the Law. So when Paul states that 'Christ is the end of the law' (Rom 10:4), he is not meaning 'end' in a sense of it having been abolished, but being focused in the person of Christ. Christ fully embodies the Law, and through His person becomes the 'telos', the goal, the focus or even the purpose of the Law. Paul makes this clear when he says the role of the Law is to bring us to Christ, the one who perfectly keeps the Law. It is on this basis alone that any one of us can regard ourselves as being a 'Law-keeper', through the one who alone was able to keep Torah. The new humanity centres on Christ the Law-Keeper.

The emphasis, then, in each covenant is different. In the Old Testament, Israel is the dominant motif, with the Law central to revelation. The ecclesia arising from within Israel, the community called to live by faith, is secondary, hidden, mysterious but present, as the writer to Hebrews makes clear when he lists the great saints of the Old Covenant. Likewise, in the New Testament, although Israel is the theatre of God's operation, the emphasis is the Kingdom of God with the calling out of the ecclesia which now extends beyond the confines of ethnic Israel, to embrace all who receive Israel's Messiah. The ecclesia, then, is comprised of 'neither Jew nor [Gentile], slave nor free, male nor female' (Gal 3:28). It is this community of the Messiah that is entrusted with taking the kingdom. So when the leadership of Israel comes under Christ's judgement in the Parable of the Wicked Tenants (Lk 20), what is taken from Israel is her exclusive claim to the kingdom, now to be given to another, who will bear the fruits of repentance. This is an indictment on Israel's leadership, and not an annulment of God's covenant with Israel as a nation. Individuals are fully entitled to enter and participate as the ecclesia in the kingdom being formed around Israel's Messiah. In its earliest years the ecclesia remained exclusively Jewish until the conversion of Cornelius and the incorporation of Gentiles into the messianic community.

Who and what is Israel?

It could be argued that the definition of what it means to be a true Israelite, a true Jew, has been extended and transformed beyond purely physical descent to Abraham, although not to the exclusion of those of such physical descent. Paul makes it crystal clear in his exposition of God's ongoing plan for the Jewish people in Romans chapters 9–11 that to be a child of God is no longer merely by natural descent from Abraham, but descent is traced through Isaac, the child of promise (Rom 9:7). The genuine people of God, the true Israel, are comprised of those who are called out as children of promise, spiritual descendants of Isaac, which although substantially from the Israelite community in the Hebrew Scriptures was never exclusively so. However, now, in Christ, all who believe are declared to be children of the promise, whether ethnic Jews or Gentiles. Again, just as Israel could be classified as 'according to the flesh' and 'according to the promise', so the church as a totality comprises both those who are nominal believers and those true believers who form the true ecclesia of God.

Just as it could be said that there is an 'Israel according to the flesh' (that is, the physical descendants of Abraham through the line of Isaac and Jacob), so there is a 'spiritual Israel' (who are the heirs of the promise and grafted into the true Israel, who also are the genuine ecclesia). It is Jesus as Messiah of Israel who brings together in His body both Jews and Gentiles. 'Israel', then, has a number of meanings which have a bearing when we seek to understand the ongoing purposes of a national Israel. On one level we have Israel 'according to the Spirit', which could also be called the true ecclesia of God, and we have Israel 'according to the flesh', ethnic or national Israel: those who trace their physical line of descent from the Patriarchs. In Romans 9–11 both levels are referred to, and we need to understand which is meant through the context of the text itself.

This hermeneutic is often not pursued when Christians disagree over the restoration of Israel, since many are very happy to be included in spiritual Israel, but far from happy that this may also involve a repentant national Israel being grafted in once more to its own Olive Tree as part of a spiritual Israel. The true ecclesia of God, then, comprises all the Old and New Testament saints of God and all who are grafted into Israel's

Olive Tree, a metaphor for Jesus Himself. It could be argued that the church is only truly the church when it reflects its Jewish Messiah, and where it truly becomes the one new humanity, Jew and Gentile, as distinctive expressions of its life. A church without any Jewish contour to it is not the church; similarly the church without Gentiles cannot be the church. It could be argued that much of the church has been in apostasy since the Council of Nicaea and subsequent ecumenical councils, when all Jewish expression was declared anathema.

The metaphor of Israel

We cannot interpret Scripture unless we interpret it through the metaphor of Israel. It could be argued that both canons of Scripture concern this one nation. Indeed without the Jews there would have been no transmission of the word of God. Ultimately every book in our Bible, with the possible exception of Luke, was written, through the direction of the Holy Spirit, by Jews. The roots of Christian belief have their origin in the Old Testament and can only rightly be interpreted through the outworking of God's purposes through Israel. The Holy Scriptures were written by Jewish prophets, evangelists and apostles under the inspiration of the Holy Spirit. The Bible is a Jewish book about a Jewish people and a Jewish Messiah who brings salvation to the Jew first and then to the nations. The Scriptures maintain throughout the missiological priority that the gospel is 'first for the Jew, then for the Gentile' (Rom 1:16). It is a nonsense that the Christian faith stands apart from its Jewish context. Take away its Jewish roots and it has nothing. As Paul reminds the Gentile followers of Jesus: 'You do not support the root, but the root supports you' (Rom 11:18).

The Vine

In Psalm 80 the psalmist addresses the Lord as 'the Shepherd of Israel'. It is one of the many uses of shepherd imagery in relation to God's care and protection of Israel. Indeed it is one of the many Old Testament images that Jesus takes to Himself when He says: 'I am the good shepherd' (Jn 10:11). Here we see Jesus deliberately linking the divine name of Yahweh, 'L'Adoni Roi', to Himself and thus saying that He is the true Shepherd of Israel.

In one of the other 'I am' sayings, Jesus makes a powerful link between Himself and Israel. In saying: 'I am the true vine'(Jn 15:1), Jesus draws on another powerful metaphor that would resonate with the Jewish people who heard His teaching. The vine is the image the psalmist adopts later in Psalm 80 when he addresses God as 'Shepherd of Israel' and says: 'You brought a vine out of Egypt; you drove out the nations and planted it' (Ps 80:8). Here we see a picture of God as vine-dresser, the one who enabled Israel to be established in Egypt, and subsequently uprooted and transplanted the nation to Canaan. The linkage between Israel and Jesus is made even more striking when we see that one of the prophecies speaks of God 'calling his Son out of Egypt'. God first sends His Son to Egypt, then uproots Him and plants Him back in Israel where, like the vine, He grows, matures and bears fruit for God's kingdom purpose for Israel. He becomes the embodiment of Israel as the vine. So although Israel continues to exist physically as a nation, its callings and attributes are, if you like, transferred to Jesus, Israel's Messiah. Jesus is not only a son of Israel, He is, as we have seen, in every respect 'Israel'. He incorporates every aspect of what Israel means within His person.

When Israel's leaders are held to account for their rejection of Jesus in the Parable of the Unfit Stewards, Jesus makes clear that one aspect of Israel's calling, her calling to bring in God's kingdom, is no longer invested in the physical nation as such, but in its Messiah, around whom the kingdom will grow and expand not only to incorporate Israel, but eventually all the nations. National Israel, in rejecting her King, also rejected her calling to bring in the kingdom, and that task was then entrusted to all who followed Israel's Messiah regardless of ethnicity. Although Jewish people were not excluded from the kingdom, Israel as a nation no longer enjoyed sole prerogative to the kingdom. Yet even in the Old Testament, Israel had never had the monopoly entirely, as Hebrews makes clear when it cites the many saints of the Old Covenant, who clearly, by their faith, were within the kingdom, if only in an anticipatory sense until the coming of the Messiah.

No wonder Jesus says that those who came after John the Baptist, the last of the Old Testament prophets, were even greater than he in the kingdom of God. The ecclesia which was part of Israel under the Old Covenant would be radically transformed under the New Covenant in the Messiah.

It was because Jesus fully embodied Israel and indeed the kingdom, and through His obedient death for the destruction of sin, that the wall of enmity which had once divided Jew from Gentile (Eph 2:14), and indeed Israel from the nations, had been broken down and the two made one in the Messiah. It is Jesus who truly brings reconciliation, through taking upon Himself the enmity and hostility of two opposing groups. However, supremely He fulfils Israel's calling to be a light to the nations.

Despite this reconciliation, both Jew and Gentile remain distinct identities, as do Israel and the nations. How else could the Jewish people have maintained a national identity throughout nearly 2,000 years of dispersion, and against great pressure to assimilate or be destroyed? How else can we explain the extraordinary restoration of Israel, except by the faithfulness of God to His covenant people, and to the irrevocability of Israel's call and gifting (Rom 11:29)?

What the New Testament does is extend the mission of Israel to be a light to the nations, through the one whom Simeon greets in the Temple with these words: 'Sovereign Lord, as you have promised, you now dismiss your servant in peace. For my eyes have seen your salvation, which you have prepared in the sight of all people, a light for revelation to the Gentiles and for glory to your people Israel' (Lk 2:29–32).

Israel and the church

The New Testament simply will not allow us to do away with Israel as a nation. Jesus is both a light to Gentiles and the glory of His people Israel; He is Saviour of the world but remains Israel's Messiah and King. While there can be an acceptable theology which allows Gentiles to be Israel after the Spirit, this is not at the expense of displacing and removing Israel according to the flesh. We have to read the New Testament with that perspective or else we shall go the way much of the church has followed in denying any ongoing need for ethnic Israel.

The major thrust of St Paul's teaching in much of Romans, but more especially in Romans 9–11, is to stress that it is not ethnic Israel that is now grafted into the church, but the Gentile believers who are grafted into Israel. Although we may argue as to what that means, the point is that the Gentiles are grafted into Israel, and not Jewish people into the church. In these chapters Paul again uses the powerful image of Israel as an olive tree, to drive home the point that the Gentile church does not stand apart from Israel, but is deeply and intrinsically linked to her. We need to remember that it is those who are non-Jewish who are the wild olive branch that has been grafted into Israel. Although some natural branches were broken off so that Gentiles could be grafted in, this does not mean that ethnic Israel has for ever forfeited her right to be grafted back in again. Indeed, as Paul makes clear in Romans 11, it is a far easier task to graft back natural branches than it is to graft in something that is contrary to nature. Where is, then, that sense of recognition and gratitude to ethnic Israel by the Gentile church, which even today finds it hard to be charitable to the Jewish people or to recognise in her restoration the faithfulness of God?

The fact that we can lay claim to the rich spiritual heritage that belongs by right to Israel should not be a source of pride and arrogance, but should create within us a humility that the Holy Spirit has 'granted even the Gentiles repentance' (Acts 11:18), and that we can be included in the kingdom of God as joint heirs with Israel, not in place of Israel.

Jesus as representative Israel

In summary, the kingdom, then, is not divorced from Israel, as many Christians seem to believe, but it finds its focus in the one who fully represents Israel, her Messiah Jesus. Jesus Himself makes clear that the Law, the heart of the Old Covenant, is not done away with, for He has come not to abolish but to fulfil the Law. The only true Israelite who has fully kept the Law becomes the cornerstone for the whole people of God and inaugurates the New Covenant which is centred in Himself. Yet as Tom Torrance writes:

> Ultimately, of course, the salvation and renewing of mankind depend on the reconciling and resurrecting power of Christ himself; but if the actual unification of world humanity is to come about, it must involve at its very centre the reconciliation of Jew and Gentile in Jesus Christ. And how is this to take place except through the vicarious role which, precisely because God's covenant with Israel is not annulled, remains very much in force? ('The Divine Vocation and Destiny of Israel in World History' from *The Witness of the Jews to God*.)

There is a deep connectedness between Israel as a people and a nation and Jesus as its representative and King, into which Gentiles are grafted, and who together become the whole people of God.

The focus of all Scripture is not then ultimately on 'covenant' or indeed on 'kingdom' as abstract concepts, but it is located in the one who embodies the kingdom, the King Himself. All Scripture finds its fulfilment not in Israel as a people group, but in the one who fully embodies Israel, her Messiah, whose very title is Yeshua Ha Mashiach in Hebrew, and Jesus the Christ from the Greek.

It has been unfortunate that much Christian theology has denied or down-played the Jewishness of Jesus in its attempt to place a barrier between Christianity and Judaism (out of which it originally arose and to which it is constitutionally rooted). It is no wonder that much of Christian, and indeed Jewish, theology is confused, because both religious traditions in some respects seek to ignore the Jewishness of Jesus. For Judaism this has been a convenient let-out from seriously addressing the person of Jesus, and for Christians it has been a way to detach Jesus from His ethnicity as a son and indeed King of Israel. Only now are we beginning to see within the Jewish community a real engagement with the person of Jesus, as they seek to disentangle themselves from the labyrinth of Christian dogmatics, which has so alienated Judaism from its true understanding of Jesus.

The legitimate way to interpret Scripture would be to assert that Jesus is the only true Son of Israel. The key to the interpretation of Scripture is only found in the person of the Messiah, but more than that, it can only be interpreted in the light of both comings of Christ to which Old and New Testaments bear testimony. This is the crunch issue and in this chapter there is no time to do justice to the whole theme of how the church has substantially nullified large parts of the Old Testament with regard to having anything meaningful to say about any continuing role for Israel.

Allegory

In Christian theology large swathes of the Hebrew Scriptures, especially the prophetic writings, are simply dismissed as having nothing to say about the circumstances of Christ's Second Coming. This is a strange conclusion to reach when the only Scriptures the early church had to make sense of Christ's first coming and indeed His second were the Hebrew Scriptures. If the Hebrew Scriptures. have been the means by which the church has made sense of His first coming, why are they set aside as having nothing to say about His second? It can only be, to my mind, because of the dualistic approach to Scripture taken by the church, both in regard to the Old Testament as merely the precursor to the New, and by the approach of splitting Scripture into what could be regarded as literal, and what should be seen as allegorical. The early church fathers, in distancing themselves from their Hebrew origins, did a great disservice to the church by introducing this divided way of viewing Scripture. It is noteworthy that in the earliest years of the church, the dominant view of interpretation was to regard Scripture as literal unless the clear context was otherwise. How much pain the church would have been spared if it had ignored the road of allegory which has led to such painful division between Jew and Christian, synagogue and church! Even now, in its refusal to imagine that any aspect of the modern restoration of Israel is of God, it has continued the hostility.

Many Christians today reluctantly recognise that the Jewish people need a safe homeland, but do so not on scriptural warrant but on humanitarian grounds in the wake of the Holocaust. Today much of their energy is focused on rebuking Israel in terms of justice. Naim Ateek indeed has entitled one of his books *Justice and Only Justice*, as if this is the only possible consideration in the conflict between Arab and Jew, Palestinian and Israeli. This totally ignores the faithfulness of God to Israel. In turn this leads us to another important dimension of how we should read Scripture.

The faithfulness of God to Israel

Sadly many who hold Israel to account for the real or assumed injustices done to the Palestinians are as selective in the use of scriptural text as they accuse of being those who would want to be critically supportive of Israel. I have been to countless meetings when Israel's biblical prophets have been drafted in to support the clamour against injustice, yet the same speakers remain silent in respect to the far greater number of texts that speak of God's faithfulness and comfort to Israel. In so doing they ignore the many promises concerning the regathering and restoration of Israel.

There seems to be a very distorted way of reading Scripture when it is acceptable to take every scripture that rails against injustice, yet regard any scripture that speaks of restoration as either fulfilled spiritually or to be allegorically interpreted – a very convenient mechanism for avoiding the more uncomfortable passages of Scripture that speak of God's faithfulness and ongoing commitment to Israel. This is often most clearly seen in some headings in certain translations of the Hebrew Scriptures, where any curses are for Israel and all the comfort and blessings are assigned to the church.

One can only assume that the early church fathers, in their desire to stress the supremacy of church over synagogue and to relate to a society strongly influenced by Greek culture and thought, had to come up with some way of interpreting Scriptures which nullified any ongoing role for Israel. Allegory and spiritualisation of the text became effective weapons in their armoury and have succeeded in disabling any serious Christian engagement in the reasons for Israel's continued existence through the long years of scattering and exile. Consequently it has led to a real struggle as to how to interpret Israel's re-emergence within the community of nations in the modern era. How sad that the very sign of Israel that Jesus spoke of as an indication of the imminence of His return has been set aside as, at best, irrelevant and at worst highly controversial by so many within the churches, and the 'blame' for her restoration laid at the door of Christian Zionists. Why is it that so many who embrace the name of Jesus have become so hostile to the notion that He may be coming again for the very nation that at His first coming spurned and rejected Him?

Important issues for the church in its relationship with Jewish people

We need to wrestle with these issues because they raise important questions concerning the underpinning of our own faith. For far too long the church has failed to examine the effects of its longstanding antipathy to the Jewish people and its own interpretation of Scripture. This failure has led to a theology which significantly diminishes Christ's person, calling and ministry. It has in turn failed to engage seriously in the reasons for removing Christ from His status as Messiah of Israel, and so has developed a theology of supremacy towards the Jewish people which seeks to rob them of their heritage and future blessing.

Why is all this so important? Those who are wanting to sideline Israel, or go down the road of a dual covenant approach to Scripture, are undermining the very foundations of the Christian faith. The Christian faith cannot stand outside its Jewish context. Remove its roots and it shrivels and dies, because it has no independent existence outside its 'rootedness' in Israel.

If, for example, we go down the dual covenant approach, what does that do to the centrality of Christ? If the Jews have their own covenant, then there are two paths of salvation: one for Jews under the Old Covenant and the other for Christians under the New Covenant. What place is there then for Christ as Israel's Messiah? As someone has remarked, if Jesus is not first and foremost Israel's Messiah, He cannot be the Christian Messiah either. Jesus Himself said at the well of Sychar: 'Salvation is from the Jews' (Jn 4:22), and supremely in the one Jew Himself. The dual covenant route is very dangerous because it significantly removes Jesus as Israel's Messiah, and gives Jewish people a let-out clause from the need to engage seriously with the person of Jesus. They can continue their own theological path of rabbinic Judaism, which has developed in parallel with Christianity and largely defined itself over and against Christianity.

This in turn has major implications for Judaism and Christianity. If they are equally valid theological routes for Jews and Christians, then Jesus has no relevance in Jewish theology, and if He is detached from the Jewish context to which He came, He is seriously compromised in His mission to be Saviour of the world. Jewish people then have every right to develop their own hermeneutic based on Scripture and rabbinic tradition, just as the church has done with its own interpretation of Scripture and Christian tradition. This scenario seriously weakens the hand of those who believe that the church has replaced Israel as the people of God, and undermines the arguments of those from that tradition who have dispensed with any need for a regathering of the Jewish people to their ancient homeland. If Christianity and Judaism are equally valid paths, then the gospel has no relevance to Jewish people and they are no longer, if they ever were, beholden to Christian theology which has done away with the need for an ongoing Jewish expression within the Christian faith.

If the two faiths are equally valid, then rabbinic Judaism is set free to develop its own theological traditions, as it indeed has, including its theology concerning the Land and the Messiah. The New Testament has no relevance or significance to them, the Scriptures remain, as they always have to Jewish people, simply the Hebrew Scriptures. The New Testament can continue to be regarded by them as heresy that can safely be ignored.

The significance of this stance cannot be overestimated. It means that although the church may wish to voice an opinion concerning the circumstances of Israel's return to the community of nations, and its impact on the indigenous people living in the Land, it has forfeited any right to hold Israel and the Jewish people to theological account, based on its own theological understanding of Scripture and church tradition.

Indeed it has significantly strengthened the hand of those within Judaism to engage with their own Scriptures and traditions which speak of the circumstances of a physical return to the Land, the manner of that return and its relationship to the coming of their Messiah. Any Christian perspective can then be disregarded. The consequences sadly are the legacy of that tradition within the church that has severed itself from its Jewish roots, dispensed with any ongoing role for the Jewish people, and failed to recognise in Judaism an equally valid faith. It has not only made Jewish evangelism unnecessary, but has also made the gospel irrelevant to Jews.

The right to pursue Jewish self-determination in whatever form it may choose to take, including its right to nationhood based on its own scriptural and theological traditions, is something that the church has no permission to challenge other than on values based on secular humanism. It is highly compromised if it chooses to challenge it from its own theological interpretation of Hebrew Scripture rooted in the supremacy of a figure, Christ, who is not acknowledged by the Jewish community, or from writings, namely the New Testament, that have no legitimacy within that same community.

The church has shot itself in the foot by its own hermeneutic, as having nothing to say that Jewish people would want to hear. Why should Jewish people recognise a Christian theological stance that denies them the right to their own aspirations to nationhood, based either on its own eschatology or on Zionism that largely looks to the Hebrew Scriptures for its legitimacy? Sadly these very same Scriptures have been discounted by much of the Christian world as having anything to say about a restoration of Israel either in the present through Zionism, or in the future when, according to Orthodox tradition, the Messiah will gather the exiles and reconstitute the state.

In short, the church displays its usual arrogance in acknowledging on the one hand the validity of the Jewish faith, yet on the other hand denying those elements of its traditions which give voice to a national or political expression of its corporate life. It still takes a supremacist view, which acts as a profound barrier to any Jewish person wanting to evaluate the person of Jesus.

It is quite remarkable that parts of the church are more than willing to recognise Muslim claims to the Land based on one very spurious passage in the Qur'an, yet deny the validity of Hebrew Scripture which speaks of the rootedness of Jewish people to the Land and of the centrality of Jerusalem and the Land to the outworking of their faith. This is another case in which the church has failed to understand that its own theology prevents a right appraisal of God's ongoing concern that His name should be honoured among the nations by the very nation that was entrusted with the Land by unconditional covenant.

Conclusion

In conclusion, then, the Christian community needs to engage seriously in the issues addressed in this chapter if it is to have anything to contribute to the polarised and somewhat sterile debate over Israel which so scandalously divides the church and even further alienates Jewish people from their own Messiah. This debate raises justifiable fears that in one aspect of its life, its nationhood, the Christian world remains as hostile and antipathetic as it has always been. A right understanding of Scripture articulated well will present Jesus in His Hebraic context and enable Jewish people to cast off the baggage of Christian antisemitism, and so come to reappraise who Jesus is and what He came to do.

ISRAEL IN THE LAND – A LEGAL VIEW

Professor Gerald Adler

(This essay is a revised version of a lecture given by Professor Adler to the Annual Meeting of Christian Friends of Israel held in Eastbourne in October 2002.)

For the past 35 years Israel has constantly been politically attacked by the nations of the world generally, and by the Arabs in particular, for allegedly occupying the West Bank and Gaza contrary to international law. Israel's response has been that the legal status of Judea and Samaria ('the West Bank') and the Gaza Strip is not 'occupied' territory, but rather territory 'in dispute'. In making the position clear, it is important to bear in mind some recent history, as well as the relevant internationally recognised treaties and agreements, including the provisions of the Palestine Mandate, which in the absence of validly enacted legislation to the contrary, may still have application today in the West Bank and Gaza.

To examine and understand the present situation from a political, economic and legal perspective, it is difficult to find a logical historical starting point. Here we have chosen to begin with the aftermath of the First World War.

The historical background

Following the Allied victory over Germany and her allies, the Versailles Treaty appeared to have settled matters in Europe, while the Peace Conference held in San Remo, convened on 24 April 1920, dismembered the Ottoman Empire. The conference, which preceded the establishment of the League of Nations, paved the way for the implementation of the Sykes–Picot Agreement and the Balfour Declaration.

In July 1920, the government and administration of the territory, consisting of some 97,740 sq. km, was entrusted to Britain by the League of Nations under a mandate, the final terms of which were only finalised some two years later. The terms of the Mandate approved by the League of Nations reflected the terms of the Balfour Declaration and 'fleshed out' the manner in which it was to be implemented. In particular it provided for the establishment in Palestine of a national home for the Jewish people, and the facilitation of Jewish immigration and encouragement of close settlement by Jews on the Land.

A number of points should be noted here. First, the primary objective of the Mandate required Britain, as the mandatory power, to facilitate Jewish immigration and to encourage close settlement by Jews on the Land, including state lands and wastelands not required for public purposes, provided that the civil and religious rights and position of other sections of the population were not prejudiced. The proviso neither confers any political or *new* civil and religious rights on non-Jewish communities nor confers rights on any non-Jewish *new communities* that might subsequently settle on the Land. Protection is given only to such non-Jewish communities *existing at the time*.

To the best of our knowledge, between the granting of the Mandate in 1922 and the present time, there has been no valid constitutional legislative enactment by any internationally recognised sovereign authority which repeals the above provisions, such as would prohibit the Jewish settlement in the West Bank.

To satisfy political commitments made by Britain to Sharif Hussein, King of Hijaz (Arabia), and his sons for their initiation of the 'Arab Revolt' against the Turks in 1916, and to relieve, in part, the financial burden of the Mandate from Britain's taxpayers, Britain delegated to Emir Abdullah (Hussein's second son) the administration of some 70,000 sq. km lying to the east of the River Jordan and excluded it from Jewish settlement (Transjordan). This constituted some 71.5 per cent of the total 97,740 sq. km which comprised the Mandate territory. The balance, of only 28.5 per cent of the Mandate territory, west of the Jordan, was to remain available for Jews to reconstitute their national home.

Those Arabs who lived on the west bank of the Jordan were to be re-settled in Transjordan once the Jewish homeland was established.

Between 1922 and 1939, acting contrary to the Mandate and to appease Arab violence and rioting, Britain not only turned a blind eye to extensive illegal Arab immigration, which should have been settled in Transjordan, but also severely restricted Jewish immigration. This contributed in no small measure to the annihilation of European Jewry. With the publication of the British government's White Paper in May 1939, it became clear to a majority of the League of Nations Mandates Commission that Britain was in breach of her obligations under the mandate in deciding to restrict the voluntary sale of Arab held lands to Jews, and more particularly, to limit Jewish immigration beyond a specific quota, without prior Arab approval. The outbreak of World War II September 1939, left Britain to deal with the situation as she saw fit without being accountable.

The end of World War II saw the resurrection in 1945 of the old League of Nations in the form of the United Nations and the emergence of over 100 new states, each giving expression to demands for self-determination and nationalism. The UN, under Chapter XII of its Charter, assumed the role of the League in regard to the various Mandates that were still in effect. Among those seeking self-determination and statehood was the Jewish population of Palestine, as represented by the Jewish Agency, and Transjordan, which obtained its independence from Britain in 1946.

The UN General Assembly in 1947, under Resolution 181, recommended the partition of that portion of Palestine remaining under the Mandate (after Britain had transferred Transjordan to the sovereignty of King Abdullah) into an Arab and a Jewish state, with Jerusalem being held under an international regime. This was accepted by the Jewish representatives and rejected both by Arab institutions in Palestine and by the surrounding Arab nations. In 1948, the British left Palestine, and Israel declared itself independent on 14 May, on which date, in response to the demands of the Arab High Committee (AHC), five Arab armies invaded the nascent state.

The successful establishment of Israel after the 1948 War, augmented by Arab propaganda of atrocities, unfortunately created the Arab refugee problem. It is alleged by Palestinians that some 600,000 Arabs were driven out (rather than fled) from the territory of what is now Israel. Notwithstanding the number of refugees who may have registered with the United Nations Relief and Works Agency (UNRWA), the true number of Arabs who may have been displaced and who can justifiably claim to have suffered from Jewish eviction from lands alleged by them to have been held 'from time immemorial' may be considerably less. Two factors need to be taken into account.

First, as a result of the 1922 and 1939 British White Papers, and particularly during the latter period of the Mandate, there is much evidence to show that the local British administration, while enforcing a blockade against Jewish immigration (contrary to the intention and express terms of the Mandate), turned a blind eye to considerable illegal Arab immigration into Palestine from surrounding Arab lands. Such Arab immigration skewed the demographic balance in favour of an even larger Arab majority than that which would have occurred naturally. If the various British governments of the time had administered the Mandate in accordance with its stated objectives, the dislocation to the Arab population in Palestine immediately before the establishment of Israel would have been considerably lessened.

Second, UNRWA defines a 'refugee' as anyone who was living in Palestine *two years* before the 1948 War and migrated to one of the areas in which UNRWA operates (Jordan, Syria, Lebanon, West Bank and Gaza Strip). UNRWA also grants refugee status to the male sons and grandsons of such refugees born after 1948. The result of this very liberal 'two-year residence' definition of 'refugee' magnifies the issue beyond that which would normally be considered in a 'traditional' refugee situation.

Both of the above factors have consequences on the character and extent of the Israeli occupation in the West Bank and Gaza, and on the possible 'right of return' of 'Palestinian' refugees into Israel proper.

It is not the intention here to deal with Palestinian claims of a right of return, but it should be remembered that the 1948 War also gave the surrounding Arab nations the opportunity to expel some 800,000 Jews from Arab lands in which they had been living, some of them for many generations, forcing them to abandon their property without compensation. The Jews were absorbed by Israel and granted citizenship without imposing a financial or social burden on the free world. In contrast many Arab refugees were forced to remain in their refugee camps, and still remain there as political pawns, supported, in the main, by international bodies and not by their Arab brethren.

Returning now to the issue of territorial control after the 1948 War, the ceasefire lines west of the Jordan River ultimately agreed upon among the belligerents left Jordan in control of Judea and Samaria, and Egypt in control of the Gaza Strip. This amounts to approximately 6,000 sq. km, being 6 per cent of the total Mandate territory. Thus, together with the 70,000 sq. km of Transjordan lying to the east of the river (71.5 per cent), Arab states now retained control of 77.5 per cent of the original 97,740 sq. km constituting total Mandate territory, leaving Israel to establish and develop a Jewish homeland in the remaining 22.5 per cent.

While it should be noted that Egypt never annexed the Gaza Strip, Jordan purported to annex Judea and Samaria ('the West Bank') in 1950. Only the UK and Pakistan recognised this act, while the other Arab states rejected it. Why no one called the West Bank territory 'occupied' when Jordan and Egypt exercised their control from 1948 to 1967 is not surprising, since from 1918 no state had successfully asserted a sovereignty that was generally recognised at an international level. There was, in law, and there still is, an abeyance of sovereignty in that territory.

On 6 June, 1967, Israel acted in a pre-emptive defensive war started against it by Egypt, Syria and Lebanon. In the ensuing 'Six-Day War', Egypt lost control of Sinai and the Gaza Strip, and Syria of the Golan Heights. King Hussein, instead of responding positively to Israel's undertaking that it would respect Jordanian territory, decided to follow his Arab brethren and attacked Israel. As a result he lost Judea and Samaria, including Jerusalem, in 96 hours.

Land for peace

At issue currently is the question as to whether the establishment by the Israeli government of settlements populated by Jews constitutes 'occupation' contrary to international law or even domestic law. It should be remembered that settlements have never been 'an obstacle to peace', as is now argued by the Arab bloc. From 1949 until 1967, when Jews were forbidden to live on the West Bank, the Arab bloc refused to make peace with Israel. From 1967 until 1977, the Labour Party established only a few strategic settlements in the territories and yet there was still opposition to peace. Only after the Likud government assumed power in 1977, committing itself to an expansion of Jewish settlement in the captured territory, did a member of the Arab bloc move towards peace. Sadat's visit to Jerusalem in November 1977 opened the way for the signing of a peace agreement between Israel and Egypt, under which Egypt recognised Israel and Israel removed all her settlements from Sinai.

In the West Bank and Jerusalem, Israel has permitted its citizens to recover lands it once owned, but abandoned following the Arab riots of the 1930s (Neve Yaakov, Atarot, Shimon Hatzdik) and during the 1948 War of Independence, and to establish new settlements in the territories now under its control. However, it is the buzz words 'illegal occupation' which have given rise to much confusion in this long-lasting conflict and created the pretext for Arab hate and violence. The term 'occupation' is of itself ambiguous. In normal parlance it could be understood to include expropriation and physical occupation of privately owned land. However Israel has made a point of not clearing Palestinians off the land they occupy for the purpose of settlement building. Neither has it taken land for any other purpose except that required for public works, like roads, or for security purposes, where Palestinian terrorists have used buildings located among a civilian population for sniper attacks or ambush positions alongside roads. In such cases the buildings have been demolished and not re-occupied by Israelis. Some settlements and houses have been constructed on land that was owned prior to Israel's 1948 War of Independence by Jewish communities or citizens.

'Occupation' could also mean the appropriation of vacant publicly owned land. Settlements have for the most part been built on barren hilltops, which have never been privately owned, populated, cultivated or otherwise physically occupied. This is consistent with Article 6 of the Palestine Mandate which, it will be remembered, encouraged 'close settlement by Jews on the land, including state lands and wastelands not required for public purposes'. Article 6, to the best of our knowledge, has never been repealed by any sovereign power having jurisdiction in the West Bank.

'Occupation' in military terms is governed by the Hague Regulations 1908. Under Article 42, territory is considered occupied when it is actually placed under the authority of the hostile army and extends only to

the territory where such authority [of the hostile army] has been established and can be exercised.

Following the 1993 Oslo Accords (detailed below) until the outbreak
of the Intifada of 2000, Israel ceased to exercise military control over
approximately 68 per cent of the West Bank territory and left 97 per
cent of the total Palestinian population to be regulated by its own
Palestinian Authority ('PA') established under the Accords. Such regula-
tion includes the exercise of exclusive jurisdiction for maintaining
internal law and order in the eight major Arab towns in the West Bank
and the Gaza Strip and the transfer to the Palestinians of responsibility
for almost all areas of civilian activity. This includes the powers of
domestic legislation, administration and enforcement of law, municipal
administration, health, safety, education, police, finance, economic and
physical planning and transportation. The PA also has authority in matters of broadcasting, and exercises control over the press and media.

Thus although Israel has retained control over population movements
between Palestinian and Israeli urban centres and the right to re-enter
Palestinian urban areas for reasons of security, Israel cannot be said to
'occupy' and control the West Bank and Gaza Strip population in the
peaceful exercise of its civilian rights. It has been alleged, improperly,
that Palestinians need special documentation to move from one town in
Area A (under Palestinian authority), through Israeli-controlled territory
to another Area A town. This is incorrect. For most people an identity
card (ID) is the only document that they are required to produce.
(Israelis, too, within Israel are required to carry IDs at all times.)
Unfortunately, there are occasions when Palestinians are delayed at
checkpoints for identification purposes. This, however, is for security
reasons alone, when Israeli forces have received reliable intelligence of a
planned incursion by Palestinian terrorists or of a suicide bomber into
Israeli territory. Such delays are not expressions of Israeli arrogance and
intended Arab humiliation, but are the direct result of the failure of the
Palestinian Authority to abide by the terms of the agreements made with
Israel.

In addition to the Hague regulations there are a number of international treaties and agreements which impact on Jewish/Israeli settlement
in the West Bank, some of which deal almost exclusively with the issue
while others only tangentially. Among the most significant are the 4th

Geneva Convention, the Khartoum Conference, UNSC Resolutions 242 and 338, the Rabat Conference, the Camp David Agreements, the Madrid Peace Conference, and most importantly the Oslo Accords.

The last two sets of Agreements have tried to resolve in a detailed manner three main points: Arab recognition of Israel as a legitimate state; 'peace' between the Israelis and the Arab belligerents; and the 'return of territory' taken by Israel in the Six-Day War. The Camp David Agreements provided the basis for the return of Sinai to Egypt, and the Oslo Accords allowed Jordan to sign a peace treaty with Israel in which settlements were not an issue.

The Oslo Accords in which the Interim Agreement is prominent also provide a detailed framework of obligations assumed by the Palestinian Liberation Organisation and Israel for the cessation of violence as a means of resolving their disputes, the establishment of Palestinian self-governmental institutions and the phased withdrawal of Israel forces as an interim measure. The Accords contemplate, as subjects to be deter-mined in 'Final Status' negotiation, the complete military withdrawal of Israel's presence in the West Bank and Gaza; the *status* of the Jewish set-tlements (not their building or their removal), Jerusalem and the return of refugees.

Let us now examine the treaties and agreements in some detail to determine the extent to which Israel is, allegedly, in illegal occupation of the West Bank and Gaza.

4th Geneva Convention

It has been asserted by some that Israeli settlement in the West Bank and Gaza is contrary to the 4th Geneva Convention, which regulates the law arising out of belligerent occupation. The Convention becomes applic-able in cases of declared war or armed conflict between *national states* who are parties to the Convention and where the whole or part of the territory under the *legitimate sovereignty* of one state becomes occupied by another state. In this regard, one should note, since the Convention was formulated in 1949 and is not retrospective in its application, any civilian claims under the Convention for protection against an 'occupy-ing' power or for compensation for injury arising before 1949 would have no legal validity.

Furthermore, a distinction has to be made between 'aggressive con-quest' and territorial disputes that arise after a war of self-defence. In the latter situation, where a prior holder of territory had seized that terri-tory unlawfully, the state which subsequently takes that territory in the lawful exercise of self-defence has, against that prior holder, better title. This is Israel's position. As has been shown earlier, after the withdrawal of the British from Palestine in 1948, sovereignty in West Bank territory and the Gaza Strip was in abeyance. Although the areas were under the control and occupation of Jordan and Egypt, the world in general (except for Britain and Pakistan), and the Arabs in particular, failed to confer any internationally recognised sovereign status. The Palestinians residing in the West Bank and Gaza in 1967 were not, nor are they today, subjects of any recognised sovereign having jurisdiction in the ter-ritory. Neither are they yet recognised internationally as having achieved the status of statehood.

Since Israel's capture of the area did not result in the ousting of any sovereign power, neither under customary international law nor under the Convention do Judea, Samaria and Gaza constitute 'occupied terri-tory'. Rather they constitute 'disputed' territory. The term 'occupation' is misleading and implies that Israel captured the territory in a war of aggression and conquest – which was not the case. The fact that Israel has voluntarily agreed to apply the Convention's humanitarian provisions of belligerent occupation within the territories does not alter the situation.

Even if it is argued that the 4th Geneva Convention does apply to the West Bank and Gaza, its provisions do not prohibit Jewish settlement. The relevant provision is found in Article 49 (6). This provides 'The Occupying Power shall not deport or transfer parts of its own civilian population into territory it occupies'. It is, however, clear from the full text of Article 49 and from its title 'Deportations, Transfers, Evacuations' that the provision is directed against *forcible transfers* of the occupying power's civilians, and it is designed to protect the *local population* from *displacement* from the occupied territory.

These conditions are absent in the case of the Israeli settlements. The movement of Jewish population into the territories is entirely voluntary, and settlements are located for the most part on what were previously barren and uninhabited hilltops (public land – consistent with Article 6 of the Mandate) without displacing existing Arab settlement, much of which is only decades rather than centuries old, as can be shown by the Mandatory Land Register. Furthermore, the growth of Jewish settlements is constrained within their originally established boundaries and they have neither been permitted nor have they in fact encroached on Palestinian villages.

As will become clear below, this situation is recognised in the Israeli-Palestinian Interim Agreement, which does *not* restrict the establishment or expansion of Israeli settlements – nor of Arab ones. It is the *status* rather than the *occupation* of Jewish settlements that is one among a number of issues to be discussed and settled by negotiation in the Final Status talks with the Palestinians. As stated earlier, it is often overlooked that Jewish inhabitation of the West Bank is a continuation of a long-standing presence. The 3,000-year-old community in Hebron existed throughout centuries of Ottoman rule, while settlements like NeveYa'akov and the Gush Etzion bloc were established under the British Mandate.

The Khartoum Conference, 1 September 1967

Following the Six-Day War of 1967, the Israel Unity government declared on 19 June 1967 that it was ready to return the Golan Heights to Syria, Sinai to Egypt and most of the West Bank to Jordan, in return for peace treaties with its Arab neighbours, the normalisation of relations, and the guarantee of navigation through the Straits of Tiran. The refugee problem would be solved by resettlement outside the borders of the State of Israel. On the same day, the USSR submitted UN General Assembly Resolution 519, calling for immediate Israeli withdrawal from all territories, with no mention of peace or negotiations. The resolution was voted down on 4 July.

In the wake of the Arab defeat, eight Arab heads of state attended an Arab summit conference in Khartoum, Sudan, held 29 August to 1 September 1967. It formulated the Arab consensus that underlay the official policies of most Arab states (with the exception of Egypt) for the next two decades and beyond: 'No peace with Israel, no recognition of Israel, no negotiations with it.'

Resolution 242, 22 November 1967 (introduced after the Six Day War)

UN Security Council Resolution 242 has two main operative provisions which have become the cornerstone for subsequent negotiations. The Resolution affirms that the fulfilment of the UN Charter principles requires the establishing of a just and lasting peace in the Middle East, *which should include the application of both of the following principles*:

(a) the 'withdrawal of Israeli armed forces from territories occupied in the recent [1967] conflict' *and*
(b) the 'termination of belligerency, together with respect for the territorial integrity and political independence of every State in the area'.

As Lord Caradon, sponsor of the draft Resolution, confirmed in 1973, Resolution 242 must be read as a whole: 'Withdrawal should take place to boundaries which are both secure and recognised . . . It was not for us to lay down exactly where the border should be. I know the 1967 border very well. It is not a satisfactory border. It is where troops had to stop, just where they happened to be that night. That is not a permanent boundary.'

Moreover, the Resolution did not require Israel to withdraw from 'all' territories. Successive British Foreign Secretaries, Michael Stewart, on 17 November 1969, and George Brown, who formulated the Resolution, on 19 January 1970 both confirmed to Parliament that the omission of these words was deliberate. As the British delegate to the UN, Lord Caradon, said: 'The 1967 borders, being the 1948 cease fire lines on the ground, were undesirable and artificial. Since the resolution also calls for every State in the area to have the right to live in peace within secure and recognised borders, it follows that the new borders will differ from the territorial lines which applied between 1948 and 1967.' Resolution 242 also calls for a just settlement of the refugee problem – but it makes no mention of a right of return for Arabs into Israel.

Taken together with UNSC Resolution 338 passed on 22 October 1973 (after the Yom Kippur War), it becomes clear that only negotiations will determine which portion of these territories will eventually become 'Israeli territory' and which will be retained by Israel's Arab counterpart. It is conceivable, theoretically, that some Jewish populated settlements could remain in the territories under Palestinian jurisdiction and subject to Palestinian law, just as many Arab villages exist peaceably within Israel proper and are subject to Israeli law.

The Arab Summit Conference, Rabat, October 1974

In essence, this Conference of the Arab leadership conferred, in a non-democratic process, legitimacy on the Palestine Liberation Organisation (PLO) as the 'sole legitimate representative of the Palestinian people'. While in no way changing the international status of the West Bank by conferring 'sovereignty' on the PLO it had the effect of transferring from Jordan to the PLO the responsibility for negotiating the return of the disputed territories with Israel. Having steadily lost ground in the fight over the political future of the West Bank, Jordan's standing was undermined by the outpouring of Palestinian nationalism sparked by the *intifada*. With Hussein's claim that the PLO leadership was forced on unwilling West Bank residents discredited, the King set the disengagement process in motion.

Although Jordan had continued its administrative and financial support to the residents of the West Bank after June 1967, King Hussein announced on 28 July 1988 the cessation of a $3.1 billion development programme for the West Bank under the pretext that the measure was designed to allow the PLO more responsibility for the area. Two days later he dissolved parliament, ending West Bank representation in the legislature. In a speech to the Jordanian people on 31 July 1988, the King announced the severance of all administrative and legal ties between Jordan and the West Bank areas, thus removing the issue of Jordanian purported sovereignty over the disputed territories from the Israeli-Palestinian conflict.

The Camp David Accords, 17 September 1978

The Camp David Accords of September 1978 established in principle a peace agreement between Israel and Egypt under which Israel was to retreat from Sinai. While the Accords did not define an autonomous Palestinian area, they also provided for a framework agreement setting up a format for negotiations for the establishment of an autonomous regime in the West

Bank and Gaza. Within the framework of these Accords, an agreement between Israel and Egypt was signed in March 1979 whereby peace between the parties was declared, with Israel surrendering control of Sinai and removing its settlements. It also led to the resolution – by arbitration – of the dispute over Taba and the establishment of full diplomatic relations.

The former matter has been implemented with Israel transferring Taba to Egypt, while unfortunately the latter has now been virtually suspended. It should also be noted that, contrary to the peace agreement, for some considerable time Egyptian authorities have permitted incitement and hate against Israel to become common practice in the Egyptian media and, in recent months, they have also failed to take steps to prevent the smuggling of illegal weapons into the Gaza Strip. Time will tell whether this tendency portends a further deterioration in Israeli – Egyptian relations.

The Madrid Peace Conference, October 1991

The break-up of the Soviet Union and the Gulf War reshaped the basic political order of the Middle East. In an attempt to take advantage of this change, US Secretary of State James Baker made eight trips to the region in the eight months following the Gulf War. The Madrid Invitation, inviting Israel, Syria, Lebanon, Jordan and the Palestinians to an opening conference, represents the result of this shuttle diplomacy. The invitation, an outcome of compromises by all sides, details the structure of the Madrid process: an opening conference having no power to impose solutions; bilateral talks with the Arab states bordering Israel; talks with the Palestinians on five-year interim self-rule, to be followed by talks on the permanent status, and multilateral talks on key regional issues, like refugees.

The Oslo Accords, 1993

These constitute a series of agreements between Israel and the Palestinian Organisation (PLO). The first is made up of letters (9–10 September 1993) between Yasser Arafat and Yitzhak Rabin, whereby Israel recognises the PLO as being the representative of the Palestinian people for the purposes of settling the dispute between them and Israel, and the PLO make a declaration renouncing the use of terrorism and violence and an undertaking to amend the PLO Covenant, which denies Israel's right to exist.

The second agreement is a Declaration of Principles on Interim Self Government Arrangements, dated 13 September 1993 (Oslo I) in which Israel and the PLO (forming part of the Jordanian Delegation) agree to put an end to the decades of confrontation and conflict and recognise their mutual legitimate and political rights. The aim of the negotiations was to establish a Palestinian Interim Self-Government Authority, and to elect a Council for the Palestinian people on the West Bank and Gaza for a transitional period of five years, leading to a permanent settlement based on UNSC Resolutions 242 and 338.

The third comprises a number of interim agreements between Israel and the Palestinians regarding the redeployment and withdrawal of Israeli troops from various parts of the West Bank and Gaza, and the scope of a continuing Israeli military presence and its relationship with the Palestinian Authority until the conclusion of a 'Final Status' agreement.

The first preparatory agreement in respect of the Gaza Strip and Jericho was signed on 4 May 1994. Attached to it were a number of Annexes which contain a framework for what appear to be final arrangements for the transfer to the Palestinian Authority of almost all areas of civilian activity and jurisdiction. These arrangements deal with security, civil affairs, legal matters and economic relations.

On September 28, 1995, the Gaza–Jericho preparatory agreement and its Annexes (now amplified) was superseded by the Israeli-Palestinian Interim Agreement and was extended to apply to the remainder of the West Bank (Oslo II). Annex I – Protocol Concerning Redeployment and Security Arrangements – designates specific areas in which the security and policing functions of the PA and Israeli military forces are to be performed, and preserve the rights of Israel to re-enter areas from which they have withdrawn in order to protect Israeli security concerns and Israeli citizens. More on this subject will be discussed below.

With the tragic assassination of Prime Minister Rabin in November 1995, Israel's democratic process took hold. Shimon Peres assumed office and was presented with the problems of settling the boundary division between the Arabs and Jews in Hebron. Peres's election defeat in 1996 prevented him from resolving the problem of Hebron, but he set the stage for Binyamin Netanyahu's government which followed, to settle and sign the Hebron Redeployment Protocol on 17 January 1997. This provided for the ultimate settlement on the ground of the division of Hebron into separate Palestinian areas and the area under exclusive Israeli jurisdiction.

In May 1999 Ehud Barak, after promising to bring Israel's dispute with the Palestinians to a successful conclusion, was elected to succeed Netanyahu as Israeli Prime Minister. Notwithstanding many breaches of Oslo II by the Palestinian Authority, particularly the encouragement rather than the cessation of incitement to violence in the media, mosques and schools, the recruitment of more police than agreed and the failure to suppress terrorist organisations, Barak resolved to complete the peace process in September 1999. He agreed to participate in Final Status negotiations at Camp David in July 2000, making one last final effort at Taba in September 2000 before the expiration of both his term as Prime Minister of Israel and Bill Clinton's tenure as President of the United States.

The outstanding issues between the parties included: the final boundaries between the Palestinian Authority and Israel; the designation of those settlements which were to become part of Israel proper and those which were to be vacated; the characteristics and nature of the future Palestinian state; the political status of Jerusalem and its municipal administration; sovereignty and control over Muslim and Jewish holy sites; and external security.

In the ensuing discussions, Barak offered to concede to the Palestinian Authority 97 per cent of the West Bank territory captured by Israel in 1967 and a sharing of sovereignty in Jerusalem. Arafat, on the other hand, demanded the right of return of between 3 and 5 million refugees and their descendants to within Israel proper, and rejected US President Clinton's proposal for joint sovereignty over Jerusalem in general and over the Temple Mount in particular. Arafat failed to put forward any alternative plans and refused to negotiate further. It does appear, however, that there was near agreement on the nature of the future Palestinian state, interim security boundaries, particularly in the Jordan Valley, and the control of airspace. Even the question of which settlements were to be vacated and which were to be included in Israel proper was almost agreed.

Israel, however, was unable to accept the PA demand for the unrestricted right of refugees to return to Israel. The relocation of this number of Arabs into Israel, which when added to the million existing Israeli Arabs, as compared with the 5 million Jews, would lead inexorably to the destruction of Israel as a Jewish state – which many Israelis believe to be Arafat's true purpose.

Justification for continued Israeli military presence in the West Bank and Gaza

The basic premise of 'Oslo' was the cessation of violence as a means of resolving disputes between the Palestinians and Israel. With the breakdown of the Camp David talks, occasioned by the rejection by the Palestinians of Israeli and US proposals on Jerusalem, and Israel's refusal to accept unlimited refugees, the Palestinians again resorted to violence. There is concrete evidence to support allegations that Arafat initiated and planned the current *intifada*, which erupted even before Sharon visited the Temple Mount and contributed to the political downfall of Barak as Prime Minister and the election of Ariel Sharon in his stead.

Unfortunately, throughout the long period of negotiation, and particularly during the current round of violence, the PA has consistently failed not only to abide by the Oslo Accords, which contain a wide range of other provisions laying the foundations of peaceful co-existence between the Israelis and the Palestinians, but has also committed acts of perfidy contrary to the 4th Geneva Convention.

Palestinian breaches of the Oslo Accords

The Palestinian Authority has committed the following major breaches of the Oslo Accords:

(a) The obligation to renounce violence and terror and to take all measures necessary to prevent acts of violence and terror against Israel.
(b) The obligation to resolve *all* outstanding issues through bilateral negotiations.
(c) The duty to refrain from and to act against all forms of incitement.
(d) The duty to apprehend, prosecute and detain terrorists.
(e) The duty to confiscate illegal arms exceeding the type and number of weapons permitted.

(f) The duty to maintain continuously joint security co-operation mechanisms with Israel to ensure public order and security.

(g) The duty to ensure that holy sites are respected and protected.

(h) The duty to ensure that no armed forces, other than the agreed number of Palestinian police, are established who, together with the Israeli military forces, operate in the West Bank and Gaza Strip.

It should also be noted particularly that incitement to violence and hatred against Israel and the Jews has continued unabatedly in the Palestinian media, the mosques and particularly in the schools, where the textbooks do not recognise even the existence of Israel.

With the full knowledge and support of the PA, quantities and qualities of explosives and weapons contrary to the agreements have been smuggled into the West Bank. Additionally the PA has failed to take steps to control the various terrorist groups that have been permitted to operate in territory transferred to the Authority. Since the breakdown of the talks nearly two years ago, and perhaps even before that, a number of members of the Authority's security organisations have participated with the terrorist organisations in planning and executing terrorist actions in Israel proper and against Israeli settlements in the West Bank.

It has also become clear that after the breakdown of the Camp David talks, Arafat and his colleagues planned a new campaign of violence, the current *intifada*, and waited for the right opportunity (Sharon's visit to Temple Mount) to instigate the violence that has now continued for over three years. (The Mitchell Report concluded that Sharon's visit was not the cause of the uprising.) Increasing violence fostered by Arafat has led to suicide bombing and deliberate targeting of women and young people, with no condemnation from the UN.

When the reign of terror became unbearable, Israel reacted. In order to minimise Palestinian civilian casualties, and by way of legitimate anticipatory self-defence, Israel instituted the targeted killing of specific terrorist leaders known to be involved directly in the planning and execution of terrorist activities against Israeli citizens. It has captured many organisers of the suicide bombers and has found incontrovertible proof of Arafat's intimate role in launching such bombings and his involvement in the smuggling of illegal weapons. Arafat's declarations of ignorance of the *Karine A* weapons ship have been shown to be blatant lies.

Palestinian breaches of international law and the 4th Geneva Convention

In addition to breaches of the Oslo Accords, senior officials in the Palestinian Authority have acted in breach of the 4th Geneva Convention and in the commission of 'perfidy' contrary to customary laws of war. In international law, it is important to distinguish between 'deception or ruses' and 'perfidy'. The Hague Regulations in the Laws of War allow ruses, but disallow treachery or perfidy, whose prohibition is reaffirmed in Protocol I of 1977.

Examples of ruses include the use of camouflage, decoys and mock operations, false signals and the jamming of communications. Perfidy, on the other hand, includes such treacherous practices as improper use of the white flag, feigned surrender or pretending to have civilian non-combatant status. In particular the shielding of military targets and assets from attack by moving them into civilian-populated areas, and the placing of armed forces in such areas, is unequivocally an act of perfidy and constitutes what is known in the Laws of War as a 'Grave Breach'.

The legal effect of such perfidy – the practice now engaged in by the PLO/PA – is to exempt the victim (in this case Israel) from the normally operative rules on targets, and to place the responsibility for civilian injury on the side that engages in perfidy. This does not imply that terrorism represents a permissible use of force under international law. By its very nature, the PLO/PA plan of violence is overwhelmingly illegal. Jurisprudential expansion of the Laws of War under Article 3 of all four of the Geneva Conventions makes the rules of war applicable not only to Israeli or American uniformed military forces; they are also binding upon the Palestinian Authority and the terrorists groups operating with PA support.

After suffering intentionally directed Palestinian attacks by terrorists using nail-studded bombs on Israeli women and children, in cafés, places of entertainment and of worship, bus and train stations, Israel has the right and the obligation under national and international law to protect its citizens against terrorist attacks originating from Palestinian territory, and is, without choice, forced to retaliate. This 'post-attack' right is codified in Article 51 of the UN Charter while 'anticipatory self-defence' is justified under customary international law.

Israel's use of force is designed only for survival and self-protection.

Its attacks are aimed specifically and exclusively against PLO/PA military targets and supporting infrastructure, including the targeted killing of known terrorist leaders and perpetrators of murder of Israeli civilians. Unfortunately, Israeli fire sometimes unavoidably kills and injures Palestinian non-combatants, creating the false impression of lawlessness on both sides.

In the light of the transfer to the PA of civilian and police control of many areas of the West Bank and Gaza, the PA has a positive duty under Oslo II to act to prevent lawlessness emanating therefrom. Recent factual evidence and documentary disclosures have shown the PA's involvement and collusion in the following acts, all of which are contrary to the Geneva Conventions:

(a) permitting the use of Palestinian Red Crescent ambulances to transport terrorists and weapons;
(b) failing to distinguish combatants from non-combatants;
(c) permitting the deliberate placement of Palestinian military targets and assets in densely populated areas in order to shield them from attack.

Instead of restraining the operations of Palestinian terror groups, including the actual participation of members of the PA security forces, the PA has allowed the areas under its control, including the UNRWA-organised refugee camps, to become seedbeds of anti-Israel terrorism. It has provided the funds to finance such activities and the activities of suicide bombers operating in Israel itself.

Indeed, even if the PLO/PA had not intentionally been engaged in treachery, any Palestinian link between protected persons and military activities places all legal responsibility for Arab injury to civilian persons and property squarely on the Palestinian Authority and its leadership.

Conclusion

George Santayana once said, 'Those who cannot remember the past are condemned to repeat it.' It is important to know the history of the Land of Israel, and the legal basis for Israel's tenancy of it, in order to assess the accuracy and veracity of the statements made by Israel's enemies. Notwithstanding the Israeli government's decision to withdraw unilaterally from the Gaza Strip, at present there appears to be no prospect of a genuine peace in the region. Incitement to hatred in the mosques, schools and media continues, as does the violence and terrorism which inevitably follows. Should Arafat's successor, Abu Mazen, be persuaded that the cessation of violence is to his advantage, it will take many years to eradicate the anti-Jewish/Israeli hate that has been inculcated into the Arab population of the Middle East over the last century.

Since its establishment, particularly after the Six-Day War, Israel has been accused of being 'racist' and having colonial aspiration characteristics that are anathema to Arab and other emerging nations. However, it should be recalled that Israel has among its citizens not only Jews but Christians, Muslims, Bahai and Druze; all with equal civil rights and whose holy places are fully respected both in law and in practice. Israeli Arabs participate in civic public life as members of the Knesset (Israel's legislature), judges in the Israeli Supreme and inferior Courts, in the free professions and in the civil service. Ethnically Israel has within its population black Jews from Ethiopia, coloured Jews from North Africa, Yemenites, Jews from India, Caucasian white Jews from Europe, as well as Arab Muslims and Christians.

As a cultural minority in the Middle East, what Israel, a country the size of Wales, seeks is not only the right of its citizens to live in peace with their neighbours, but to be able to express, as a majority within its own territory, its history, its own varied Jewish culture, social, religious and secular customs, values and practices without having to justify and expose them to exceptional international scrutiny and approval.

Taken from an unpublished article by Professor Gerald M. Adler Ll.M J.S.D (Yale).

Author's Note: This article does not take into account the legal aspects of three major events which have recently occurred in the Israel-Palestine conflict: the construction of the terrorist security barrier; the advisory opinion rendered by the International Court of Justice on the legality of the 'wall' and Israel's implementation of its disengagement plan to remove Jewish settlements from the Gaza Strip. Each of these events has extensive legal implications which could not be addressed in this paper.

CHRISTIANS, ISRAEL AND THE STRUGGLE FOR PEACE

Geoffrey Smith

Israel is the third most commonly used name in the Bible. It occurs over 2,000 times in the Old Testament and 70 times in the New Testament. For the Puritans in the seventeenth century the theme of Israel was a thread of covenant theology that runs right through the Bible. They rediscovered the love in the heart of God for the people of Israel and the significance of Israel as a principle of faith.

Three views in church teaching

Biblical Zionism

The biblical case for the restoration of Israel was being made by Christians in England long before the term 'Zionism' was coined by Natan Birnbaum in 1885. Biblical Zionism is simply the affirmation of the Jewish people's right to self-determination in the Land of their fore-fathers – a right endorsed by the United Nations in 1948, similar to the right offered to the Palestinian Arabs in 1937 and 1947 under the partition proposals. In relation to Israel there is the added dimension that the regathering and restoration of the state is in line with the witness of the Hebrew prophets. For Christians in the Puritan tradition this fulfilment of prophecy was to be welcomed by the church, which itself has grown from Jewish roots. But tragically, those roots had been severed between the first and third centuries. The severance gave rise to replacement the-ology and a different understanding of Israel.

Replacement theology

From the church's side, the breach between church and synagogue was formalised by Constantine's recognition of Christianity as a state religion. After the Church Council of Nicaea in CE 325 he wrote to the churches, insisting they should hold nothing in common with the Jews. For hundreds of years church teachers followed the traditions of the early fathers that the church had replaced Israel in the purposes of God. According to that teaching, Jesus had fulfilled in Himself the covenant promises of 'Israel' and the concept of Israel was enlarged to embrace all people who have become followers of Christ, while dispossessing those who did not recognise Him as Saviour. Thus the Jewish people were dispossessed of their inheritance and replaced by the church – very different from Paul's picture in Romans 11 of the church 'grafted in' to the olive tree of Israel. So two very different views of Israel became established in the church by the seventeenth century. They were to lead to quite opposed views in the church regarding the restoration of Israel in our time.

Recognition and dialogue

In the twentieth century a third school of thought was added, strengthened by biblical criticism, wartime reflections and the Holocaust, or *Shoah*, as it is known to Jewish people. Through his personal experience on the eve of the First World War, the Jewish theologian Franz Rosenzweig concluded that Judaism and Christianity are both partial truths in history, equally valid for their respective communities. This theology was further developed by his friend Martin Buber in his philosophy of dialogue. Dialogue was also the key to the establishment of the Council of Christians and Jews in 1942. After the Second World War, as Christians came to recognise that the Shoah was part of their history too, perspectives in both Catholic and Protestant churches were radically changed. There was a growing realisation that God loves the Jewish people as Jews and not just as potential Christians. This does not mean that everything they do, or Israel does, is right, but there is a valid call to repentance for past attitudes and persecution, and to Christian solidarity with the Jewish people today.

Restoration of the Jewish state

To Christian lovers of Israel in the Puritan tradition of Bible teaching, the restoration of the state in 1948 was indeed a miraculous fulfilment of God's covenant promise to His people. There had been a continuous history of Jewish settlement in the Land since biblical times, but the regathering of the exiles was a further fulfilment of prophecy. In the years that followed, they came from Russia, the land of the north, from Ethiopia in the south, from India in the east and from Europe and America in the west. Referred to as *aliyah*, this was the beginning of the fulfilment of what Isaiah, Jeremiah, Ezekiel, Amos and Zechariah had foretold, coming to pass in our generation.

From 1948 to 1967 Israel survived constant conflict with its neighbours. Then in May 1967 President Nasser of Egypt ordered troops into the Sinai. UN forces withdrew and Nasser closed the Straits of Tiran to Israeli shipping, denying Israel access to the Red Sea. This was an act of war. On 26 May Nasser declared: 'We intend to open a general assault against Israel. This will be total war. Our basic aim is the destruction of Israel.'

The Israeli government did not wait. It took action against Egypt's airforce, destroying 300 of Nasser's 340 combat aircraft within three hours. Nevertheless, Jordan was duped by Nasser into believing that Egypt would soon be victorious, and entered the fray alongside Egypt and Syria. In six days the fighting was over. Egypt was defeated and the Jordanian forces had been driven back across the Jordan River, leaving the West Bank in Israeli hands. This West Bank is the territory now so much in contention between Israel and the Palestinian Authority.

In the aftermath of victory, Israel hoped to use the West Bank as a bargaining chip. It did not annex the newly occupied territory, but many in Israel hoped to exchange it with the Arab powers for a recognition of the State of Israel and peace with secure boundaries. But such hopes for peace were quickly dashed. The Arab states began to re-arm and at the August 1967 Arab League meeting in the Sudan, adopted as their political position 'the three nos', principles by which the Arab states were to abide, namely: 'No peace with Israel, no recognition of Israel, no negotiations with it.'

An opportunity for negotiation was lost which could never so easily be regained, as on the Israeli side the ideology of *Gush Emunim* (the Block of the Faithful) had strong resonance among the right wing of Israeli politics, and led to the rapid growth of Jewish settlements in the occupied areas. These became a first line of defence for the state, in some cases securing hilltops in strategic locations, such as Alfei Menashe, which commands a view of most of Israel's coastline, and important sites of Jewish history, such as Hebron, one of five biblical Cities of Refuge and the tomb of Abraham, Isaac and Jacob; Shiloh where the Ark of the Covenant rested for 200 years and Tekoa, home of the prophet Amos.

The struggle for peace

The UN Resolution 242 which followed the 1967 war (and was re-affirmed in Resolution 338 after the Yom Kippur War in 1973) has been the baseline for all subsequent peace negotiations. Resolution 242 called for the application of two principles:

(i) Withdrawal of Israeli armed forces from territories occupied in the recent conflict.
(ii) Termination of all claims or states of belligerency and respect for and acknowledgement of the sovereignty, territorial integrity and political independence of every state in the area and their right to live in peace within secure and recognised boundaries free from threats or acts of force.

Both clauses are important, and from Israel's viewpoint implementation of one is dependent on acceptance of the other. In 1967 Israel offered the first, but the Arab nations refused the second. It was a pattern to be repeated in 2000 when President Clinton tried to broker an agreement. Israel's Prime Minister Barak offered 96 per cent of the land claimed by the Palestinians plus additional land from Israel to make up the total, but Chairman Arafat would not agree to the termination of all claims. He walked away to launch the second *intifada* and the campaign of terror through suicide bombing.

The struggle for peace is over the application of these key principles, but any settlement involves far more than a territorial dispute. There is the difficulty for Islam of recognising the sovereignty of any non-Muslim government over land formerly ruled by a Muslim power. There is the problem for Arab ideology of accepting a non-Arab state within the Arab world, where the concept of pluralism is resisted; whether among the Maronites in Lebanon, the Copts in Egypt, or the native African population in Sudan. There was the dimension of Cold War rivalry in which each side had its proxies in the region. There are the rights of refugees on both sides of the dispute: some 700,000 Arabs were displaced from Israel in 1948 and have been kept with their descendants in refugee camps ever since, while in excess of 800,000 Jews were displaced from Arab lands and absorbed into the new state. Finally, there is the issue of Jerusalem – symbolically so important to Jews, Christians and Muslims.

Nevertheless, in 1979 Israel and Egypt had signed the Camp David Accords under which Egypt recognised Israel's sovereignty in exchange for territory claimed by Egypt. In 1995 a peace agreement between Israel and Jordan was signed on similar terms. Anwar Sadat of Egypt paid for the first with his life – assassinated by Islamic militants. Prime Minister Rabin of Israel paid with his life for the attempt to enlarge the peace – assassinated by Jewish extremists. The death of Chairman Arafat in 2004 opens a new chapter.

Christian intervention strategies

Where are the Christians in all this? The three theological viewpoints outlined at the start of this chapter are reflected in three intervention strategies in Middle East affairs. For the spiritual heirs of the Puritans with their biblical theology, the use of the oil weapon by the Arab states, forcing 13 countries to relocate their embassies away from Jerusalem, triggered a strong reaction. In 1980 the International Christian Embassy Jerusalem (ICEJ) was established as a declaration of support for Israel with Jerusalem as its eternal capital. From its inception, the Embassy arranged an annual Christian celebration of the Feast of Tabernacles, bringing thousands of Christians from many nations to Jerusalem in an outpouring of support. Another Jerusalem-based organisation is Bridges for Peace, founded in 1976 to support Israel and build relationships between Jews and Christians worldwide. In 1985 Christian Friends of Israel was also formed as an expression of love to the Jewish people and to provide them with practical assistance, while teaching Christians in

the nations about Israel and their Jewish roots. In 1991 Ebenezer
Emergency Fund began as the doors of the former Soviet Union suddenly opened to permit the return of Jews to Zion, and Christians
caught the vision of chartering ships to bring the immigrants home, just
as Joanna Cartwright had requested of Cromwell's parliament back in
1648. These four organisations are examples of many evangelical societies founded in this period who stand with Israel, while at the same time
offering aid to Arab Christians.

By contrast, those Christians who followed the teaching of replacement theology saw no special significance in the restoration of Israel in
1948. They focused more clearly on the plight of Palestinian refugees,
encouraged to flee from Israel by the Arab powers so their armies could
destroy the state at birth, and then kept for generations in squalid
refugee camps and used as a political pawn to pressure the West. For
organisations like Christian Aid and War on Want they were a natural
focus for aid. Their efforts were assisted by local partners who saw political pressure rather than development aid as the key to change.
Supported by government grants as well as Christian charity, Christian
Aid and other charities put increasing weight into political advocacy for
the Palestinian cause. However, such one-sided publicity does little to
help the Palestinians see themselves as other than victims, or capable of
influencing their own development through the restraint of violence.

The third strategy of Christian involvement – interfaith dialogue – arose
out of the perceived failure of the Oslo Peace Accords signed in 1993.
Why had this peace attempt failed to get anywhere, though strongly supported by Washington? A strong point was the attractive vision of
economic advantages for both sides as part of a peace dividend. So what
went wrong? Was it because it failed to recognise the spiritual dimension
to the conflict? Could spiritual leaders on both sides be involved in finding a solution? George Carey, then Archbishop of Canterbury, himself an
evangelical, was willing to see if interfaith dialogue between Christian,
Jewish and Muslim leaders could point the way to reconciliation. Under
his chairmanship, the Alexandria Process became a parallel track to the
diplomatic talks aimed at reviving the Oslo Peace Process. They faced massive obstacles of understanding and logistics, but with the help of Canon
Andrew White (the Archbishop's special envoy) they made remarkable
progress in developing trust between the participants.

All three groups have an ongoing commitment with varying degrees of involvement by local Arab Christians in Israel and in the Palestinian Authority. There are also approximately 8,000 messianic believers in Israel from a Jewish background who are strongly loyal to the Jewish state. In addition, there are Orthodox and Catholic Christians with Jewish partners, who have emigrated from the former Soviet Union. Many of these local Christians are involved in grass-roots peacemaking initiatives that cross racial boundaries. One such Christian initiative from Israel's side is *Shevet Achim* (dwelling in unity) which brings Palestinian and Iraqi infants needing open-heart surgery to Israeli hospitals. In Jerusalem, Tel Aviv and Haifa, doctors and nurses give their time freely to provide life-saving paediatric care not available in Gaza or Iraq. Another Christian initiative, this time from the Palestinian side, is *Musalaha* (reconciliation), which arranges camel treks into the desert, bringing together people from Israel and the Palestinian territories. Partnered in twos with a camel, they depend on each other, and their understanding of 'the other' begins to change.

In both Christian and Jewish teaching, peace will not be fully achieved till Messiah comes. Indeed the fact that the world has evidently not been living in peace for the last 2,000 years is one of the strongest Jewish arguments against recognising Jesus as Messiah. For Christians to say that the prophecies He did not fulfil in His first coming will be fulfilled at His return seems to most Jews to be merely an escape clause. But the expectation of Messiah's coming has been affirmed by generations of orthodox Jews in their prayers: 'I believe in the coming of the Messiah, and even if he tarries, still I will wait every day for him to come.'

And what should we be doing until that day comes? For Jewish people there is an imperative – *tikun ha olam* – to make the world whole. For Christians there is the instruction Paul gave to Timothy: 'First of all I urge that entreaties and prayers, petitions and thanksgivings be made on behalf of all men, for kings and all in authority in order that we may lead a tranquil and quiet life in all godliness and dignity.'

What kind of quiet life and dignity is it for Israelis living in the desert town of Sderot to be attacked randomly by Kassam rockets fired from the Gaza Strip? What kind of quiet life and dignity is it for the 700 victims of suicide attacks against Israel in the ten years from 1994 to 2004, killing teenagers, women and children, and the thousands more who struggle with physical and mental injuries? And we must also ask: what kind of quiet life and dignity is it for Palestinian families whose homes are destroyed in the search for tunnels bringing rockets and grenades into the Gaza Strip, and for thousands more who queue for hours at checkpoints while they are searched for terrorist weapons?

To state that innocent people suffer on both sides does not imply moral equivalence between terrorists and those who defend against terrorism. But it does mean our prayers and concern are needed for both sides and for creative strategies that will isolate the terrorists or bring them to co-operate in civic society.

Pathways to peacemaking

For more than 50 years Israel has sought a peaceful solution to this conflict. In 1947 the UN proposed to partition Palestine (under the British Mandate) into two independent states: Israel and Palestine. The Jewish leaders accepted the UN plan, even though it gave them less land than they wanted, but the Arab nations rejected it. Again in 1967 Israelis tried hard to negotiate a settlement with Arab leaders in the West Bank, but moderate Palestinians were unwilling to conclude any agreement in the face of the refusal by the Arab leadership at Khartoum to negotiate with Israel. In 1993 Israel entered the Oslo Accords and agreed to negotiate a comprehensive peace agreement on the basis of 'land for peace'. These Final Status negotiations began at Camp David in 2000 and culminated at Taba in 2001 when Israel proposed the establishment of an Independent Palestinian state in virtually all of Gaza and the West Bank. Under American pressure, Israel offered that the capital of that state should be East Jerusalem.

However, Chairman Arafat insisted on the right of Palestinian refugees to return not only to a Palestinian state but also to the State of Israel, where their numbers would have swamped the Jewish state. Unable or unwilling to compromise on this claim, he could not agree to the creation of a Palestinian state as marking the end of the conflict, and went away to launch the second *intifada*. In March 2002 there were 37 separate attacks on Israel in 31 days; 135 people were killed. Israel had to take action against suicide bombers.

Terrorism and the security barrier

No government could resist a call for action when faced daily with pictures of its civilians killed in buses, shopping malls and restaurants, when the emergency services have to retrieve body parts from roofs and bus shelters. To fence in every school and community would be a retreat to the ghetto. The alternative was to separate the main areas of Jewish population from the source of terrorist attacks by a physical barrier. The idea of a security fence had been mooted, but up to that time was not supported by any major political party: the left saw it as an obstacle to co-existence and the right as abandoning the settlers in Judea and Samaria. It would cost a fortune and generate hardship, but the slaughter of innocent civilians could not continue.

The security barrier was started around the northern end of the disputed territories in 2003 and immediately the percentage of terrorists blocked from entering Israel rose. In 2004 a UN report acknowledged that 'terrorist attacks inside Israel' dropped 83 per cent in the first half of the year. However, the international community had raised a storm of protest at Israel's action in defending its citizens against terrorism.

At the UN, an emergency special session of the General Assembly in December 2003 requested an *advisory* opinion from the International Court of Justice on the legality of the 'Wall'. It is in fact a temporary barrier, 95 per cent of which is made of wire-mesh fencing and only 5 per cent of actual wall (and that only in urban areas or along highways subject to sniper fire). If terror is stopped, the barrier could be removed. But the dossier of 88 documents provided to the court by the UN was totally silent on the subject of Palestinian terrorist attacks. Similarly in Britain, a Parliamentary Committee invited evidence on the humanitarian and economic consequences of the barrier, but did not see fit to enquire into the causes for its construction.

'To save lives' is too obvious an answer, yet Israel can point to a reduction of 90 per cent in the number of murder attacks inside Israel, a decrease of 70 per cent in the number of people killed and a reduction of 85 per cent in the number wounded, comparing the average in the year before the fence to the months after. However, a land grab was in the minds of Israel's critics. 'We can understand why Israel, fearful of its security, wants to build the barrier,' concluded the parliamentary report.

'But any such security fence should be constructed on Israeli, not Palestinian, land.' So was the UN report correct to argue: 'There is no compelling evidence this could not have been done with equal effect by building the wall along the Green Line'?

A number of questions are prompted by these seemingly reasonable objections. First, exactly what is the boundary between Palestinian and Israeli land, and, second, when was it agreed? The so-called Green Line follows the Armistice line, where the respective armies stopped fighting in 1949, but was never recognised as an international boundary. UN Resolution 242 called for negotiations between the parties to establish 'secure and recognised boundaries'. If they believed the Green Line to be this, surely they would have said so. Again, the Oslo talks called for negotiations between the parties on this matter, and the 'Roadmap' requires a halt to Palestinian violence as the first step in a process leading to recognition of provisional boundaries. When violence is halted, boundaries can be negotiated with the Palestinians, as they have been with Egypt and Jordan. Until then, it is not clear exactly what is Israeli land and what is Palestinian land.

The League of Nations, in Article 6 of the Palestine Mandate, required the Mandatory power to establish close settlement by Jews on public land and wasteland throughout this area. Britain split off 70 per cent of the Mandate on the other side of the Jordan for the Arab population. Political positions are vocal, but there will be no legal clarity on what is Palestinian land to the west of the Jordan until boundaries are negotiated between the parties. In the meantime, Israel took into account that the Green Line passed so close to Tel Aviv airport that a terrorist with a shoulder-launched missile (as was used against an Israeli aircraft at Mombasa) could threaten departing planes unless the security fence was sited beyond the Green Line.

The actual route of the fence was determined according to topographical and security features and was open to argument by Palestinians in the Israeli Supreme Court. What other government in the region would have left itself open to such challenge under the rule of law? In practice, the Israeli court upheld several complaints and ruled that inconvenience to Palestinians, including difficulties in school journeys, had to be balanced with security considerations. The Israeli government immediately announced it would accept the judgment and moved the fence accordingly.

Proportionality is not an easy principle to apply. When terrorists in Gaza fire four rockets indiscriminately against the Israeli township of Sderot, would a proportional response be to fire four rockets into Gaza from just beyond its border, or to go into Gaza, seek out the terrorists and destroy the tunnels by which their munitions are imported? The first would result in more loss of life than the second more targeted approach, yet the second is widely criticised.

The opinion of the International Court of Justice, however, went beyond the principle of proportionality, to deny Israel the right of self-defence under Article 51 of the UN Charter, on the grounds that the armed attack against it was not caused by one state against another. When nation after nation has signed up to a war against terror, is Israel the only nation to be denied the right to defend itself against armed terrorist organisations committed to the destruction of its homeland? Such discrimination against Israel's right to defend itself is clearly political and not judicial, and must be rejected as antisemitic.

As Christians in the nations we have no right to tell the sovereign State of Israel what it should do, but we have a duty to stand with her as the only democracy in the Middle East and to oppose terrorism and anti-semitism wherever it is found. We must also reject loudly and clearly the moral equation of Palestinian terrorist action on the one hand with Israeli action to defend its citizens from terror on the other. Islamic terrorists deliberately attack civilian targets – passengers on a bus or train, people in a café, teenagers at a disco. Israeli soldiers target the terrorists and do their utmost to avoid civilian casualties, even at the risk of exposing their own troops to greater danger. This distinction is so often obscured in the Western media, which simply refer to the cycle of violence as if there were no moral difference.

Inevitably, the tension of confrontation and the need for constant watchfulness cause distress; houses are removed in Gaza to force back the terrorists who use them as cover to attack Israeli positions; nerves snap, so lives are lost in tragic errors. So is there any way to move beyond containment of terror to a peace process?

An opinion poll in the West Bank at the end of 2004 showed that the majority of Palestinians want a negotiated agreement with Israel, to end the conflict by peaceful means. Similarly, polls in Israel show that the majority of Israelis would be prepared for withdrawal from the disputed territories, if they could be assured the result would be peace. So why is it so difficult to resolve the conflict?

At root there is a lack of trust. The fact is that the Palestinian Movement, Fatah, began before 1967, with the aim of destroying the State of Israel as a whole, even before it occupied the disputed territories. Maps in Palestinian schoolbooks still ignore the existence of Israel and claim a Palestinian state to the Mediterranean Sea. Fatah now declare they have given up this objective, but Hamas have not. They boycotted the election for a Palestinian prime minister and so are not bound to the result. How can Palestinians be sure that a cessation of violence would result in withdrawal of Israeli troops, or Israelis be sure that withdrawal from the territories would truly be the end of the conflict? Is it surprising that neither side wants to take the first step? In the next section we examine four policy options and their constraints.

Option 1: the status quo

Israel wants peace, but needs a partner for peace with the political will and power to stop terrorism. Without that precondition there will be no effective movement towards peace. However, the status quo cannot satisfy either side, and is increasingly difficult to defend internationally, unless there is some clear policy direction to bring hope beyond it. In the short term the status quo risks acute economic hardship for Israel, as well as for the Palestinians, and a security disaster. In the medium to long term it carries a growing risk of destroying the Jewish state.

Both in the British parliament and in the International Court at the Hague, the criticism of Israel's security barrier has focused on its consequences rather than the onslaught of terror that was the reason for it in the first place. One-sided though this is, it has led in both Britain and the Hague to calls for international trade sanctions against Israel – a call which was taken up in the United Nations General Assembly when the Court's advisory opinion was received. The British government turned down the recommendations of a Select Committee to this effect, and it may be expected that the American administration would use its veto in the UN Security Council to block a trade embargo there. But support from both these quarters is crucially dependent on Israel making diplomatic progress to resolve the conflict. Sticking to the status quo would almost certainly result in further support for trade sanctions in the General Assembly, severe damage to the Israeli economy and hardship for Jews and Arabs alike.

With regard to security, Israel is even more concerned by the nuclear threat from Iran than by the terror on its doorstep. Iran's first nuclear reactor at Bushehr is due to enter service in 2006 and additional nuclear plants are planned. Although Iran claims these are purely for peaceful purposes, it has been none too forthcoming with the international agencies and has developed Shehab-3 missiles, capable of reaching all areas of Israel. To counter this threat, Israel needs international assistance.

The strongest threat to the status quo comes, however, from inside – the demographic time bomb. The population of Israel is 6.8 million people, of whom approximately 5.5 million are Jewish and 1.3 million are Israeli Arabs. In addition, there are 2.3 million Arab people in the West Bank and 1.3 million in Gaza, making a total Arab population of 4.9 million in Israel and the disputed territories. If all these Arab people were included in an Israeli state it would lose its Jewish majority in 10 to 15 years, given the higher birth rate of the Arab population. 'We shall win the war on our beds' is one powerful Palestinian claim.

Israeli settlers in Gaza and the West Bank have a vote in Israeli elections. If the Arab population were denied this right when they become a numerical majority in the combined area of sovereign Israel and these administered territories, the result would be incompatible with Israel's democratic character. Only another massive wave of immigration could postpone that tipping point beyond 2020. The search is therefore for an alternative policy that not only meets the aspirations of nationhood by the Palestinian people, but also preserves the character of a Jewish homeland. To split off the bulk of the Arab population into some form of elected administration for a Palestinian entity living as neighbours to Israel would be a way of achieving both goals.

Without such a change of policy, the status quo of a Jewish state could only be retained by denying the vote to some, while allowing it to a racial minority within the same geographical area. Alternatively there might be some fancy franchise, for example in a two-chamber legislature, where the consent of both chambers was required for legislation and the electorate for one chamber was restricted to the Jewish population. It is hard to imagine that international opinion would agree to such a blocking device. So the demographic reality is one factor that drives Mr Sharon's policy of disengagement in Gaza, and Jewish support for a two-state solution.

Option 2: a two-state solution

Western policy was summed up very succinctly by Tony Blair in his speech to the Community Security Trust, London, dinner on 26th February 2003: 'If we want to tackle terrorism we also have to bring peace to the Middle East. We know the outcome. Two states based on the twin principles of an Israel secure within its borders, and a viable Palestinian state.'

In April 2003, a 'Performance-based Roadmap to a Permanent Two-State Solution to the Israeli-Palestinian Conflict' was handed over to the two parties and published by the Quartet (the United States, the European Union, the United Nations and Russia). In essence this envisaged the recognition of the State of Israel by the Arab states and the cessation of conflict in return for Israel's withdrawal from areas occupied since 2000, agreement on provisional borders and recognition of a Palestinian state.

This process was envisaged in three phases, the first of which (targeted for completion by June 2003) required reciprocal declarations at the outset. At Aqaba, the Palestinians issued an unequivocal statement reiterating Israel's right to exist in peace and security, and calling for an immediate and unconditional ceasefire. For its part the Israeli leadership issued an unequivocal statement affirming its commitment to the two-state vision of an independent, viable, sovereign Palestinian state living in peace and security alongside Israel.

Going on from there, both sides were to undertake visible steps towards making their declarations a reality. Specifically, the Israelis were to dismantle settlement outposts erected since March 2001, freeze all settlement activity and undertake no actions undermining trust. The Palestinians were to arrest individuals and groups conducting and planning violent attacks on Israelis anywhere, dismantle the terrorist infrastructure and start the confiscation of illegal weapons. Institutional reform of the Palestinian Authority was to be accompanied by budgetary support.

Arab states were to cut off public and private funding of groups supporting and engaging in acts of violence. As confidence increased in Palestinian security measures, the IDF would progressively withdraw from areas occupied since September 2000. It was assumed that the Palestinian people would then have a leadership acting decisively against terror, and willing and able to build a practising democracy. They could then proceed to Phase II, with an international conference and the creation of a Palestinian state with provisional borders.

From the start, however, the Palestinians argued that they could not comply with these terms and dismantle the terrorist infrastructure without causing a civil war. Instead they proceeded to negotiate a *hudna*, or ceasefire, with the terrorist organisations rather than confront them. At the same time Israel was pressed to make concessions regarding release of prisoners and the security fence, neither of which is mentioned in the 'Roadmap'! Israel withdrew troops from Gaza and Bethlehem, and was on the verge of handing over two further towns to Palestinian control, but in the first month of the 'ceasefire' there were over 100 attacks against Israelis.

Israel's attempts to deal with active terrorist leaders in areas still under its control led to massive retaliation against civilians in Israel. Two suicide bomb attacks in September 2003 brought the peace process to collapse. Arafat's promises to reform the structure of the Palestinian Authority always fell short of handing control of security to his prime minister, and corruption in the Palestinian Authority was rampant. The US secretary of state warned that if the parties gave up the 'Roadmap' they would go 'over the cliff'. But documentary evidence linking Chairman Arafat to terror attacks against civilians in Israel convinced the Israeli government they no longer had a partner for peace.

While international support for the 'Roadmap' turned largely to lip-service and hope, Israel committed itself to unilateral action in defence of its civilian population by building the security barrier, and to a policy of disengagement from Gaza to be completed in 2005. The first of these measures cut the number of deaths from suicide bomb attacks by 90 per cent in the first six months of 2004 as compared with the same period in the previous year. The second – withdrawal of troops and settlers from Gaza – was projected as a unilateral step in line with both the 'Roadmap' and UN Resolution 242. It was supported by a majority of Israelis, according to opinion polls, but was vigorously opposed by the settlers themselves and by members of Sharon's own Likud party.

In a visit to the United States, Mr Sharon won support from George Bush for his policy of disengagement. In return, he secured a statement from the American president with two crucial points: first that the return of Palestinian refugees should be to a future Palestinian state and not to sovereign Israel, and second that in drawing the future boundaries between the two states, recognition should be given to developments on the ground, thus implicitly giving approval to the incorporation into Israel of the major settlements at Ariel and Ma'ale Adumim. This, however, was not enough to placate the opposition in his own party, which called a special conference to defeat the policy of disengagement or withdrawal from Gaza.

It is a difficult issue for biblical Zionists as well as for Jews. In July 2004 close to 200,000 Israelis formed a human chain from the Western Wall in Jerusalem of 90 kilometres (or about 56 miles) to the Jewish settlements in the Gaza Strip. It was a massive demonstration against government policy. About 3 per cent of the population of Israel took part, equivalent to a demonstration by 2 million people in Britain.

The demonstrators had at heart two arguments: (i) that biblically, Gaza belongs to the Jewish people as part of the Land of their inheritance, and (ii) that strategically, withdrawal from it will not bring peace in the Middle East. To counter those arguments, the supporters of withdrawal point out that through most of history Gaza was occupied by the enemies of Israel – Philistines – and there is little of ancient Jewish heritage in this small strip of land. Also, even if disengagement does not bring peace, separation of Jews and Arabs in this area will remove a source of continuous friction.

The fact is that the biblical borders of Israel differed from one historical period to another. God's promise to Abraham is the Land of Canaan, and the boundaries of that Land are defined in different ways at various times. The Jewish people cannot exist in cyber space – they need a real homeland in Israel with secure borders. Yet if they had not been prepared to be pragmatic about its boundaries, the State of Israel would not exist today. Since 1967 the administration or relinquishment of territory acquired in a defensive war brings many moral dilemmas. Surprisingly, Jesus never taught directly about the rights or wrongs of occupation, even though Israel in His time was occupied by the hated Roman administration. So Christians today must wrestle with these issues in prayer and discussion, seeking to apply the values of a heavenly kingdom to the realities of earthly politics.

Option 3: a one-state solution

So long as progress in implementing the two-state option is blocked by the failure of the Palestinian Authority to rein in terror and disagreement in Israel about a unilateral withdrawal, a one-state solution gains momentum. This would cover the whole of Israel, Gaza and the West Bank in one political unit. It is not officially espoused by either side, but is increasingly projected by Palestinians in discussions. Although it is not Israeli policy, it might become the unintended consequence of the status quo, unless there is movement towards an alternative policy direction.

For many biblical Zionists it is at first an attractive option. Indeed, some may ask why Israel did not annex the territories and create this Greater Israel in 1967. Joel 3:2 shows the Lord's judgement against those who divide His Land: 'I will enter into judgment against them.' A one-state solution would avoid that judgement, but the dynamics of population growth presented above suggest that a one-state solution would lead quickly to the demise of a democratic Jewish state. The current growth rate of the Arab population so outstrips the Jewish growth rate that without a massive increase of Jewish immigration, the majority of people within the wider boundaries would be of Arabic descent by 2020 at the latest.

Already Israel has the highest Jewish population of any country, so the prospects of future immigration are limited. With an Arab majority the way would be clear for the return of up to 4 million refugees, whether to Haifa or to Lod as much as to the West Bank, thus overwhelming Israel. While the rhetoric of Islamic militants calls for the Jews to be thrown into the sea, the tradition of Islam is more tolerant to Judaism so long as it accepts the subordinate role of a dhimmi class and the imposition of Sharia law. But that is not the future the Jewish people see for themselves in Israel. There are already 22 Arab states and only one Jewish state. A wrong choice would put its future existence at risk.

For biblical Zionists and Jews to advocate this option, before the coming of Messiah, requires an immense leap of faith. Is it worth insisting on the wider boundaries of biblical Israel at the risk of losing a Jewish state? We may indeed pray for this at 'the restoration of all things', when His Law goes forth from Jerusalem, but is it how Israel should operate in the meantime?

Option 4: a comprehensive Middle East agreement

This, of course, is the dream of politicians! But is it feasible? The perspective from inside Israel is often of an embattled nation, but from across the Jordan things look different. Israel is at peace with two of its Arab neighbours. Peace with Egypt has been secured – a cold peace maybe, but with a significant leader in the Arab world. Peace with Jordan secures a second frontier. For King Abdullah, with Iraq in turmoil on one side and a Jordanian population of whom 70 per cent are Palestinians, there is much to be gained from stabilising the Israel/Palestine conflict on the other side of the kingdom. When King Hussein of Jordan backed Iraq in the first Gulf War, Jordan had to absorb an influx of Palestinians expelled from Kuwait and Saudi Arabia. Now Jordan would rather close its border than risk a further influx from Israel and the disputed territories to add to the numbers of unemployed Palestinians in its refugee camps or townships.

In the Palestinian Authority there was widespread disillusionment with corrupt leaders, but no one commanded strong support on the street as a successor to Arafat. The constitution of the Palestinian Authority set out an interim leader, but with the risk of chaos as radical groups competed for power. In practice, apart from the old guard of Abu Mazen and Abu Ala, most strong men who might follow Arafat had their power base either in Gaza or in Jericho/Ramallah and not in both.

In the eyes of some observers, Menachem Begin made a mistake in not insisting on the return of Gaza to Egypt's control in the Camp David Accords of 1978. Twenty-five years later, Mr Sharon's attempt to extricate the IDF from Gaza through disengagement talks seems to depend heavily on Cairo's role in talks between Palestinian factions, and Egypt's willingness to help maintain order if Israel withdraws. Avoidance of a breakdown in civil society or of the takeover of Gaza by Hamas is in Egypt's interest as well as Israel's. In the light of the marriage of King Hussein's son and successor to a Palestinian, one might ask: was it equally a mistake of King Hussein to renounce any Jordanian interest in the West Bank?

We cannot turn back the pages of history to solutions that Egypt and Jordan declined to be drawn into before. But it is clear that their active support is crucial to the development of a Palestinian state in these areas. For Jordan, the extent of such involvement will be influenced by the role of Syria. The recent account by Itamar Rabinovich, Israel's chief negotiator on that front from 1992 to 1995, shows that Ehud Barak as Israel's prime minister saw Israel-Syria negotiations as a more hopeful starting point than direct negotiations with the Palestinians. Is there scope here for Israel to negotiate with its neighbours in a wider Europe, while retaining the transatlantic alliance? In 2003 the European Union launched its European Neighbourhood Policy offering states beyond its borders participation in various programmes (but not the institutions) of the EU, in order to strengthen the rule of law, good governance and respect for human rights. Egypt, Israel, Jordan, Syria and the Palestinian Authority were among the potential partners in these negotiations with the EU in 2004.

Putting a conflict into a wider framework where partners of both sides can work together is one method of conflict resolution. Would it work here? Israel has strong economic and technological ties with Europe, but could she trust her European partners in such crucial negotiations when Europe was the root of poisonous antisemitism in the last century? If such talks were to succeed, some might still wonder if they were not more likely to result in the false peace described by Ezekiel rather than ushering in the messianic age. Is that a risk peacemakers should be willing to accept?

There is no easy political solution to the problems of the Middle East. While Israel must defend its citizens from terrorist attack, it is committed to the search for a peaceful resolution that will provide security with dignity and a quiet life to Israelis and Palestinians alike. But militant Islamic groups will not accept any compromise solution. Four times the offer of a Palestinian state in co-existence with Israel has been turned down by Palestinian representatives – in 1937, 1947, 1967 and 2000. Now, antisemitism is on the rise again across Europe. Anti-Israelism is rising in the media, in the universities and in the trade unions.

Jews are not alone in facing persecution: The church is suffering in Asia and northern Africa where it confronts militant Islam. For reasons that have nothing to do with Israel, Christians are being killed for their faith in Nigeria, where several states are adopting Sharia law, and in Indonesia and the Philippines. Over the last ten years, many thousands of Christians have been killed in the Sudan and hundreds of thousands made homeless. Christians are also under pressure in Lebanon, Egypt and Iraq. The result in the Middle East is a new openness of Jews and Christians to each other, as minority faiths in a region of conflict, but a wariness of political solutions which would leave both communities open to the persecution Christians in Iraq face since the liberation of that country by the Western alliance.

JUST PEACEMAKING THEORY

Fred Wright

In the hearts of people today there is a deep longing for peace. When the true spirit of peace is thoroughly dominant, it becomes an inner experience with unlimited possibilities. Only when this really happens – when the spirit of peace awakens and takes possession of men's hearts, can humanity be saved from perishing.

Albert Schweitzer (1875–1965)

In addition to ethical dimensions of war, there are ethical dimensions to peace. It is worth considering what is meant by the term 'peace'. Peace may be understood in two ways. First, 'negative' peace, which simply means the absence of violence, generally brought about by non-peaceful methods such as coercion rather than co-operation. In international terms, peace is considered to exist during a cessation of violence and hostility, bearing a resemblance to Theucydides' comment. The negative form of peace is often brought about by third parties such as the UN, as imposition backed by force. In reality what happens is that a just decision is imposed, rather than resolution or reconciliation taking place. Negative peace very often is non-sustainable and may provide the seedbed of resentment that may lead to further conflict in the future. The second way of defining peace is 'positive' peace, which relates to the Hebrew term 'shalom', implying rest, wholeness, well-being and, implicitly, reconciliation and restoration. When reconciliation is not possible, separation and resolution is possible with a minimum of hostility and acrimony.

Just Peacemaking Theory (JPT) was pioneered by Glen Stassen of Fuller Seminary, along with 23 Christian ethicists, scholars of international relations, specialists in conflict resolution, theologians, one New Testament scholar and a handful of leaders in Peace Action, who worked for five years to create a Just Peacemaking Theory. The theory in some ways developed from a sense of the inadequacy of the debate between Just War Theory and pacifism. Debates dominated by those paradigms inevitably focus on whether or not to make war, while ignoring the issues of making peace, not least until all avenues have been exhausted. JPT focuses on initiatives aimed at reducing international or civil tensions and develops initiatives that may lead to justice, reconciliation and a secure peace. JPT is regarded by some as an expansion of the Last Resort category of the Just War Theory, in that it exhausts possibilities for peace before the commencement of hostilities. As such, JPT deserves a separate category. It is not a pacifist position; rather it attempts a return to biblical values.

Stassen and the group suggest that there are ten practices for abolishing war and for Just Peacemaking, which follow below with adaptation and conflation by the writer:

1. *Non-violent direct action*: lobbying, boycotts, protest marches, strikes, freedom of information readily available. Tactics employed by Ghandi and Martin Luther King are held as prime examples. A little-known example that made considerable impact to the unfreezing of the Cold War and the collapse of the Soviet control on East Germany, was the non-violent protest of the East German churches. Further work should be carried out to assess the impact of the large prayer meetings and the torch-light processions in Leipzig.

2. *Co-operative conflict resolution*: developing initiatives for partners in peace. Capital should be made of the decline in the utility of war; the priority of trade and the economy over war; the strength of international exchanges, communications, transactions and networks; and the gradual ascendancy of liberal representative democracy and a mixture of welfare-state and laissez-faire market economy. The fourteenth Dalai Lama commented: 'Peace, in the sense of absence of war, is of little value to someone who is dying of hunger or cold. Peace can only last where human rights are respected, where people are fed, and where individuals and nations are free.'

3. *Acknowledgement of responsibility*: addressing past offences and grievances, real or imagined, developing empathy, offering repentance and forgiveness, identifying individual and corporate responsibility for the tensions that have led to aggression. The South African Truth and Reconciliation Commission was initiated in an attempt to bring reconciliation. It remains to be seen if its work is, and will be, effective.

4. *Advance democracy, human rights and religious liberty*: encouraging democratisation of states and the political order and legislature. Activities to enhance human rights, religious liberty and civil liberty.

5. *Foster just and sustainable economic development*: against the worst trends within sustainable development, serves the needs of the present without threatening the needs of the future. Providing adequate material, technical and economic resources to those in need, and to those who have need to learn to control resource usage and prevent future exhaustion with a view to future self-sufficiency.

6. *Working with co-operative forces, both established and developed*: working in concert with the international authorities such as the UN, the EU and NATO. There have been suggestions that an international committee of experts in arbitration be set up to be an agency in international conflict resolution.

7. *International efforts*: collective international efforts for peace and human rights, including but not limited to the UN, NATO and the EU, need to be developed and strengthened.

8. *Independent initiatives*: as negotiation between authorities can be slow and laborious there is scope for independent action by prominent individuals or groups. This may lead to reciprocal initiatives from the opposing side and develop a 'peace race'. The ex-US president Jimmy Carter was awarded the Nobel Peace Prize in 2002 for his decades of untiring effort to find peaceful solutions to international conflicts, to advance democracy and human rights, and to promote economic and social development. Christian Peacemaker Teams composed of members of the Mennonites, the Church of the Brethren, and the Quakers visited Iraq to undertake such initiatives in 2002.

9. *Reduction of offensive weapons and arms trade*: the restriction of weapons of mass destruction is a cost-effective way of limiting warfare.

10. *The development of grass-roots peacemaking groups to facilitate the above*: Paul Schroeder, the eminent diplomatic historian, suggests: 'This makes just peacemaking into a task for action by ordinary citizens individually and in groups to sustain, criticize, goad, influence, reform, and lead the many kinds of voluntary associations, governmental and private, which can contribute to transcending the contradictions and managing and overcoming the conflicts of an anarchic international society.'

The major strength of JPT is in what Stassen terms transforming initiatives. Jesus gives three examples of transforming initiatives in Matthew 5:38, 41. All three are probably the most quoted in the search for peace, or more correctly the search for pacifism.

In reality when one understands the meaning of the passage to those who heard the teaching, a rather dramatic scenario unfolds which is anything but pacifist, passive or non-responsive. Rather it is a radical series of transforming initiatives. The three elements are the teaching of the *lex talonis*, an eye for an eye and a tooth for a tooth, the second concerns someone 'suing the coat off your back' and the third 'walking the extra mile'.

Lex talonis, the principle of 'an eye for an eye' (Ex 21:24; Lev 24:20; Deut 19:21), which was also a principle of Roman law, is considered to have begun with the Babylonian law code of Hammurabi (twentieth century BCE). Its purpose was to restrain vengeance. In Jesus' time, Jewish courts often permitted a payment of money instead of physical violence, but the basis was still retribution. The discussion is the introduction to the turning of the other cheek. A key to understanding this element of the passage is in the construction *me antistenai to ponero*, generally translated as the substantive 'do not resist evil'. Clarence Jordan points out that the dative *to ponero* can be instrumental, and, therefore, can be rendered 'by evil means'. The decision to employ the instrumental or the substantive must come from the context. To employ the substantive would suggest that Jesus Himself tolerated evil. In reality Jesus repeatedly confronted evil, but He did oppose evil means of revengeful violence. Therefore contextually the instrumental 'do not resist by evil means' would be consistent. In a similar manner Paul exhorts his readers: 'Do not repay anyone evil for evil . . .' (Rom 12:17ff). In Jewish culture the type of striking here is more by way of an insult than a full-blown physical attack, as to smite the left cheek one must employ the back of the hand. The backhand slap was a customary method of reminding an inferior of his status. The matter was so much a part of life that there was a raft of legislation concerning the matter. If one struck a societal equal in this manner there was a legislation to impose fines and penalties (Mishna, *Baba Qama* 8:6). The transforming initiative is that of 'offering the other cheek' to be smitten and rendering the smiter disempowered on the one hand and standing one's own ground on the other. By not acknowledging the smiter's superior position, the individual is in a situation that to continue they would have to move from a slap to a more violent blow, and thus undermine their own position and also render themselves open to a charge of assault.

The second example of the transforming initiative concerns once again a legal and societal dimension. The drama is set in a court scene where Jesus advises: 'If someone wants to sue you and take your tunic, let him have your cloak as well' (Mt 5:40). The 'cloak' was an outer garment, also used as a cover for sleeping. The Jewish legislation as laid down in Exodus 22:26 and Deuteronomy 24 allowed for a poor person to offer his cloak as surety on a loan. A humanitarian clause was attached that demanded that the garment given as security was to be returned at night, so that the individual would not suffer the effects of the elements. The 'tunic' was a Jewish undergarment with sleeves. For a poor man to give up both would, in most instances, leave him naked. What lies behind Jesus' seemingly irresponsible advice to stand naked before the accuser and the court, is the Jewish concept of nakedness. One who is naked is not the one put to shame, but rather the one who is responsible for that nakedness, and those who witness it. In a sense it is also a prophetic action that exposes the nakedness and shame of those involved. Once again, rather than being a passive response it is a most vigorous one!

The third transforming initiative concerns the 'extra mile'. A Roman soldier might legally require a Jew to transport his baggage for the distance of a thousand paces (*milion*), translated as one mile. The measure was to keep the vast army mobile, and the relatively short distance was considered not to be so much of an imposition that it would cause deep-seated resentment among the population. Jesus' advice, if one is impressed into this service, is to undertake the transforming initiative of offering to carry the soldier's effects a further mile. The action changes the position of the one carrying the effects from one who is weak into one who is strong, and neutralises the power of the one who made the initial demand.

The teachings of the Sermon on the Mount, rather than teaching non-resistance and a seedbed for pacifism, teach not to retaliate against oppressive authority, but how to respond justly and defiantly to unjust power and domination.

Critique

JPT has been received in some areas as a positive contribution to the debate of Just War and pacifism, while others, particularly in the Roman Catholic tradition, have dismissed it as another academic fad.

One of the strengths of the Just Peacemaking Theory is that there is an emphasis on the role of the individual and small, sometimes informal, groups as agencies for potential change, especially by transforming initiatives. In domestic terms, lobbying groups can be effective in winning individual support of members of the legislature and parliamentarians in general. There is also value in such initiatives in smaller conflicts and perhaps in civil conflicts. When it comes to conflicts where in the eyes of one party they are fighting an ideological war, where they consider themselves to be working on a sanitising programme, such initiatives are generally not only despised by the party that is being approached, but also the well-intentioned are paraded as part of the propaganda apparatus.

A singular weakness in all theories of Just War and Just Peacemaking is an assumption that people in different cultures and at different stages within the historical process can be assumed to have the same, or at least similar, sets of standards of behaviour. Positive values in one society can be seen as extremely negative values by another. The Christian emphasis on love, forgiveness and reconciliation contrasts starkly with the values of honour, power and revenge in Islam.

An area that seems to present immediate difficulties is the area of acknowledgement (3 above), in particular forgiveness and reconciliation. In the area of forgiveness an immediate tension is: 'Does the New Testament have a viable social ethic? Can you draw a viable social ethic, namely the question of forgiveness, from the New Testament? Then, can religiously based ideas be articulated in a way that they are politically relevant and usable in a society where there is not a common religious basis?' (J. Bryan Hehir, 'An Ethic for Enemies: Forgiveness in Politics', *Woodstock Report*, March 1996, No. 45.)

The teaching of forgiveness, and the benefits thereof, is nowhere better articulated than in Jesus' teaching in Matthew 18. In the religious world, and in particular Christianity, in the micro sense the healing of personal conflicts by repentance and the release of forgiveness has proved to be the ground for reconciliation and is shown to be both cathartic and providing a basis for re-establishing relationships. In the macro sense it could be argued that forgiveness has only succeeded within the community of the church, or probably more properly within the communion of individual groups within the church. Hannah Arendt, the Jewish philosopher, reflecting on the teaching of Jesus, pointed out that although His teaching of forgiveness was couched in religious language and set within a religious context, the empirical importance of forgiveness in social and political life had been underestimated, not only by secular but also by religious thinkers.

As all wars have ended with a peace conference, with the exception of those that ended from exhaustion or lack of fighters, terms of peace need attention. Within the category, thought must also be given to some measure of penalty for wrongdoing, as forgiveness and recompense are not incompatible. The tension arises when recompense (sometimes referred to as reparations) is spiteful, vengeful and causes disabilities present and future, and is damaging to the party charged with recompense. The provisions of the Treaty of Versailles following the end of the First World War at the insistence of the French, produced a seething resentment in the German nation. For recompense to be meaningful it should be done willingly by those called upon to engage in it, and elements of mercy within the proposals should always be considered and included.

Probably the most forthcoming single statement on peacemaking is the charming but somewhat optimistic statement of Muriel Lester: 'The job of the peacemaker is to stop war, to purify the world, to get it saved from poverty and riches, to heal the sick, to comfort the sad, to wake up those who have not yet found God, to create joy and beauty wherever you go, to find God in everything and everyone.'

SECTION III

The third section concerns Jewish believers in Yeshua in the Land of Israel. Jewish Christians have not been generally appreciated, either by the church in general or by their community, and have been regarded with suspicion within the Land. The Jewish believer has suffered greatly through history. St Jerome (331–419) despised them as being neither something nor nothing. During the Inquisition new believers, whether genuine or not, were always under suspicion, and it has often been the case that when a Jewish person comes to faith in Jesus as Messiah there is an insistence that he assimilate, or denounce Judaism as being inherently evil, as is illustrated in various church confessions for Jewish believers. Messianic fellowships are valuable, but they also stand as an illustration of the Gentile churches' failure to provide adequate resources and understanding for the needs of the Jewish believer. There can on the other hand be a tendency, because of the tragic history of Christian – Jewish relationships, for some Jewish people to accept Jesus and not the church, and as such they tend to struggle along without the benefit of fellowship. The problem is exacerbated by Christian anti-Israelism, which is perceived most often as being a manifestation of continuing institutionalised anti-semitism.

Murray Dixon opens the section with a consideration of the momentous events of the nineteenth and early twentieth centuries that led to the founding of the State of Israel. Gershon Nerel reflects on the Jewish believers in Yeshua in the Land up until 1967 in an insightful presentation. The theme is picked up from that point by Ken Burnett, an elder statesman of Israel-related ministries and founder of Prayer for Israel, in a personal retrospective.

NINETEENTH-CENTURY MIDDLE EAST ENIGMA

Murray Dixon

The nineteenth century was destined to bring sweeping unexpected changes to the Middle East region, sowing seeds that were to mature into full blossom during the twentieth century, leaving a challenging legacy for the twenty-first century.

Two dramatic eighteenth-century events changed the Jewish future, determining events of the nineteenth century. The Enlightenment in the West had opened the ghetto door, changing Judaism, especially among the youth, more dramatically than anything previously. The Enlightenment broke the strictures of confinement to religious communities and the subsequent French Revolution broke open the gates of the ghetto.

Jewish emancipation

In *Declaration of the Rights of Man* in the 1790s, Thomas Payne seemed to offer freedom for the Jews. God, who was no longer needed, was displaced by man, who was master of all, and science was his tool. The ripple effect of the French Revolution provided the Jew with new hope: equal rights. It was the dream of many Jews, who simply wanted to be accepted, to live normal lives like anybody else. They wanted to assimilate, to be Frenchmen, Englishmen, Germans – they wanted to be accepted as nationals of the land in which they lived.

Social acceptance of the Jewish people resulted in a loss of identity. Jewish communities had always remained closely knit and separate from the non-Jewish population. This was partly the result of religious practice but was also forced upon them by antisemitism. They shaved their beards and swapped their distinctive religious clothing for Western garb. Many were baptised, the so-called 'passport to civilisation'. And they were absorbed into Christianity, agnosticism or atheism. They assimilated.

The Jewish Reformation in the East took a different path. Where the West had adopted a Gentile Enlightenment, a Jewish Enlightenment had to be created to emancipate the Jews of the East. It came to be known as the *Haskala*. Unlike the West, which produced secular humanism, it was expressed in terms of the orthodox religious tradition. The disciples of the *Haskala*, known as the *Maskilim*, expanded the *Haskala* among Eastern Jews. By 1837 Rabbi Judah Alkalai was suggesting that though the full occupation of the Promised Land must await the coming of the Messiah, meantime the task could be started by men. Alkalai was instrumental in the forming of *Hovevei Zion*, the Society of Lovers of Zion, which first gathered together pioneers with a vision for settlement in their ancient homeland as a necessary preparation for the redemption.

Jewish nationalism

The spark of Jewish nationalism arose not from the West but from the East. It did not at first come from persecutions; that came later. Rabbi Alkalai wrote:

> It is written in the Bible: 'Return, O Lord, unto the tens of thousands of the families of Israel' . . . But upon what should the Divine Presence rest? On the sticks and stones? Therefore, as the initial stage in the redemption of our souls, we must cause at least 22,000 to return to the Holy Land. This is the necessary precondition for a descent of the Divine Presence among us; afterward He will grant us and all Israel additional signs of His favour.

Others wrote on similar lines. The funding essential for this development was expected from Jewish financiers. Sir Moses Montefiore and Baron Edmond de Rothschild responded to the challenge. Between 1884 and 1900 Rothschild spent $6 million on the purchase of land and houses for the immigrants, on training, machinery, livestock and waterworks, on the construction of dispensaries, synagogues and homes for the aged. In Russia the *Hovevei Zion* had groups springing up in many places during the 1870s. Their basic belief was 'that there is no salvation for the people of Israel unless they establish a government of their own in the Land of Israel'.

The eruption of antisemitism by the end of the nineteenth century dispelled the myth that assimilation provided the answer for Jewish security. Theodore Herzl, an assimilated Jewish lawyer from Vienna, was convinced the future for the Jews was to be found in assimilation. Herzl was assigned to report on the court martial of a Jewish French army captain, Alfred Dreyfus, who was sentenced to life imprisonment for treason in 1895. Shocked at the resurgence of antisemitism, Herzl realised the secure future of the Jews could only be in their national homeland. Within a year he had published *The Jewish State*, in which he presented detailed plans for the establishment and government of the Jewish nation. In 1897 he convened the First Zionist conference at Basle and there founded the Zionist Organisation, which gathered widespread support as Jewish people recognised the winds of hatred were again blowing. The Congress adopted the resolution defining the aim of Zionism: 'The aim of Zionism is to create for the Jewish people a home in Palestine secured by public law.'

After the Congress Herzl wrote in his diary: 'Were I to sum up the Basel congress in a word – which I shall carefully refrain from uttering in public – it would be this: in Basel I founded the Jewish State. If I were to say this out loud today, everybody would laugh at me. In five years, perhaps, but certainly in fifty years, everybody will agree.' On 22 November 1947, 50 years later, the United Nations voted for the partitioning of Palestine, permitting the Jewish people to establish their state, which they did six months later on 14 May 1948.

The challenges of the Promised Land

The groundswell of Jewish interest for a homeland exploded as persecution erupted in Eastern Europe. Zionist leaders emerged to prepare the way. The situation for Jews of nineteenth-century Russia was particularly harsh. Nearly a century before, they had been forced to live in a region known as the 'Pale of Settlement' and give up their professions and trades to work on the land. In less than two centuries, 600 laws against the Jews had been enacted. In 1881, when Czar Alexander II was assassinated the Jews were blamed. Within weeks intense pogroms swept the land to solve the 'Jewish problem'. In 160 towns and villages Jews were killed and their property destroyed. By 1894 there was a plan to destroy the 6 million Jews of Russia.

A Jewish doctor, Leon Pinsker, a leader of *Hovevei Zion*, called for a second exodus. He wrote: 'Let us obtain bread by the sweat of our brow on the sacred soil of our ancestors.' In 1881 he began a movement of Jews back to their ancient homeland. From that beginning until 1914, over 65,000 Jewish refugees fled from Russia, Romania and Poland to settle in their ancient homeland, Eretz Israel, then in southern Syria part of the Ottoman Empire.

Until the twentieth century, Eretz Israel remained under Ottoman control. The 400 years of Turkish misgovernment had encouraged recurrent warfare between local pashas and had permitted Bedouin robber bands to terrorise the country's 400,000 inhabitants. Trade was minimal. The entire region was agriculture-based but stunted in its growth by tax farmers, by army recruitment, forced labour, drought and locusts.

Tax farmers enjoyed great power, and because of the increasing weakness and corruption of the government, the peasants had practically no legal protection. A few Arab effendi (landlord) families – like the Al-Husseinis, Nashashibis and the Khalidis – accumulated large landholdings and then continued to exploit the unfortunate peasant migrant. It was to these families that the Jewish immigrants paid high prices for inferior land.

While the flood of Jewish immigration was stimulated by persecution in Eastern Europe, they came not as individuals but in organised groups or *aliya* waves. Between 1882 and 1903, 25,000 arrived. Among these were Zionist leaders like Leon Pinsker from Odessa, Perez Smolenskin and others who had planned organised settlements in the ancient Jewish homeland when they called for mass immigration.

Ze'ev Dubnow was among the first group to arrive in 1882. His letter of 1 November 1882, to his brother, expresses the pioneering idealism many young Jewish immigrants felt:

Do you really think that my sole purpose in coming here was to take care only of my own affairs? No, my ultimate aim, and that of many others, is great, vast, and boundless, but it cannot be said to be beyond reach. The ultimate aim is to take possession of the land of Israel and to give back to the

Jews the political independence of which they have been deprived for 2,000 years. Do not laugh, this is not an empty dream.

In 1918, the Arab leader Sharif Hussein foresaw the effect of this zealous enthusiasm evident in the Jewish immigrants, which starkly contrasted with Arab neglect of the land: 'The resources of the country are still virgin soil and will be developed by the Jewish immigrants. One of the most amazing things until recent times was that the Palestinian used to leave his country, wandering over the high seas in every direction. His native soil could not retain its hold on him.'

Chaim Weizmann, leader of the Zionist Organisation who was to become Israel's first president, explained to the United Nation's Special Committee on Palestine (UNSCOP) in 1947 the reason for the immigrants' zeal:

As soon as the Jew comes into contact with his country he begins to feel as if he has returned. The country releases energies, activities in the Jewish people which are not released anywhere else. I shall not say that one feels this at once. But there are sentiments which grow in every one of us, and the rocks, marshes and sands of Palestine become a Jewish possession into which we pour our sweat, our blood, our effort and ingenuity in order to make it what it is.

On an earlier occasion Dr Chaim Weizmann was in discussion with British Foreign Secretary Arthur Balfour regarding the possibility of the Jewish people being settled in East Africa as a homeland. Weizmann reported the conversation: 'Suddenly I said: "Mr Balfour, supposing I were to offer you Paris instead of London, would you take it?" He sat up, looked at me and answered: "But Dr Weizmann, we have London." "That is true," I said. "But we had Jerusalem when London was a marsh."'

This raises the question of the political agenda that influenced Britain's thinking on the whereabouts of the Jewish homeland. In 1902 a suggestion was proposed to resettle persecuted Russian and Polish Jews in the Sinai Desert at El Arish. Prime Minister Joseph Chamberlain had been influenced by Theodore Herzl to support Zionism. Chamberlain's biographer, Julian Amery, wrote:

Herzl's arguments had undoubtedly made a deep impression on Chamberlain. Hitherto his interest in Zionism had been chiefly humanitarian; he now saw in it some positive opportunities for British policy. By supporting Zionism, Britain could enlist the sympathies of world Jewry on her behalf. She could also secure Jewish capital and settlers for the development of what was virtually British territory. Looking, moreover, to the future, a Jewish colony in Sinai might prove a useful instrument for extending British influence in Palestine proper when the time came for the inevitable dismemberment of the Ottoman Empire.

Access to, and protection of, the Suez Canal was fundamental to British shipping routes to her empire in India and the South Pacific and of course to the Mesopotamian oilfields.

A successful community experiment

In 1909 seven pioneers of the second wave of Jewish immigrants, who had been working as employees of the Palestine Land Development Company's farm on the shores of Lake Galilee, were permitted to experiment on a new style of communal farming. Unlike private plots the farm was shared and worked upon by all the members as a team. All possessions and equipment were purchased and held not by the individuals but as a community. The experiment was clearly a success. Others joined this community, known as a kibbutz, named Degania Alef. A second neighbouring kibbutz commenced, Degania Bet, in 1913. Degania was often referred to as the 'Mother of Kibbutzim'.

The kibbutzim multiplied. Their membership was voluntary and they were originally all agricultural settlements. They provided security for new settlers, who contributed their working and organisational skills to the welfare of the kibbutz. Everybody had a place and a contribution. The kibbutzim were an attraction to many of the early Jewish settlers, who were refugees with meagre possessions but often highly skilled. Members who were immigrants from many nations were unified in these tightly knit communities where the work was hard, the life difficult and the facilities minimal.

Land was purchased by the Jewish National Fund, later to be owned by the government of Israel. Rarely was land privately purchased. The kibbutz movement is unique to the Zionist labour movement and has played a pioneering role in the economic, political, cultural and security activities of the emerging Jewish nation. From the kibbutz movement developed the Histadrut in 1920, whose aim was the creation of a new Jewish working society in the Land.

Kibbutzim were usually established near borders or exposed parts of the country. They were surrounded by strong fences with watch-towers, to protect themselves, and the Jewish community at large, from marauders bent on stealing the fruit of the harvests and equipment, and even from murder. During the Arab riots and uprisings that later developed, the kibbutzim played a significant role in defence. From the kibbutzim emerged the early Jewish defence force and, at the birth of the Jewish state, leaders in the armed forces.

The effendi families felt threatened by the growth of Jewish communities developing the land. Thousands of peasant migrants were attracted to the Jewish communities for employment, which generally provided them and their families with improved standards of living. In 1898 the fields of Zichron Ya'akov were tended by more than 1,000 Arabs working for 200 Jews. In Rishon l'Zion, 38 Jewish settler families provided labour for over 300 Arab migrant families encamped in nearby huts. By the time the First World War broke out in 1914, 54 Jewish towns and settlements had been developed in addition to the Jewish and Arab towns of Jerusalem, Jaffa, Hebron, Haifa, Gaza, Tiberias and Safed. Palestine had a population of 500,000 Arabs and 90,000 Jews.

Conflicting promises

It was not until the birth of Zionism that pressure for the re-establishment of a Jewish state and a return to Israel gained ground among the Jews of the diaspora. The Turks tolerated the initial agricultural settlements. It was only when faced with military defeat at the hands of Britain in the First World War that they responded with persecution. The declining power of the Ottoman Empire coincided with the birth and growth of Zionism, which made the future control of the region a matter of keen debate among the great powers. Matters came to a head in the First World War, when, to appease the Arabs, the Allies agreed to control the Holy Land themselves.

Ibn Ali Hussein of the Hashemite house of Sharifs (descendants of the prophet Muhammad) was appointed Sharif of Mecca in 1908, making him the supreme Muslim spiritual leader. He agreed to the Jewish immigration that had begun in 1882, as long as it was confined to providing a home for persecuted Jewish refugees. However, he clearly stated that the Arabs would never agree to a Jewish state in the region.

Sir Henry McMahon, British Ambassador to Egypt, corresponded with Sharif Hussein in January 1916, seeking Arab support against the Turks in taking the Ottoman Empire. This agreement was interpreted by the Arabs as promising them independence after a successful war. This interpretation, of course, was in conflict with the later British promise to the Jews of a Jewish national homeland in the region as promised in the Balfour Declaration.

Sharif Hussein had his own agenda. His dream was to unite all Arab lands under his rule, with his sons serving as viceroys in the various regions: Ali, his first-born, in the Arabian peninsula; Abdullah, next in line, in Iraq; and Faisal, the third son, in Greater Syria which, according to Hashemite plans, was to include Lebanon and Eretz Israel as well. Sharif Hussein's son, Faisal, on behalf of the Arab kingdom of Hejaz, made an agreement with Chaim Weizmann, representing the Zionist Organisation, in January 1919, permitting Jewish immigrants to settle in Palestine 'on a large scale and as quickly as possible . . . upon the land through closer settlement and intensive cultivation of the soil'. It was agreed that Arab peasant farmers already in the area would be protected 'and shall be assisted in forwarding their economic development'. Protection for 'the free exercise of religion' and assurances that 'the Muhammadan holy places shall be under Muhammadan control' were given.

At the signing of this document, typed in English, Faisal wrote a provision in Arabic at the end before signing it. The translation of that provision reads:

Provided the Arabs obtain their independence as demanded in my Memorandum dated 4th of January, 1919, to the Foreign Office of the Government of Great Britain, I shall concur in the above articles. But if the slightest modification or departure were to be made [in relation to the demands in the Memorandum] I shall not be bound by a single word of the present Agreement which shall be deemed void and of no account or validity, and I shall not be answerable in any way whatsoever.

These concerns had been included in a letter from Foreign Secretary Arthur Balfour to Lord Rothschild, the leader of the Zionist Federation, dated 2 November 1917. Later this letter was dubbed 'The Balfour Declaration':

Dear Lord Rothschild

I have much pleasure in conveying to you, on behalf of His Majesty's Government, the following declaration of sympathy with Jewish Zionist aspirations which has been submitted to, and approved by, the Cabinet.

'His Majesty's Government view with favour the establishment in Palestine of a national home for the Jewish people, and will use their best endeavours to facilitate the achievement of this object, it being clearly understood that *nothing shall be done which may prejudice the civil and religious rights of existing non-Jewish communities in Palestine*, or the rights and political status enjoyed by Jews in any other country.'

I should be grateful if you would bring this declaration to the knowledge of the Zionist Federation. [Author's emphasis]

The Balfour Declaration was raised to the status of a treaty when it was embodied in the Mandate for Palestine and Mesopotamia conferred upon Britain by the League of Nations at the San Remo Conference on 25 April 1920. Britain was now obliged to 'be responsible for putting into effect the declaration originally made on November 2nd 1917, by the government . . . in favour of the establishment in Palestine of a national home for the Jewish people'. They were to 'use their best endeavours to facilitate' Jewish immigration and to encourage Jewish settlement on the Land. The British were given 'full powers of legislation and administration', indicating it was not the purpose of the Mandate to establish self-government by either Arabs or Jews. Each year Britain was required to submit a report to the Permanent Mandates Commission of the League of Nations.

The Mandate established in public law the restoration of the Jewish home in Palestine and also protected the rights of those already resident in the Land. But there was no mention anywhere of the prior arrangement between Ambassador McMahon and Sharif Hussein.

The problem of failing to define the area known as 'Palestine' was destined to be the source of major problems which would not only cause

Britain to withdraw but would affect Jewish–Arab relations until today. Britain's White Paper of 17 May 1939 was more crippling to Zionism than any other British document. *The Palestine Post* headlined the event: 'New policy winds up mandate and Jewish national home.' It took another nine years, till 14 May 1948, before Britain actually left Palestine. On that day David Ben Gurion proclaimed the existence of the State of Israel following the United Nations' favourable vote the previous November.

Partitioning the land

Before the Mandate for Palestine was awarded, the Arab population violently expressed its disapproval, on the grounds that it would permit increased Jewish immigration and land purchase. Violence erupted during a Muslim religious festival in April 1920 only weeks before the San Remo Conference. Within a short time large numbers of Jews and Arabs were killed and hundreds injured. The Arab view was quite simple: they wanted an independent state with an Arab majority.

During 1921, Colonial Secretary Winston Churchill visited Palestine to investigate the problem of the rioting. He reaffirmed his support of the Jewish national home, then published a White Paper in July 1922 with his answer to the problem: divide Palestine down the Jordan River thereby creating 'Transjordan', which Britain would continue to administer through a government led by Abdullah as a part of Britain's Palestine Mandate; restrict the Jewish national home to the area west of the Jordan; avoid a predominantly Jewish state; limit Jewish immigration to the 'economic capacity of the country'.

Avoiding a predominantly Jewish state was defined in the White Paper:

Phrases have been used such as that Palestine is to become 'as Jewish as England is English'. His Majesty's Government regard any such expectation as impracticable and have no such aim in view . . . When it was asked what is meant by the development of a Jewish National Home in Palestine, it may be answered that it is not the imposition of a Jewish nationality upon the inhabitants of Palestine as a whole but the further development of the existing Jewish community . . . in order that it may become a centre in which the Jewish people as a whole may take . . . an interest and a pride. But in order

that this community should have the best prospects of free development
. . . it is essential that it should know that it is in Palestine as of right not on
sufferance.

Transjordan, which comprised 76 per cent of Palestine, was exclusively for
Arabs; no Jews were permitted there. It provided a Palestinian Arab state.
This decision to partition Palestine established a principle that was to
become the basis of future attempts to bring a peaceful solution to the
problem. The Passfield White Paper of 1930 was much harsher than
Churchill's treatment; it appeared to reject the purpose of the Balfour
Declaration and the terms of the Mandate award. The 1937 Peel
Commission recommended partitioning Palestine west of the Jordan River
into two separate states: one Jewish and one Arab, with a British controlled corridor from Jaffa to Jerusalem. The Jews reluctantly accepted
this plan. The Arabs rejected it. Then in 1947 the United Nations voted in
favour of partitioning Palestine with different boundaries, offering the
Jews and the Arabs their own states, with Jerusalem an international zone.

Churchill's plan provided comparative peace until a major riot erupted
in Jerusalem during 1929. In a short time 133 Jews were killed and 399
wounded, with 178 Arab casualties, including 87 dead. By mid-October
1937, violence surpassing the level of the previous year raged through
Palestine, with attacks on Jewish settlements and buses and the murder of
Jewish civilians. For the first time British patrols also were cut down by
snipers. The British had 20,000 troops stationed in Palestine and 10,000
more on the way. By November some 1,300 casualties had been sus-
tained, including 197 Arabs, 80 Jews and 28 British personnel killed. The
cost to Palestine tax payers was nearly 6 million Palestinian pounds.

The Jews operated their own defence force, the Haganah, and
Captain Orde Wingate, a British officer, helped train them in guerrilla
warfare. From July to November 1938, when the uprising was at its
fiercest, about 16,000 local and imported guerrillas were involved in the
insurrection, and they succeeded in paralysing civil authority outside the
nation's larger cities and in the Jewish agricultural areas. The rebels had
virtually taken control of the Old City of Jerusalem. The fighting among
Jews, Arabs and British ultimately claimed several thousand lives and
inflicted tens of millions of pounds in property damage.

Then came the White Paper of 1939.

The rise of Arab nationalism

A Jewish national homeland in this region defied Islamic theology. In the seventh century the explosion of Islam out of the Arabian Peninsula swept the entire Middle East. Muhammad's teaching was that the Arabs were the 'chosen of the nations' and that his new religion was to dominate the world for Allah. In barely 100 years from the death of Muhammad, in 632, an Arab empire had been founded, which extended to the Mediterranean Sea, across North Africa and then towards Europe. Under their rule a 'golden era' unfolded as they conquered a large portion of the unknown world and gave it a new civilisation.

The Turks were not Arab, although Islamic, and their domination of the Arabs since 1517 in the Ottoman Empire had always been a source of humiliation. In 1908 Arab nationalism broke out. The timing of the British and French offer of independence after World War I was optimum. It was the British and the French who drew the boundaries creating Iraq, Kuwait, present Syria, Jordan and Lebanon. But those in the region that came to be known as Palestine were left waiting for their independence.

A portion of Ibrahim Yaziji's poem, 'Ode to Patriotism', provides us with a taste of rising Arab nationalism in the second half of the nineteenth century:

> Arise you Arabs and awake,
> The calamity is in full flood
> And covers your knees.
> The Turks are looking at you contemptuously
> Usurping your rights.
>
> Only the quarrelsome
> Can win against the Turks.
> How often you think good of them,
> Though they are vicious in their hearts.

The rising Arab nationalism was a reflection of the aims of Islam. Embedded in Muslim expectation were the past glories of Islam's 'golden era' during the Abbasid Dynasty spanning the eighth to the thirteenth centuries.

Islamisation was the product of unifying the masses of conquered countries by the adoption of the religion of Muhammad. Generally speaking, every country that became permanently Arabised became permanently Islamised, although there were countries like Persia and Afghanistan that were Islamised but not Arabised.

Two worlds were created: the Muslim world and the Arab world. The world of Islam reached out into India, China and the western extremities of Africa. The Arab world was confined to those countries where Arabic was made the national language, where Arab culture was adopted and where pure Arab intermarriage had taken place. Appropriately the term 'Arab' no longer refers to just the nomadic tribes who inhabited the Arabian Peninsula but to all citizens of the Arab world. This was a period of great Arab power, maintained by formidable armies, when Muslim trading reached to Russia, Germany and Scandinavia, at a time of intellectual awakening which was drawn from the knowledge of many peoples, and then absorbed into the Arab Empire: ancient Greek learning, philosophy, medicine, mathematics, astronomy, architecture and engineering.

A significant change in the Arab world began in 1517 when Selim I, an Ottoman Turk (a non-Arab), conquered Egypt and assumed the Islamic leadership as Caliph. Under his successor, Suleiman the Magnificent, the Turkish power reached its height as he swept through the Arab world, conquering the sacred cities of Mecca, Medina and Jerusalem, then Damascus, the first capital of the Arab Empire, and Baghdad, the science centre.

German interest in establishing colonies in Asia led to close contact with the Sultan of the Turkish Empire. In 1883 a military mission arrived to modernise the Sultan's army. German finance and engineers built a railway in the north of Turkey which finally reached down past the holy places of Mecca and Medina almost to Aden and then planned to reach through Baghdad to Basra on the Persian Gulf, skirting the boundary between Turks and Arabs.

The despotic power of the Turkish sultans inspired a widespread desire among the Arab population, and others, to be free of their yoke. In 1908, a revolution broke out under the leadership of the Committee of Union and Progress composed of Turks and Arabs. This was the beginning of the rise of Arab nationalism. Secret Arab nationalist soci-

eties emerged whose objective was to restore Arab power to the Arab
world and with it the religion of Islam. Sharif Hussein, a strong Arab
nationalist, was appointed to the powerful Islamic post of Grand Sharif
of Mecca. The foundation was laid for the Arab awakening.

Ibn Ali Hussein was born in Istanbul, Turkey, in 1853 of the Hashemite
house of Sharifs (descendants of the prophet Muhammad) that had ruled
Mecca since the tenth century. He spent some time in Arabia as a boy, but
the Turks kept him in Istanbul for most of the first 50 years of his life.
Following the Young Turk revolution of 1908 he was appointed Sharif of
Mecca. In this capacity Hussein took part in the movement seeking Arab
independence from the Ottoman Empire. The British encouraged him to
motivate the Arabs in a rising against the Turks during the First World
War. As a result he proclaimed the Arab revolt against the Turks in 1916.
Although he took the title of King of the Arab countries, the Allied powers only recognised him as King of the Hejaz. Hussein's forces and those
of T. E. Lawrence and other Allied officers played an important part in
driving the Turks out of northern Arabia, Transjordan and Syria.

Hussein was bitterly disappointed by the British, who promised him
Arab independence in return for Arab support in the assault against the
Turks. After the war, British commitments to the French and to the
Zionists superseded these promises, resulting in a major conflict of inter-
ests in the region, providing the basis of the conflict in the Middle East.
Hussein agreed to Jewish immigration to Palestine as long as it was pro-
viding a home for persecuted Jewish refugees, but clearly stated that the
Arabs would not agree to a Jewish state in the region. Ibn Saud of Arabia
finally won Mecca in 1925 and Hussein was exiled in Cyprus until his
death in 1931. The British appointed his son Abdullah as King of
Transjordan and his son Faisal King of Iraq.

An Islamic worldview provides the larger context for these events.
Islam sees the world in two sectors. *Dar el Islam* (the house of Islam)
is that sector of countries governed by Islam, such as Iran and Sudan.
Dar el harb (the house of war) is the remainder of the world, which
Islam intends to submit to its own authority and power. Usually the
transformation of *dar el harb* is by *jihad*, popularly translated 'holy
war', which includes any method that will achieve its goal. It could be
war, or oil pressure, or propaganda. 'Peace' as defined by fundamentalist
Islam can only be enjoyed within Islamic-governed territory; it is not

able to be shared with non-Islamic nations. So there can be no peace while the Jewish state exists – precisely the statement of Sharif Hussein to Ambassador McMahon in 1916.

Jerusalem, the eye of the storm

For the Jewish people, Jerusalem has been, and continues to be, the heart of Zion. It is the Holy City associated with their identity and history dating right back to Melchizedek blessing Abraham. David united Israel by establishing Jerusalem as its political and military capital, and then brought the Ark of the Covenant to its first permanent resting place. This most sacred national and religious symbol of Israel was brought to Jerusalem, making this city the capital of Israel's faith. Jerusalem was to be the spiritual capital of Israel for all time. Later Solomon built the Temple there.

Even in dispersion the Jewish people honoured Jerusalem, longing to be there. Rabbi Levi Isaac, who lived in Berditchev, expressed the yearning to be in Jerusalem in his betrothal contracts at a time when there was no possibility of him or the bridal couple being there: 'The wedding will, God willing, take place in the Holy City of Jerusalem. But if, Heaven forbid, because of our sins, the Messiah will not have come by then, the wedding will take place in Berditchev.'

Every diaspora family has concluded its Passover meal with the declaration of anticipation: 'Next year in Jerusalem!' And the psalmist declared: 'If I forget you, O Jerusalem, may my right hand forget its skill. May my tongue cling to the roof of my mouth if I do not remember you, if I do not consider Jerusalem my highest joy' (Ps 137:5–6).

Haj Amin al-Husseini, who rose to become the Mufti of Jerusalem in the 1920s, was related to Sharif Hussein and was the uncle of Yasser Arafat. Arafat's mother was a cousin to Haj Amin. The Husseini clan is one of the oldest and most aristocratic families of the region. They claim their descent from Hussein, son of Caliph Ali and his wife Fatima, daughter of Muhammad. Al-Husseini saw to it that the Dome of the Rock became the focal point of Arab nationalism. He was given supreme religious and political authority, enabling him to use the Temple Mount to fire up the bloody anti-Jewish riots of 1920, 1929 and 1936. Fanatical preachers incited the masses, who went out to execute their deeds of hatred with the shouts '*Allu akbar*' (Allah is great) and '*Idbah al Yahud*' (Slaughter to the Jews). Later al-Husseini joined the Nazis.

Historically a pattern has emerged showing that when Jerusalem has been in Islamic hands Jerusalem's sanctity plays an insignificant role, but when Jerusalem is not under Islamic control, Islam's religious fervour for Jerusalem intensifies. This was evident during the Crusader period and also since the rebirth of Israel. Jerusalem was never the capital of the Arab Empire.

The Muslim response to the United Nations resolution to partition Palestine in November 1947 marked an escalation of the battle for Jerusalem. The Muslim spiritual leader of al-Azhar University in Cairo issued a religious ruling (*fatwa*) that called for a 'jihad to save Palestine and to defend the al-Aqsa mosque'.

Muslims changed the name from Jerusalem to Al Quds, which means the City of Holiness. Legend has it that Muhammad rode on his two-winged white horse, al-Buraq (the bright one), to the seventh heaven, where he was met by Abraham, Isaac, Joseph, Moses and Jesus, and received their blessing to become the last prophet of God. Historically, however, Muhammad never went to Jerusalem. He died in 632 CE and it was another six years before Jerusalem fell to the Arabs under Caliph Omar. Islam's claim to the Temple Mount rests solely upon this legend.

The Qur'anic statement 'Praise be unto him who transported his servant by night from the sacred mosque to the farthest mosque . . .' has subsequently been interpreted to include Jerusalem as the third holiest site of Islam after Mecca and Medina.

In 691 CE Caliph Abd al-Malik built the Dome of the Rock on the Temple Mount. The building and its inscriptions state a religious purpose. That purpose is that Islam is not only a challenge to Byzantine Christianity but that it has eclipsed it. The Dome of the Rock and the adjoining Aqsa Mosque constitute the first great religious building complex in the history of Islam. It marked a new era. Islam was no mere successor to Christianity, but a new universal dispensation. The place, the style and above all the ornamentation of the Dome of the Rock reveal its purpose. The style and scale were intended to outshine the Church of the Holy Sepulchre. The place was Jerusalem, the most sacred city on earth to both the predecessor religions, Judaism and Christianity.

The choice is significant. Jerusalem is never mentioned in the Qur'an.

Even the name 'Jerusalem' does not appear in early Muslim writings. When the city is mentioned at all it is called Aelia, the name imposed by the Romans to the city to obliterate its Jewish and Christian associations. Later they replaced Aelia with Al Quds – 'the (city of) holiness'. The site was the Temple Mount, the scene of major events in both Jewish and Christian sacred history. The actual spot was the rock on which, according to rabbinic tradition, Abraham prepared to sacrifice his son, and on which in later times the Ark of the Temple had rested.

The Dome of the Rock is the new Temple dedicated to the religion of Abraham, replacing the Temple of Solomon, continuing the revelations given to the Jews and the Christians and correcting the errors into which they have fallen.

Conclusion

Frustrated, Britain returned the Mandate to the United Nations and left Palestine. The Jews accepted the opportunity and established their state. Today Israel's Jewish population almost exceeds that of any other nation. The Arabs refused their opportunity for independence. For them to have established their state would have recognised the right of the Jewish state to land, which, they claim, should be included in the Palestinian state. History has proved the truth of Sharif Hussein's statement to Ambassador McMahon in 1916 that there can be no peace while the Jewish state exists. The legacy inherited by the twenty-first century offers no simple answer to a question many international leaders have hoped to solve and thereby enhance their prestige. Israel's God issued a warning that international leaders would be wise to heed:

'I am going to make Jerusalem a cup that sends all the surrounding peoples reeling. Judah will be besieged as well as Jerusalem. On that day, when all the nations of the earth are gathered against her, I will make Jerusalem an immovable rock for all the nations. All who try to move it will injure themselves.' (Zech 12:2–3)

FROM DEATH TO LIFE:
The Restoration of Jewish Yeshua – Believers in the Land of Israel

Gershon Nerel

Introduction

The emergence of the Messianic Jewish (Hebrew Christian) self-identity between the years 1917 and 1967 is a unique phenomenon in the history of the 'Yishuv' in Eretz-Israel, the Land of Israel. By 'Messianic Jews' it is meant Jews who voluntarily decided to embrace faith in Yeshua (Jesus) of Nazareth as Son of God and Redeemer, or as in one single case, to be discussed later, merely as Messiah and Prophet. The originality of this segment in Israeli society – which in Mandatory Palestine numbered circa 120 persons and roughly 150 around 1967 – was that they insisted on *not* being regarded as 'converts to Christianity', but rather stressed their being called 'Completed Jews' or 'Messianic Jews'.[1]

The chronological scope between the years 1917 and 1967 is an eventful period of 50 years, significantly marked by the transition of Jerusalem from one political hegemony to another: from its capture in 1917 from the Ottoman (Turkish) Muslim Empire by the British Christian Empire, and the reunification of the city in 1967 by the Israelis. Since Jerusalem always had a particular place in Old and New Testament exegesis, it also naturally held a central place within the contextualising views of Messianic Jews.

Within the time spectrum of these two events in 1917 and 1967, representing two salient 'crossroads', one finds a most formative half-century within which modern Messianic Jewish thought in Eretz-Israel was shaped. In fact, Messianic Jewish hermeneutics of biblical prophecy had as its focus both Jerusalem and the people and Land of

Israel at one and the same time. The Messianic Jews viewed and interpreted not only regional affairs in the Middle East, but also sought to trace prominent eschatological happenings within a world perspective and history.[2]

Complexity of nomenclature

The issue of nomenclature is one of primary importance within the history of the movement. When examining the terminology used in Messianic Jewish circles, it becomes crystal clear that they rejected any approach that might have classified them as Christians *per se*. Even the term 'Hebrew Christians', and especially within an Eretz-Israel context, was not always accepted among them. As Jews who followed the Messiah of the New Testament, they preferred to be called simply 'Messianic Jews'.

In Mandatory Palestine we do not find a uniform definition or term used by Jewish believers in Yeshua (whom we shall refer to as JBY) for their own self-identity. Most of those who were mainly connected to English-speaking churches and missionary societies, like the British London Society for Promoting Christianity Amongst the Jews, also known as the 'Church's Ministry among Jewish People (CMJ) and the American Christian and Missionary Alliance (C&MA), did use among themselves the term 'Hebrew Christian'. This term was already well known within the Anglo-Saxon Protestant world, at least since the second half of the nineteenth century.

However, more than semantic difficulties arose when the term 'Hebrew Christian' was used in Eretz-Israel. 'Hebrew Christian' conveyed mixed meanings when translated into colloquial Hebrew within a Hebrew-speaking milieu. JBY were aware of the fact that the title 'Hebrew Christian' was often understood as meaning complete separation from anything connected to Jewishness or a Judaic background, while this was not their intention in using the term.

Ambiguity also arose when the term 'Hebrew Christian' was understood to be related to the concept of restoration. JBY did express clear aspirations for restoring for themselves an archaic and authentic Hebraic nationality. This 'archaic nationality' was found actually in the first century CE and related to the first JBY in Jerusalem. Moreover, modern JBY also wished to attach to themselves literal biblical prophecy and biblical spirituality. However, they dropped the prefix 'Hebrew' and replaced it with the term 'Jew', in order to be related to the heritage of the Jewish world. In the Eretz-Israel milieu a term like 'Messianic Jew' enabled JBY to identify themselves both with modern Jewish nationality and with biblical Judaism, as being distinct from rabbinical Judaism.

By the adoption of the term 'Messianic Jews', JBY in Eretz-Israel also rejected the term 'Jewish Christians' or 'Judeo-Christians'. The difficulty they faced was mainly with the proper noun 'Christian', especially when it was translated into Hebrew נוצרי. They strongly rejected any possible equation between themselves and Gentile Christianity as manifested in church history. In their writings we find a profound desire not to become 'Gentilised' by any terminology or by any other inducement from non-Jewish followers of Jesus. Yet at the same time, they were compelled quite often to reject accusations from Gentile circles that they had, so to speak, some hidden or even apparent intentions to 'Judaise' the Gentile Christians through their 'Jewish inclinations'. De facto, those accusations reflected Gentile Christian suspicions that JBY had planned on purpose to regain 'theological hegemony' over Gentiles, as it was in the first century.[3]

When the majority of JBY consented to define themselves as Messianic Jews, especially following the establishment of the State of Israel in 1948, it gradually became evident that within mainstream Jewish thinking the term 'messianic' could hardly be adopted exclusively for themselves. Historically, the term 'messianic' was derived from 'Messiah' (Christos, משיח), and was also linked to diverse holders of ideologies denoting a particular 'Messiah' or Saviour. Such 'Messiahs' or 'messianic situations' could range from the sphere of religious persons or territorial concepts to completely secular concepts relating to non-religious socialist utopias.

The 'Hebrew Catholics'

From a theological perspective, a basic similarity is found between Messianic Jewish belief and various Protestant evangelical teachings based on the New Testament alongside the Old. Yet at the same time, when relating to JBY, we need to point also to another group: Jews who, following their baptism within the Roman Catholic Church, preferred to call themselves Hebrew Catholics. Most of these Hebrew Catholics, however, would object to being called Messianic Jews, and prefer to be known as Christians (נוצרים). Such differences of nomenclature do not reflect merely semantic preference. The acceptance of the term 'Christian' (נוצרי) by Hebrew Catholics manifests a clear universalistic approach, a policy of integration into the Catholic Church. Some of them even aspire to become an approved and 'quasi-independent branch' within the universal Catholic Church.[4] The Messianic Jews, however, by rejecting the use of the Hebrew term 'נוצרי' ('Christian') wished to express their disconnection from the *Gentile* church's history of the past nearly 2,000 years. They rejected the term נוצרי because it was linked to anti-Jewish Christian history.

However, most JBY endeavoured to restore a historical and genuine self-identity as Jewish followers of Yeshua. Although they identified themselves with the first-century JBY, they were still divided in principle on how to shape and manifest such an identity vis-à-vis synagogue and church alike. In the context of the historical divisions between Catholics and Protestants, it became obvious that Messianic Jews would constantly differentiate themselves from Hebrew Catholics – and vice versa. Such dissimilarity was quite evident, although each group openly struggled against the assimilation of its members into the institutional Gentile churches. In fact, both groups also denounced traditional Christian antisemitism, and insisted on maintaining a unique status, as Jews, among all other followers of Jesus, especially in still being part of the biblical chosen people.

Hebrew Catholics and Messianic Jews form *de facto* two modern Yeshua movements. In our context it is indeed interesting to perform a systematic comparison between Messianic Jews and Hebrew Catholics. Such a 'mechanism' may add to the illumination of specific issues that characterise the global restoration of JBY.[5]

Striving for corporate emancipation

The attitudes of JBY towards establishing their own corporate institutions are observed not only on a national level with strong territorial roots, but are also reflected through their theological thinking. This is seen, for example, when they come to define those persons who would qualify to join their circles officially.

Basically, Messianic Jews in Mandatory Palestine were part and parcel of the Protestant missionary organisations located in central towns like Jerusalem, Jaffa, Haifa, Safed and Tiberias. A constant tendency was found among them to leave these Gentile institutions, and even to avoid the use of traditional theological terminology; e.g., to drop the word 'church' (כנסייה) and to use instead terms like 'Assembly' (קהילה)) or 'Alliance'(אגודה).

No doubt the ongoing Hebraisation within their circles, as in the society surrounding them, such as the daily use and 'indigenisation' of the Hebrew language, influenced their way of thinking. So did their growing awareness of the need to develop a genuine Messianic Jewish mentality which would distinguish itself from any characteristics or customs that would, so to speak, Gentilise them and cause them to lose their Jewish heritage and identity.

The outcome of this tendency was that JBY constantly attempted to develop new forms of grouping by themselves in order to better express, as well as maintain, their unique identity. Thus, they strongly insisted on shaping a distinct Jewish identity, that embraced the belief in Yeshua as Messiah and Son of God within their own phraseology.[6] However, they faced difficulties and misunderstandings, particularly with those expatriate Christian missionaries who were ministering in the Land and yet could only with difficulty grasp such 'separatist' or even so-called 'self-exalting' Jewish believers in Yeshua.

Thus, for example, a special attempt to establish an independent Messianic Jewish congregation can be traced in Jerusalem between the years 1925 and 1929. However, in English they called themselves 'Hebrew Christians', but in colloquial Hebrew and in Hebrew texts they used the term 'Yehudim Meshihiim' ('Messianic Jews'). The founders of this congregation were two Jews, Hyman Jacobs and Moshe Immanuel Ben-Meir, and a Norwegian missionary, Dr Arne Jonsen. Jonsen and Jacobs published a statement of principles to serve almost as an enlarged creed or manifesto. This proclaimed their aspirations to restore the original and national entity of JBY as described in the New Testament. By this they expressed strong awareness of their need to observe the Jewish national customs and holy days originating in the Old Testament, particularly circumcision, the Sabbath and Passover.[7]

There were heavy pressures exerted on them from their Gentile mission boards overseas. The supporters of Dr Jonsen in Oslo and the board of the Chicago Hebrew Mission in the USA that supported Jacobs compelled them to keep Sunday and the Sabbath as *two days* for divine worship. The Sabbath was not to remain the single day for their weekly worship. Theological pressure was also put upon the leadership of this congregation, and they were accused of being Judaisers who experimented at keeping only the Sabbath day or stressing the observance of Jewish festivals according to the Jewish calendar. Pressures of this kind, followed also by financial and personal inducements, finally blocked any possibility for such a revolutionary congregation, which at the same time was regarded, in a dialectical way, as a reactionary congregation. Therefore, this first attempt to form an *independent* Messianic Jewish congregation in twentieth century Jerusalem did not survive more than four years.

Both Jonsen and Jacobs were obliged to face investigators who came to Palestine to learn first-hand about their 'Judaising' tendencies. At last Jonsen had to leave the country and Jacobs became an itinerant evangelist in Palestine.[8] Ben-Meir, who returned from the Moody Bible Institute in Chicago after studying there between the years 1927 and 1931, found the congregation disintegrated. He then occupied himself with fresh attempts to found larger territorial organisations of JBY covering Palestine and the Middle East, rather than starting new local assemblies of JBY. Thus, the solution of Ben-Meir, and Jacobs as well, for shaping a genuine Messianic Jewish self-identity in Eretz-Israel was transferred from the local level to the wider regional level. They also had great hopes of crystallising such an identity through co-operation with the International Hebrew Christian Alliance (IHCA).[9]

In 1931 the first regional grouping founded by Messianic Jews was named in English – for their Gentile constituency – 'The Hebrew Christian Fellowship of Palestine'. However, in their internal Hebrew texts they used the term 'Messianic Jews'. In principle, their theological goal was to achieve an interdenominational fellowship without any kind of subordination to the traditional churches and mission organisations in Palestine. Among their proclaimed aims, just the principal ones should be mentioned: '. . . To unite Messianic Jews in Palestine and Syria; to establish and support urban branches; to witness corporately both to Synagogue and Church concerning the fulfilment of Israel's messianic hope in Jesus; to introduce Jewish thought to Gentile Christians and the Gospel to Jews; to cooperate with the IHCA'. They also bypassed any controversial issues in order to provide a wide common ground for as many of them as possible to join their Fellowship.

In 1933 the Fellowship changed its official title and adopted a new name: the Hebrew Christian Alliance of Palestine and the Near East. The requirements for admission to the Fellowship/Alliance were as follows: 'Expression in public of faith in Messiah Jesus as personal Saviour and Lord; belief in the divinity of Messiah Jesus; belief in his sacrificial death and resurrection; acceptance of the Old and New Testaments as the word of God and as the rule for their faith and lives.' However, neither the issue of the Trinity nor the topic of baptism was mentioned as a stipulation for membership in that organisation. The reason for that was the desire to present the broadest theological spectrum as a possible doctrinal basis in order to permit maximal membership by avoiding doctrinal confrontation on very problematic issues.

Abram Poljak was another active and influential personality among Messianic Jewish circles in Mandatory Palestine. In one of his early books titled *The Cross in the Star of David*, he endeavoured to launch a unique world movement that would crystallise a clear and solid identity for those Jews who believe in Yeshua. However, instead of focusing on a special Eretz-Israeli Messianic Jewish identity, Poljak ended up in English and German speaking countries, where he promulgated the idea of reciprocal coexistence between Jews and Christians through regular dialogue between them. Just like other leaders, such as Moris Sigel, Pauline Rose, Jacobs and Ben-Meir, Poljak was struggling to create a *corporate* witness of JBY in the Land. Like his colleagues, Poljak emphasised the need to institutionalise these activities. He implemented this mainly through publishing various articles in his magazine *Jerusalem*.[10]

Insecurity among Jewish believers in Yeshua

Not every Jewish believer in Yeshua in Mandatory Eretz-Israel was willing to expose himself in public as such. A few dozen so-called 'Nicodemus Jews' (see John 3:1–2) tried to keep secret their belief in Yeshua and for decades lived in this context with an underground mentality. Their main fear was that they would not be tolerated by normative Jewish society, and they dreaded the possibility of jeopardising their positions at work, and even being stigmatised as traitors. Later, within the State of Israel, the phenomenon of Nicodemus Jews did not disappear. Alongside those who publicly declared their faith in Yeshua, many others endeavoured to remain in the shadows. While examining the relationship between the open and the closed groups of JBY, it became evident that they were characterised by constant tensions. Usually the former strongly criticised the latter as being fainthearted and opportunistic.

When the British Mandate over Palestine came to an end in 1948, the Jerusalem Anglican ecclesiastical authorities raised the issue of the future of JBY when the Jewish state would become a fait accompli. Their major concern related to those JBY who were linked to the 'double British enemy'; namely the British missionaries and the British government. Therefore, Operation Mercy (or Operation Grace, as it was also termed) was launched to evacuate from the country all Hebrew Christians who preferred not to remain within the anticipated new Jewish state. The operation was organised as a kind of spiritual Dunkirk, transferring about 80 persons to Liverpool in England.[11] Most probably, a strong motivation behind this operation was in the association of ideas relating to a modern equivalent of the first-century Jerusalem community exodus to Pella in Transjordan shortly before the destruction of the Temple in CE 70.

The first decade in the State of Israel

However, not all JBY left the country then. About a dozen remained, among them Shlomo Ostrovsky, Abram Poljak, Pauline Rose, Moshe Ben-Meir and Hayim Haimoff. As a result of this operation, a profound disunity was created among JBY. The majority followed the Gentile ecclesiastical policy; namely that JBY should gradually assimilate within the non-Jewish church society. The minority aspired to shape and maintain a unique identity within Jewish society as an integral segment within the Jewish state. No doubt this difference of outlook was rooted in the theological education and thought of individuals who had key positions within JBY circles.

A major consequence of Operation Mercy was that, with the departure of those evacuees in 1948, a community of JBY in Eretz-Israel ceased to exist, and a new situation emerged. Operation Mercy caused generation discontinuity, and also interrupted the sequence of group overlap, i.e. caused the disintegration of local fellowships and actually produced a clear distinction between Gentile church identity on the one hand and national congregation identity on the other hand.

Following the establishment of the State of Israel in 1948, a new era began in the history of JBY in the Land. Those very few who remained, reinforced by new JBY who moved into the Land through the massive *aliya* (immigration) waves of the 1950s and 1960s, together formed a new foundation for local believers. They worked strongly to eliminate their minority status within the expatriate minorities of churches and missions in Israel. In fact, gradually they did become a self-determined ideological minority on their own.

Various efforts were made to establish their own independent fellowships in Israel. Thus, for example, the Union of Messianic Jews was founded already in 1950, and later it was replaced by the Israeli Messianic Jewish Alliance organised in 1954. However, both the Union and the Alliance were disbanded after a few years, mainly because of personal and theological disagreements. A central issue in those conflicts was whether to permit, on the one hand, the involvement of non-Jewish Christians, e.g. from the local missions and churches, and on the other hand to permit the involvement of representatives from organisations like the IHCA.[12]

In reaction to attempts to create independent and genuine corporate entities of JBY, leaders among the churches and missionary organisations in Israel decried them as manifesting renewed tendencies of Judaising the Gentiles who belonged to the universal body of believers in Jesus. Furthermore, fears were also expressed in the same circles in reaction to the possibility of having a modern Jewish-Israeli Protestant bishop in Jerusalem. Such a development, so non-Jewish church leaders reasoned, would undermine the traditional authority and prestige of the existing Gentile ecclesiastical leadership. An independent and authoritative Jewish bishop, sitting on the See of James (Yaakov), brother of Jesus in Jerusalem, could, they reasoned, decrease Gentile spiritual prerogatives not only in the Holy Land but in the global Christian milieu as well.

After the Israeli Union and the Alliance had collapsed and disappeared in the 1950s, another organisation was formed, this time by Hebrew Catholics, in 1957, which still exists. The Society of St James and its constitution were approved as a unique branch *within* the Roman Church, and were actually incorporated into the Diocese of the Latin Patriarchate of Jerusalem.[13] Hebrew Catholic members of this Society on the one hand both adopted a Hebrew translation of the Latin Rite and subordinated themselves to the Catholic hierarchy, yet on the other hand they still hoped to renew the original 'primitive' Jerusalem influence of JBY within the church universal.

While among the supporters of the Society one could find Hebrew Catholics like the late Daniel Oswald Rufeisen, Bruno Hussar and Rina Geftman, one could also find opposition to it within the same circles. The late Carmelite monk Elias Friedman, of Jewish origin, for example, opposed the Society in principle for legitimising assimilation of JBY within the Gentile church. This, according to Friedman, comes without developing an autonomous Jewish identity of JBY, and without preserving their unique election and apostolate.[14]

Another attempt to establish a genuine congregation for expressing the self-determination of Messianic Jews in Israel was through the official registration of the Israeli Messianic Assembly – Jerusalem Assembly. Although this entity was nominally registered at the Ministry of Interior in 1958, in practice it did not become, as it was initially intended, *the* national body representing the consensus of Messianic Jews in Israel. De facto, this Assembly functioned mainly as a local congregation in Jerusalem. The founders of this Assembly, among whom were Ze'ev (Shlomo) Kofsmann, Eva Kronhaus and Rachel Grinberg, explicitly expressed their desire that through their Assembly they would revive and restore characteristics of the first-century Jerusalem congregation of JBY.[15] Thus they actually wished to bridge a gap of almost 2,000 years of history and mentality. In their theology, and particularly in Christological definitions, most of them deliberately preferred to avoid reference to any traditional ecclesiastical creed. Thus they refused to adopt any creed, such as the Apostles' Creed, the Nicene Creed and the Athanasian Creed. However, they were aware of the fact that obviously their non-Jewish Christian brothers in faith, both in Israel and abroad, did expect them to do so.

Nevertheless, they insisted on using New Testament terminology exclusively, without mentioning, for example, the concept of the Trinity in the formal text of an approved creed. In other words, they were convinced that when coming to Christological definitions, the use of the Hebrew language would naturally make a substantial difference. Thus, for example, within the one concept of 'Messiah' (משיח), they argued, the divinity as well as the humanity of the Saviour were reflected.[16]

Liturgical thought and practice

Dealing with liturgical thought and practice, two major topics deserve special attention: the celebration of feasts and rituals, and hymnology. Keeping the Jewish Sabbath had a special significance for JBY; Sunday observance was treated by Messianic Jews as unbiblical. Hebrew Catholics, however, still kept the Sunday liturgy as the rule within the Latin Church. Some JBY, however, also discussed among themselves whether to formulate a particular Messianic Sabbath Liturgy, including special prayers connected with lighting two Sabbath candles, as practised in many Jewish homes. People like Poljak and Ben-Meir even initiated a unique Sabbath Yeshua Liturgy, combining Jewish traditions and biblical texts in order to find some common ground with normative Judaism. Others, like Hayim Haimoff, rejected such tendencies by arguing that liturgies of this kind are extra-biblical and therefore irrelevant for JBY.

While Hebrew Catholics mainly celebrated Easter according to the church calendar, always on Sundays, Messianic Jews almost unanimously held to the concept that Passover should be celebrated only according to the Jewish calendar. Ben-Meir even elaborated a text of 'A Messianic Jewish Hagadah', incorporating into it verses both from the standard Jewish traditional Hagadah and the New Testament. Furthermore, the celebration of the Jewish Passover also provided Messianic Jews with a unique opportunity to justify the practice of the Lord's Supper by using only matza, the unleavened bread. In contrast to Hebrew Catholics, Messianic Jews rejected the doctrine of 'transubstantiation' and celebrated the Lord's Supper basically as a symbolic act of remembrance. They argued that this reflected a New Testament theology and not merely a common Gentile Protestant theology.

As to the feast of Christmas, in Mandatory Palestine and early days of Israeli statehood, most JBY celebrated this event. Later, however, only a few of them celebrated Christmas, and even they did not attribute particular importance to the date of 25 December. Rather they focused on celebrating the message and act of incarnation. Unlike Hebrew Catholics who followed the Latin Christmas ritual without dispute, among Messianic Jews one could find both those who justified the practice of a Christmas tree and decorations, and others who only emphasised the preaching of an edifying Christmas message accompanied by Christmas carols. Messianic Jews also disapproved of the traditional custom of 'visitation' by the legendary figure of Santa Klaus. In JBY circles, Chanuka, however, was also celebrated alongside Christmas. In Mandatory Palestine individuals like Ben-Meir emphasised the importance of correlating the two feasts in order to link Christmas to the Jewish national aspect of the feast of Chanuka. Haimoff, however, ignored not only the feast of Chanuka but also the feast of Purim as irrelevant to the 'messianic programme'.

The hymns that were sung in services of Messianic Jews during the years 1917–67 were usually traditional church liturgical hymns translated from the English and/or the German into the Hebrew language. Most of the translation work was done by Moshe Ben-Meir, who also privately published three Hebrew hymnal manuals, among them *Shirat Yeshurun*, which included some of his original hymns in Hebrew.[17] De facto, their hymnal corpus in the Hebrew language actually presented a special kind of creed by itself, focusing on the issue of salvation, which was based on the life of the Messiah: his birth, teaching, crucifixion, resurrection and Second Coming. Thus on the one hand most JBY aspired to detach themselves from traditional Gentile hermeneutics and theological creedal formulas; on the other hand, through the adoption of traditional church hymns translated into Hebrew, they sensed no difficulty or menace vis-à-vis their identity.[18]

Attitudes towards the return of the Jews to Zion

Following the parable of Yeshua about the blossoming fig tree (Mt. 24:32), JBY like Ben-Meir, Ostrovsky, Haimoff and Kofsmann often preached that the interpretation of this parable lies with the national restoration of Israel to her ancient homeland. Such persons considered their own times, and the twentieth century as a whole, as the predestined period for the fulfilment of biblical prophecy regarding the return of Jews worldwide to Eretz-Israel.[19] Furthermore, they also taught that

Israel's restoration to its Promised Land had clear eschatological implications, and that the ingathering of the Jews and the establishment of a
sovereign state would precede the Second Coming of the Messiah and
the establishment of His millennial kingdom on earth.

Among Hebrew Catholics as well, and especially those represented by
Elias Friedman and Daniel Oswald Rufeisen, the notion prevailed that
the return of the Jews to Zion had theological significance. In such
renewed national context they taught that JBY had a unique calling and
vocation, and should be regarded as the real remnant of Israel that
would become a spiritual nucleus bridging synagogue and church, and
even a spearhead for combating idolatrous and apostate theologies that
had infiltrated the 'Ecclesia ex Gentibus'. Friedman, however, did not
expect all Jews to return to the Land, but only a small minority of them,
while the majority would remain outside Israel. Both Rufeisen and
Friedman did point out, as against the traditional Catholic position, that
the Jewish nation remained the elect nation according to God's plan,
which still has a unique universal mission to influence the Gentiles.
Friedman even used the term 'Catholic Zionism' as an ideology dealing
with Hebrew Catholics belonging to a revived Hebrew branch of the
church – with no less spiritual authority than the first apostles in
Jerusalem.

Thus Catholic Zionism would mean that the Holy Land becomes the
'National Vatican City for Israel'. Therefore, in Friedman's mind,
Catholic Zionism vis-à-vis secular Zionism would enable the spiritual
nucleus of Hebrew Catholics in the Land both to 'purify apostate
Christendom' and to attract and influence the rest of the Jews and motivate them to turn to Yeshua. According to Friedman, the two Ratisbonne
brothers Alphonse and Theodore, converted to Catholicism in the nineteenth century, were the forerunners of Herzlian Zionism in the Land.

However, for both Friedman and Rufeisen it was crystal clear that the
resurrection of Yeshua symbolically prefigured the national restoration
of the Jews in Eretz-Israel. The analogy they made between the Shoah
(Holocaust) and Golgotha was obvious: just as Yeshua suffered the
agony of crucifixion and death and rose from the dead after three days,
so the Jews were restored in their sovereign state three years after they
suffered the agony of the Shoah and under a death sentence from Nazi
persecutors seeking to implement 'the Final Solution'.[20] In fact, all JBY

in the Land stressed the interpretation that the historical phase of the 'fulfilment of the Gentiles' (Rom 11:25)[21] had arrived and the end-time position of JBY should be manifested not only locally in Eretz-Israel but throughout the universal church.

The verdict of the Supreme Court

The formal denial of Rufeisen's Jewishness according to the Law of Return by a verdict of the Israeli Supreme Court in 1962 led to various reactions within JBY circles. Rufeisen himself started a life-long campaign to obtain recognition of his Jewishness *within* the Catholic Church as a Hebrew Christian. For this, he relied upon the Jewishness of the early church, and proclaimed that he himself and those in his status were the direct heirs of the original Jewish church. His Zionism concentrated on identifying himself with Jewish Christianity in Eretz-Israel. However, his conservative opponent, Elias Friedman, supported the verdict of the Supreme Court, saying that Rufeisen had indeed lost his Jewish identity and should be regarded as a Christian Israelite. Yet both Friedman and Rufeisen strongly objected to the total assimilation and disappearance of JBY within the Catholic Church, as had been the case throughout church history.[22]

Reacting to the same verdict, Ben-Meir and Haimoff argued that Rufeisen represented to the Supreme Court the traditionally despised figure of the converted Jew, especially when he was wearing his friar's brown robe. However, both Ben-Meir and Haimoff used this opportunity to encourage JBY in the Land to focus on their Jewish identity and strengthen it. Thus, for example, they thought it would be imperative that JBY become totally independent from 'churchianity' and detach themselves from church customs and hermeneutics, limiting the dispute between themselves as JBY and normative Jewish society to the one single issue: the crucified and risen Messiah and Son of God.

In other words, in all other matters except faith in the blood atonement of the Messiah and Son of God, they wished to formulate a biblical way of exegesis that would neutralise accusations against them as having become traitors to their Jewish heritage. Keeping the Jewish Sabbath and Feasts, as well as practising circumcision, expressed for them the central and authentic Hebraic-Jewish national features of their faith.

Attempts to establish settlements

On the agenda of JBY in Eretz-Israel we also find various attempts to found colonies of their own. Thus, for example, in the 1920s a small hen farm was established near Motza in the Judean Hills near Jerusalem. Then in the 1930s the IHCA planned to establish a unique Hebrew Christian colony near Gaza, where 2,000 dunams were purchased for this purpose. There was also another option to purchase land near Acre (Akko). All these attempts failed. Notwithstanding these failures, we may point out the prophetic motives of the participants in attempting such settlement projects in order to be practically involved in the process of Jewish restoration and colonisation of the Land. By trying to establish their own settlements they actually laboured to present a Messianic Jewish alternative to the dominant prototype of secular Zionism.[23]

Outside mainstream JBY, the settlement called Ir Ovot, founded in 1966 by the late Simha Pearlmutter in the Arava in the Negev, still exists. In fact, this is a 'one person' settlement, limited to the wife and children of Pearlmutter. Also called K'far Yeshua, it became better known because of archaeological excavations in the region which led to the unearthing of the biblical town of Tamar. It did not, however, significantly affect the local Israeli body of JBY, but remained exclusively the residence of one man and a part of his family. Pearlmutter strongly criticised the New Testament as pagan and idolatrous literature. For him, Yeshua was only the suffering and 'potential' Messiah, and was far from being the Son of God or having any divine attributes.[24]

Eschatological implications of the Six-Day War

The Israeli victory in the 1967 Six-Day War and the reunification of Jerusalem were soon interpreted by JBY as a significant 'sign of the times' preceding the Second Coming of Yeshua and the establishment of His millennial kingdom in Zion. Ben-Meir, Poljak, Ostrovsky, Haimoff and Kofsmann repeatedly taught that full Jewish hegemony in Jerusalem meant the end of the 'times of the Gentiles' (*Kairoi Ethnon*), and that Gentile global spiritual leadership would begin to be replaced by JBY.[25]

Furthermore, Jerusalem's reunification symbolised for them the approach of the satanic Antichrist who would rule the world. In their chiliastic hermeneutics, such JBY considered the Six-Day War as also preceding the eschatological battle of Gog and Magog, which would introduce Messiah Yeshua's millennial reign in Zion over the whole world. Jerusalem would then become the centre of the world, and God's promises to Abraham, Isaac and Jacob would be completely fulfilled.

In the wake of these end-time speculations, leaders like Ben-Meir and Haimoff also stressed that JBY should serve in the Israeli Defence Forces (IDF) as loyal citizens of the state, and if competent, even as officers. Thus, in comparison to the situation in 1948, when most JBY fled the country, in June 1967 many of them participated in the fighting on various fronts. Thus, their 'Messianic Zionism' in 1967 was not merely a theoretical and 'heavenly Zionism' but a practical one as well.[26] Actually, those few like Poljak, Ostrovsky, Haimoff and Ben-Meir who did not join the exodus of JBY from the Land in 1948 raised a new generation of JBY in Israel which developed a strong patriotic Zionism as part of their eschatological theology. Zionism, therefore, was not 'courted' by JBY as a pragmatic or opportunistic ideology, 'a tool for achieving legitimation by normative Jewish circles', but was rather grasped as an immanent component of their theology. Thus, considering those who held to the concept of a 'heavenly Zion' only, as well as those who found a unique balance between their loyalty to both 'earthly' and 'heavenly' Zion, one finds that the beliefs of both groups were rooted in their diverse understanding and applications of biblical prophecy.

Epilogue

In summary, this paper draws a comprehensive mapping of the history and theology of Jewish believers in Yeshua in Eretz-Israel during the lifetime of two generations that witnessed the British Mandate over Palestine followed by the establishment of the State of Israel. The following conclusions are clear:

1. In Mandatory Palestine there was a minimum of interaction between the Jewish mainstream and the small minority of JBY, which also lived as a minority within a minority in the Gentile church and missionary circles. This tendency, however, was basically changed after the establishment of the State of Israel.[27]

2. JBY developed a strong sense of the need to prevent their total social, cultural and theological assimilation within Gentile circles.[28] They rejected the 'gentilisation' tendencies that prevailed in the past. At the same time, JBY developed no aspirations to 'Judaise' the believers from the nations.

3. JBY focused on bridging the psychological gaps between themselves and the Jerusalem first-century disciples of Jesus as recorded in the book of Acts in the New Testament. Their strong consciousness of historical affinity with the first disciples of Jesus strongly shaped their identity.[29]

4. JBY almost unanimously accepted the canonical Holy Scriptures comprising the Old and New Testaments as a fait accompli, and made no attempts to canonise new texts. On the other hand, they insisted on their right to provide new and independent scriptural interpretations, mainly as a community rooted in the Hebrew language. The revival of the Hebrew language in their circles has given momentum to new tendencies among them to redefine theologies and even historical creeds.[30]

5. Their attempts to achieve organisational independence from missions and historical churches in the Land, as for example within their home fellowships, contributed to their success in shaping their collective self-identity. However, such developments were visible mainly after the Six-Day War. Through such organisational developments, we may regard the intellectual and social history of JBY in Eretz-Israel in terms of a movement, and not only in terms of theoretical theology.[31]

6. It should be noted that usually JBY were not deterred by accusations their opponents made against them that they were 'corrupt missionaries'. In their declared statements and writings, as well as their deeds, most of them constantly emphasised that they had a civil right and a natural human right to share their faith with others. They actually ignored social and legal pressures to cease from the open dissemination of their beliefs. Responding to traditional rabbinic attacks against them, they often claimed that they had in conscience the obligation to 'maintain a candlestick of witness' for Yeshua, even if they were delegitimised by normative Judaism.

The topic of this presentation is not an esoteric issue. As it is wide open to anyone interested in messianic patterns of thought and practice, it provides much material for drawing historical, theological and social comparisons between JBY and other messianic groups past and present. Thus, for example, current comparisons between modern JBY and Chabad messianic thought already reveal new dimensions that have hardly been considered until now.[32]

Notes

1. This paper is an updated English synopsis of my PhD dissertation *'"Messianic Jews" in Eretz–Israel (1917–1967): Trends and Changes in Shaping Self Identity'*, 1996 (in Hebrew), which was carried out under the supervision of Professor Gedalyahu Guy Stroumsa, from the Department of Comparative Religion, the Hebrew University of Jerusalem (see *Mishkan*, vol. 27 (1997): 11–23). For further comparisons see also my article 'Continuity and Change Among Messianic Jews in Eretz–Israel: Before and Following the Establishment of the State of Israel', in *The Messianic Jew*, vol. 66 (1993): 77–83 (Hebrew Version in *Me'et Le'Et*, vol. 81–82 (1995): 23–27). See also recently Dan Cohn–Sherbok, 'Modern Hebrew Christianity and Messianic Judaism', in Peter J. Tomson and Doris Lambers-Petry (eds), *The Image of the Judaeo–Christians in Ancient Jewish and Christian Literature* (Mohr Siebeck, Tübingen 2003), pp. 287–98 (Wissenschaftliche Untersuchungen zum Neuen Testament, 158); and Pauline Kollontai, 'Messianic Jews and Jewish Identity', in *Journal of Modern Jewish Studies*, vol. 3 (2004): 195–205.

2. See, for example, Agnes Waldstein, 'The Fig Tree and All the Trees', in *Jerusalem* (Jewish Christian Community), vol. 124 (January 1957), pp. 3–5; cf. Gershon Nerel, 'Israel at Fifty: Messianic Jews in the Land', in *Shalom* (CMJ Magazine, UK), 1998, pp. 9–10.

3. See, for example, Gershon Nerel, 'Modern Assemblies of Jewish Yeshua–Believers between Church and Synagogue', in S. N. Gundry & L. Goldberg (eds), *How Jewish is Christianity? Two Views on the Messianic Movement* (Zondervan, Grand Rapids 2003), pp. 92–107.

4. See recently Leon Menzies Racionzer, 'Hebrew Catholicism: Theology and Politics in Modern Israel,' in: *The Heythrop Journal*,

vol. 45 (2004): 405–415.

5. See Gershon Nerel, 'Bishop Jean-Baptiste Gurion and Two Modern Yeshua-Movements', in *Mishkan*, vol. 40 (2004): 57–63.

6. See, for example, Gershon Nerel, 'Creeds Among Jewish Believers in Yeshua between the World Wars', in *Mishkan*, vol. 34 (2001): 61–79.

7. Kurt Hjemdal, 'Arne Jonsen – A Pioneer in Israel (1924–1929)', in *Mishkan*, vol. 20 (1994): 39–40.

8. Gershon Nerel, 'The Formation and Dissolution of a "Messianic Jewish" (Hebrew Christian) Community in Jerusalem in the 1920s', in *Proceedings of the Twelfth World Congress of Jewish Studies, Division E* (Contemporary Jewish Society, Jerusalem 2001), pp. 19–29 (Hebrew).

9. See also Frederick Levison, *Christian and Jew: The Life of Leon Levison, 1881–1936* (The Pentland Press, Edinburgh 1989), pp. 163–223.

10. See a collection of articles in *The Jewish Christian Movement* (Patmos Publishers, London 1955).

11. Gershon Nerel, '"Operation Grace" Before the State of Israel was Born: The Evacuation of JBY from the Land', in *Zot Habrit*, Organ of the Messianic Jewish Alliance of Israel, vol. 20 (2004): 11–12 (in Hebrew), with a photograph of list of evacuees.

12. For additional data see, for example, Heikki Nurminen, 'Eighty Years of the Finnish Evangelical Lutheran Mission (FELM) in Israel', in *Mishkan*, vol. 41 (2004): 63–67.

13. 'The Hebrew Speaking Communities', in *Jerusalem* (Diocesan Bulletin of the Latin Patriarchate), Year 9, no. 3–4, June–August 2003, pp. 131–32.

14. In general, see Elias Friedman, *Jewish Identity* (The Miriam Press, New York 1987), especially pp. 89–95. See also Judith Bratten, 'Through the Hebrew Catholic Year', in *The Hebrew Catholic*, no. 72, Fall 2000, pp. 17–23.

15. See Per Østerbye, *The Church in Israel*, Gleerup (Studia Missionalia Upsaliensia XV), Lund 1970, *passim*; and Menahem Benhayim, 'The Messianic Movement in Israel – A Personal Perspectice (1963–1998)', in *Mishkan*, vol. 28 (1998): 10.

16. See, for example, *Halapid* (The Torch), Organ of the Israeli

Messianic *Kehila* (Assembly), vol. 1, Jerusalem, 1 January 1960 (in Hebrew).

17. Concerning distinctive messianic music see also Haya & Menachem Benhayim, *Bound for the Promised Land* (Jerusalem 2003), pp. 144–45.

18. During the last two decades Israeli JBY organised prolific conferences on messianic music. These produced many new songs in Hebrew. See, for example, the song booklets titled *Zimrat 2002* and *Zimrat 2004*, compiled and published by the Messianic Jewish Alliance of Israel.

19. For later developments, compare David H. Stern, *Messianic Jewish Manifesto* (Jerusalem 1988), pp. 217–233. See also Gershon Nerel, 'Attitudes of Messianic Jews (Hebrew Christians) towards Zionism, 1866–1948', in *Proceedings of the Eleventh World Congress of Jewish Studies*, Division B, vol. 2 (Jerusalem 1994), pp. 115–122 (Hebrew).

20. See Nechama Tec, *In the Lion's Den: The Life of Oswald Rufeisen* (Oxford University Press, Oxford/New York 1990), pp. 167–70.

21. This is based on the book of Joseph Shulam & Hillary Lecornu, *A Commentary on the Jewish Roots of Romans*, Lederer, Baltimore 1998, p. 378.

22. See, for example, Daniel Oswald Rufeisen, 'Hebrew Christians between Early and Later Christian Traditions', in Torleif Elgvin (ed.), *Israel and Yeshua* (Festschrift Caspari Center, Jerusalem 1993), pp. 49–55.

23. See, for example, Moshe Immanuel Ben-Meir, *From Jerusalem to Jerusalem* (Excerpts from a Diary), Netivyah, translated by Amikam Tavor (Jerusalem 2001), pp. 95; 145–47 (in Hebrew).

24. Simha Pearlmutter, *The Tents of Shem* (A Messianic Jewish Manifesto to the Post-Holocaust Church), Waterskins Publishing, Brisbane, Australia 1987.

25. See Gershon Nerel, 'Haim (Haimoff) Bar-David: Restoring Apostolic Authority among Jewish Yeshua-Believers', in *Mishkan*, vol. 37 (2002): 59–78.

26. Concerning the ideal of 'Heavenly Jerusalem' among JBY before World War II see Gershon Nerel, 'Zion in the Theology of Leon Averbuch and Shabbetai Rohold', in *Mishkan*, vol. 26 (1997): 64–71.

27. See, for example, Kai Kjaer-Hansen & Bodil F. Skjøtt, 'Facts and Myths About the Messianic Congregations in Israel' *Mishkan*, vols 30–31 (UCCI/Caspari, Jerusalem 1999), *passim*.

28. See also, for example, Yaakov Ariel, 'Evangelists in a Strange Land: American Missionaries in Israel, 1948–1967', in *Studies in Contemporary Jewry*, vol. 14 (1998): 195–213.

29. For an elaboration on this topic see, for example, Gershon Nerel, 'Primitive Jewish Christians in the Modern Thought of Messianic Jews', in Simon Claude Mimouni & F. Stanley Jones (eds.), *Le judéo–christianisme dans tous ses états* (Cerf, Paris 2001), pp. 399–425.

30. See Gershon Nerel, 'Eusebius's *Ecclesiastical History* and the Modern Yeshua–Movement: Some Comparisons', in *Mishkan*, vol. 39 (2003): 75–76; *Idem*, 'The "Flagship" of Hebrew New Testaments: A Recent Revision by Israeli Messianic Jews', in *Mishkan*, vol. 41 (2004): 49–56.

31. Some preliminary efforts in this direction have already taken place in Turkish Palestine. See Gershon Nerel, 'Hebrew Christian Associations in Ottoman Jerusalem: Jewish Yeshua-Believers Facing Church and Synagogue', in *Revue des Etudes Juives* (REJ, Paris), vol. 161 (2002): 431–457.

32. See also, for example, Joel Marcus, 'The Once and Future Messiah in Early Christianity and Chabad', in *New Testament Studies*, vol. 47 (2001): 381–401. I thank Jorge Quinonez for drawing my attention to this reference.

CAN THESE BONES LIVE?

Ken Burnett

'Why don't you pray for your own people, the Jewish people, Israel?' enquired OM Israel Team Leader, Larry Goldberg, right in the middle of the June 1967 Six-Day War, as it later became known. I retorted: 'Why? What's so special? Why pray for Israel at all?' At that time I already had a more than packed twelve-hour day, six-day week in my busy restaurant! The nooks and crannies of my days were filled with 'good' Christian things, one of these being to bring the young people from the streets around into our homely restaurant, via the Sunday night outreach, each week of the year.

Yes, it was true: I was of fully Jewish stock as far back as my ancestry went. But my inward (and subconscious) quest for God at the age of twelve, while preparing for Bar Mitzvah at the fashionable orthodox synagogue in Central London, had eventually ended with disillusionment. Two years of attendance at Gt Portland Street had left me dissatisfied, and I had gone into a kind of spiritual vacuum. So, in spite of the love and care of parents, my later teens in business with them, and friends, I became more distant from Judaism rather than drawing near; I eventually began to steer clear of Jewish connections. Neither did I want to get involved with 'religion', so my later years (1940–46) in the Armed Services saw me as Jewish if and when the Christian chaplain visited my squadron, but absent if the rabbi happened to come round – which he did from time to time, even during my time in Burma!

It was at the end of that time of spiritual vacuum that I had a dramatic and shattering encounter with the Lord. Through my being drawn to Christ by His fragrance in a restaurant employee (a lovely believer who

189

later became my wife), I had begun a deep personal search to find that life. Almost immediately afterwards, I came under a sudden and most devastating conviction of sin which, in turn, led on to nights and nights of copious tears, of which no one else knew but myself.

I was then inexplicably drawn to go and see a film, *The Inn of the Sixth Happiness* (the life of Gladys Aylward), in which 'Gladys' reads the 23rd Psalm to children in danger in China. That reading hit me like a sledgehammer, bringing what seemed to be a veritable explosion inside of me. All this in the back seat of the Odeon cinema in my home town back in 1959! This led me into the Bible and into finding what I had unwittingly been looking for 28 years earlier: a personal relationship with and an inward knowledge of God. (I came to John 6:37 and 'Him that cometh to me I will in no wise cast out (AV)', which the Holy Spirit made personal to me.)

So, it was this radical new purpose for living with which I was still coming to terms in 1967, some eight years later. What did it mean for me (even though of Jewish stock) to be 'a disciple of Christ, the Messiah', in the midst of Christians of Gentile origin, who seemed to really care and whose zest for the things of God I shared? What was I to do with the challenge from God's servant to tune in to and to give attention to God's specific will for my life? I asked myself again: '*Why* pray for Israel?' I had had no teaching at all on the subject, but I had been in 'good' Christian work. In my close contact with Operation Mobilisation, I had learned to pray in depth and at length for almost every other country – India, Austria, China, France, Spain, Mexico, Belgium – but why Israel?

While such were my thoughts in 1967, today in 2005 – 38 years and many spiritual battles further on – I pause, look back, and reverently realise that it has been the Lord Himself who has overruled all the initial ignorance, self-will and arrogance, and who gently and imperceptibly lifted all my strong reluctance to get involved; my reluctance to take up any weapon of prayer or spiritual warfare for even my own nation – my own kinsmen of the flesh! I had neither the ability, the desire nor even the knowledge of how to begin such a task. Today I realise too that what love I now have for my own people has come not simply from my ancestry, but rather from God Himself. It is He Himself who has implanted this into my being. It is of Him and it is for Him. I know this without a shadow of doubt.

The catalyst

Out of the blue, ten months after I began studying the word of God to specifically seek Him as to His purposes for Israel (i.e. in May 1968), I was unexpectedly asked to convene a Christian meeting in Bromley, my home town in Kent. A Japanese Christian minister (Rev. Otsuki), someone of whom I had never heard before, was briefly visiting from Japan with a delegation of Japanese believers. On arrival, his preaching proved to be as fire. His words were spirit and life – powerful, penetrating and convicting. The sense of God's holy presence was awesome. I was just one among the many there who felt unclean in the presence of these holy people. We did not need to be told we were in the presence of God.

Rev. Otsuki related how he had had a personal vision from the Lord back in 1939. He had been commanded to pray three times a day for Israel! And, in obedience to that, by some 30 years later (1968), he had established 80 churches throughout Japan, all the members of which were born again, all were Spirit-filled and all prayed for the nation of Israel. He had also developed a precious relationship with the government and people of Israel, visiting regularly with a large Japanese Christian choir of high, professional standard, bringing encouragement and the comfort of the prophetic scriptures through their open-air performances.

The visit of this Japanese delegation was the catalyst to my first visit to Israel in February 1969. I turned from a heart of indifference to a burning desire to see what God was actually doing in the Land of which these Japanese Christians had been singing and testifying.

The church in Israel – 1969

My previous immersion in OM-type discipleship led me in this very first visit to enquire what was happening within the indigenous church in the Land (as opposed to the multitude of foreign churches). I discovered that it was largely a status symbol for Christian denominations to have a church in the Holy Land, particularly in Jerusalem. Here is a verbatim report from that very first visit (February 1969):

> All churches are foreign-mission sponsored; there is no local Israeli church
> . . . These are somewhat exclusive, keeping largely to themselves. The United

Christian Council, acknowledged in some measure by the Government, represents 22 different recognised groups of all shades of Christian belief, doctrine and emphasis, from Anglican to Pentecostal. Does this cause confusion to the Jew? For the Christian it is self-defeating, especially with the history of much persecution in the name of Christ . . . while most Jews in Israel are not religious at all, nearly all Jews, whether religious or not, will oppose open witness by Christians . . . some violently. Consequently, most foreign and Hebrew Christians are afraid to witness openly for Jesus. For the Hebrew Christian it is particularly difficult.

Little wonder then that in 1969 the only two congregations that were partly indigenous – and which had at least some concern for the local people and the Land – were very much 'Brethren' in style, with nothing to distinguish them from the Western church, nor to identify them with the people whom they were there to serve. Everything, even the hymns, came from abroad.

At that time (February 1969) there was a sense of spiritual violence in the air, the enemy contesting the spiritually aggressive ministry here, more than anywhere else in the world. [Believers of every kind were too timid to even give out a tract] . . . It was hard (then) to be a Christian in Israel, harder still for an evangelical, even harder for a Messianic (Hebrew Christian) . . . The Government recognises Israeli atheists and Israeli communists, and it tolerates Arab Christians, but not Hebrew Christians. There is a sad lack of nationals who could assume a wise and unifying role to the various groups in Israel – a great need for non-ambitious, spiritual Hebrew Christians.

The Messianic Message in its true essence is not alien to the Land. It belongs there, it began there, and one feels that there is some strange divine purpose in the return of the Jew to that Land of his birth.

Sprinkling clean water

Within this background, the one who has not ceased to call Himself the God of Abraham, Isaac and Jacob was, silently and steadfastly, keeping His promise to Israel to 'take you out of the nations; I will gather you from all the countries and bring you back into your own land. I will sprinkle clean water on you, and you will be clean . . . I will give you a new heart and put a new spirit in you . . . I will . . . move you to follow my decrees and be careful to keep my laws . . . you will be my people, and I will be your God' (Ezek 36:24–28).

One of the most dedicated and godly of the several men whom God chose to sprinkle the clean water – to distribute the inspired word of God – upon Arab and Jew was a Finnish missionary called Kaarlo Syvanto. He had been led by the Lord to acquire Israeli citizenship in 1947, just before the political rebirth of the State of Israel in May 1948. By the time I met him in February 1969, and in spite of government hindrances, he had already distributed tens of thousands of Bibles and Testaments in Hebrew, Arabic and a score of other languages.

The word of God has its own power and (as in my own case) it can speak in a dramatic, life-changing way directly to men and women and even children. Kaarlo's work was rewarded in many, many ways. And although the Spirit of God has still so much to do in that Land, it is quite staggering to see what has been achieved through the seed-sowing of men like Kaarlo Syvanto, whose work continued for over 40 years, until 1992.

When I first met him in February 1969, I sat entranced while he spoke to me for nearly five hours without a break, telling of what God had done and was doing in Israel, of what the Bible said of Israel's troublesome but glorious future, and the world blessing that is to follow.

Prayer for Israel . . . and the shepherds

As a consequence of this encounter, inspired once more by Gentile believers, I returned to the UK after only eight days in Israel, loaded with so much prayer fuel that it seemed needful and appropriate to have a prayer meeting in the upper room over my restaurant (known as the Golden Rendezvous). This first (and initially intended to be the only) prayer meeting saw us sharing specific prayer which, in essence, has continued down to this very day, and which the Lord has continued to answer. The Spirit of God has taken this prayer-cry, expanded it, deepened it and spread it through many others in a multitude of ways to subsequent organisations. This was the prayer of 1 March 1969:

> Pray for a band of men whose heart God has touched with a love and fervour to make Him known in the Land – so rich with His presence in the past. It could be that the immediate future might see a re-awakening of that witness.

To put it mildly, it is astonishing to consider that (with the worldwide church in general still in total ignorance and often in strong animosity to what God is actually doing and has promised to do in Israel) God has remained faithful in giving, to date, the clean heart, the new spirit and His Holy Spirit to well over 100 messianic fellowships in the Land! They in turn are representative of almost every one of the 100 nations from which the Jewish people have returned – from east to west, from north to south.

While the particular focus the Lord gave initially for prayer was (and still is) that of intercession for messianic and Arab fellowships and believers in Israel (they being God's front-line troops), many other groups have since been raised over the last 30 years to pray for other aspects of what He is doing there.

This is the hand and the Spirit of God, the unfolding word of God; what is at stake is not so much the future of Israel, but the holiness of God's great name (Ezek 36:23). This same prophetic book says no fewer than 65 times: 'Then the nations [Gentiles/Goyim] shall know that I am the Lord', or 'then they [Israel] shall know that I am the Lord'. In other words, when God unveils the fact that it is He (not politicians or army generals) who is sovereign behind the scenes, and when He takes away the veil from the Jewish heart, both the nation and the rest of the world will recognise who has been and who still is at work.

It is fitting to emphasise that neither with those who prayed, nor with the men and women and shepherds raised in response to this prayer, was the 'perfection' of those vessels the key to what has happened, but rather do we see the faithfulness of God using weak but nonetheless *consecrated* vessels to accomplish His will, demonstrating that He is the covenant-keeping God of Israel, fulfilling His word before our eyes. The 'dry bones' are being prepared for the second influx of divine breath. Soon they will stand on their feet, a spiritually reborn, mighty, great army. Not the IDF – Israel's Defence Force – but the GDF: God's Divine Few, the remnant of Israel!

With little or no travelling or teaching ministry other than the Prayer for Israel prayer bulletins which began early in 1969, the Spirit of God wonderfully opened other hearts up and down Britain (and then abroad) to this fledgling work of prayer. Those with praying hearts arose, and prayer groups began to bud and blossom, pleading for the Lord to raise shepherds and to bring Jewish people to Himself.

The Negev

Some of the earliest and strongest prayer arose for the small drug rescue work that had begun in beach outreach to the drop-outs in Eilat, at the southernmost tip of the country back in 1969. While contact initially with this work was slender, it was steady, through a valiant woman of prayer and vision, Irma Walsh. Although little known, she was the visionary who initiated thousands of Bible study bookmarks going out across the globe, explaining how and why to pray for the nation of Israel. The beach work itself, launched by a Dutchman known as Jonathan, saw Dutch-speaking John Pex rescued from the drug scene in 1969.

John and his Jewish wife, Judy, were so transformed that they have devoted all their years since to following the same vision. As a result of their zeal and consecration, more Israelis and other people have found the Lord in Eilat than in any other part of Israel. One of the most steady and fruitful works in the country in the last 36 years has been the open invitation to their Sabbath evening meal, and the constant beach outreach run from their 'hostel' base in the coastal resort of Eilat. Many fine Christian workers initially found the Lord there. Today they are serving Him and reproducing themselves in other parts of the country.

Hundreds of temporary immigrant workers have been going back to their respective countries as born-again believers, often as evangelists, having come to the Lord in Eilat. Once, it was cynically asked, 'Can anything good come out of Nazareth?' Today, asking the same of Eilat in the south, we can give an unqualified and resounding 'Yes'. For example, there are hundreds, probably thousands, of Chinese people now (to name but one of many nationalities) with their names in the Lamb's book of life, who found the Lord just by being in Israel. Have you ever seen this reported in the Christian press?

Today there are at least six fellowships (or satellites) in central and northern Negev alone as a direct result of the indigenous (no foreign missions) evangelism in Eilat. In particular, the Russian Jews who have been streaming in from the north since well before 1991 have been deeply impacted.

Beersheva

Beersheva is known as the Gateway to the Desert and, up until the mid-1990s, the developing messianic fellowship here had probably had more prayer than any other fellowship in Israel. Many spiritual battles preceded its gradual rooting and grounding. Every inch of ground has had to be fought for. Originally this fellowship was more an offshoot of a fine Finnish mission, based in a Bible bookshop. The Finnish mission themselves were the 'foster parents' in many ways in those early years, very caring and instrumental in their support.

More recently growing into a large independent messianic congregation, the fellowship (also in friendship with Arab believers) has launched into family events and is a 'parent' congregation to a sprinkling of smaller satellites over a fairly wide area. This is but one example of the work of the God of Israel, fulfilling His promise of restoration to much more than mere existence in the Land, but to His spiritual restoration, His sprinkling of clean water, His implanting of the clean heart to His people, one day to be the head and not the tail (Deut 28:13).

From early uncertainty of direction and function, the congregation at Beersheva emerged from its 'chrysalis' into its own messianic identity. Its name today, 'Inheritance of Jesus' (*Nachalat Yeshua*), seems symbolic for the nation (Ps 135:4). Its Messianic Jewish leader (Howard Bass) is one of the many answers to that earlier founding prayer '. . . for a band of men whose heart God has touched with a love and fervour to make Him known in the Land – so rich with His presence in the past'.

Growth, change and 'Israel Soup'

Typifying what occurred in other parts of Israel between 1969 and the early 1980s, in Beersheva there was an ongoing transition from the Western 'Brethren-type' hymns and worship to something which more and more harmonised with the spirit and culture of the Land. Jews from many languages, countries and cultures still continue to flow into Israel, so the process of change goes on. But, being a conglomerate of some 100 nations, and constantly worked upon by the Spirit of God, Israelis today have been called by some 'Israel Soup'! The Beersheva congregation typifies this 'soup', with their biggest component by far (as elsewhere in Israel) being Russian Jews from the land of the north.

There are nine language groups to cope with (Hebrew, Russian, English, Spanish, Arabic, Romanian, Dutch, Korean and Chinese). Today, main translations are into Russian, English and Spanish. In 1969 it was English and Romanian. While more recently it has been possible to acquire the special equipment needed for multi-translating, many earlier years of difficulty have been endured at Beersheva and elsewhere to over-come and to establish the fledgling mixed congregations. It is commonplace today to be able to translate simultaneously to two or three or more lan-guage groups, but the battles for vision, faith, perseverance, personnel and finance for the equipment have had to be fought. The struggle exists while immigration continues, but a generation of Hebrew-speaking (for-mer) Russians is in the making. Language has been perhaps the main battleground to face. In the final analysis, it is important to realise that this is far more a spiritual battle than a matter of the intellect.

Russian (and other) Jewish immigrants

One of the omissions in the early days of Russian immigration (early 1980s) was the tendency to pray Russian Jews 'out of' Russia, but not 'into Israel'. There was little emphasis on praying them through and over the many hurdles, such as settling them into Israel's totally different cul-ture and regime, and grasping its new language and alphabet. To a degree these aspects have come to be faced over the years, but for the incoming Russian believers, it is still not easy to adjust from Russian-style faith to the Israeli.

In the earlier years, it seemed that the Russians were somewhat of a burden to the body of Messiah, but today they have become a big bless-ing, constituting not only some 50 per cent of the believers within the Land, but being responsible for most of the musical and vocal talent within the congregations. Several times the Lord emphasises that He is bringing them from the land of the north (Jer 31:8; 16:15; 23:8), so with one-sixth (a million) of Israel's present population being from Russia, and with vast numbers of Jews still scattered and hidden in the north, the repeated scriptural references seem to carry special significance.

The Lord has been preserving for Himself this large remnant in 'the land of the north', in the main free from the traditionalism and Judaism that have characterised most Jews and with little to 'unlearn' in that realm. Therefore they have been better candidates for the word of God, far more open to the biblical Judaism that acknowledges Jesus as the 'Lamb of God that taketh away the sin of the world' – the very first portrait by which the Lord Yeshua was personally introduced to His own people by His cousin, John the Baptist.

From the influx of existing Russian Jewish believers, and the Russian Jews who have so hungrily come to faith from within the Land, a new zeal and vibrancy for God has arisen, healthily permeating the whole messianic body in Israel, and doubling it in size since 1991. Well might the prophet write: 'When I act, who can reverse it?' (Is 43:13).

From beyond the rivers of Ethiopia

Among the many silent miracles since Israel's national rebirth in 1948 has been the home-gathering of the Ethiopian Jews. Whether or not the rabbinic tradition is valid that they stem from the tribe of Dan is uncertain, but attention has been drawn to them in two major, highly secret operations. Prompted by the tyranny of the Communist dictator, Mengistu Halie Mariam, the Israeli government financed: (1) Operation Moses (1984–85), seeing some 10,000 escape and (2) Operation Solomon, seeing a further 14,400 escape, in a totally amazing 36-hour period (25–26 May 1991), which hit world headlines. Although this remnant was destitute and penniless, unskilled and uneducated, and riddled with rejection and fear, suspicion and mistrust, hard-pressed Israel nonetheless took on the continuing responsibility for them.

Through his lifelong link with Ethiopia, one of the men behind the scenes who has played such a vital role at high levels in fostering this *aliyah* (emigration) has been 'Gerald', who remains such a trusted and steadfast friend to the whole remnant, the thousands of Ethiopian Jews in Israel and in Ethiopia. Through Gerald, I was personally privileged in 2000 to meet in an unforgettable way so many of this godly remnant in Ethiopia.

However, in Israel to this very day, finding security as they do in their very strong Ethiopian culture, the Ethiopian believers still stand largely separate from the Israeli messianic body. With their own capacity for reverent worship being far beyond anything else in Israel (something we could all well emulate), they nonetheless enter little into aspects such as the keeping of the Feasts of Israel, fellowship with other believers and sharing at national conferences. This is a universal trait for Ethiopians, not limited to Israel.

Another feature of Ethiopian culture, a tendency to central control, has kept their six major congregations from normal localised pastoral oversight, although there are welcome signs that this may change. But coupled with this, there is an attractive beauty of Ethiopian character, personality and physique. The Ethiopian Jews have their own unique contribution to make to the messianic body, particularly in their style of worship.

Israeli Jewish orthodoxy has not been slow to stir up the unsaved Ethiopians to publicly and strongly oppose the Ethiopian Jewish witness. As among other believers in Israel, this has led to unfair dismissal, hardship, false accusations and ostracism. Through the developing, often violent and frightening opposition to the messianic witness, maturing strength has been trickling into the body in general. One leading Ethiopian believing woman, sacked from her job because of her faith, has since become a fine teacher, encourager and 'mother' for other Ethiopian women. These tests of violent persecution have served not only to highlight potential leaders from within the body, but to bring a publicity for the gospel that could be had no other way. This continues today.

The very word 'messianic' never appeared in the Israeli press until the mid-1980s, and then only gradually. Although the Orthodox Jews at times also use the term in a different sense, it has had widening public usage in recent years to refer to the Jews who actually believe in Jesus as Lord, a phenomenon that no Jew would even acknowledge, let alone mention publicly, until after the Six-Day War! So, just as persecution served to spread the faith in the first century, it is the same today.

In passing, it is not incongruous to mention that while it is difficult for the Jewish believer in Israel, it is even harder, and certainly far more dangerous, for a Palestinian believer to stand or to witness for the Lord. Some of these have been thrown into prison and severely tortured for their faith, and this in greatly added measure where the Lord has given them a love for, and an understanding of, Israel. Some of these Palestinians have stood fast and lost their lives in the process. God has been opening eyes to discern His biblical end-time purposes for Israel and the church. It is increasingly costly to stand for this truth in any part of the world today.

It is interesting to recall that at the very start in 1969 there was resistance from messianic leaders in Israel against the thought of their needing help in prayer from abroad. There was resistance from within the church in Israel against the thought of any messianic witness taking place within the country. And there was certainly strong resistance from abroad against any vestige of a thought of there being a messianic witness within Israel. One easily forgets the long road that has been trodden down through the years.

Galilee of the Gentiles

From being able, 36 years ago, to count the messianic fellowships on one hand, today it is not possible to enumerate them. There are too many, and they increase all the time. Perhaps Galilee gives the greatest encouragement, with its examples of large fellowships; of lively, thriving flocks that have come through many successive spiritual battles (and which are by no means over); of congregations that have died and come back to life; and of others that have fought and faltered through their struggles and the fierce opposition. Growing unity between Arab and Jew is seen more here than anywhere else in Israel – many being members of the same fellowship. But all of this combines to bring a present volume of praise and worship to God that has been absent for 1,900 years. This is the Lord at work saying: 'I will build you up again . . . O Virgin of Israel. Again you will take up your tambourines . . . on the hills of Samaria' (Jer 31:4–5); 'Winter is past; the rains are over and gone. Flowers appear on the earth; the season of singing has come, the cooing of doves is heard in our land' (Song 2:11–12).

One of the biggest struggles has been to find premises in which Hebrew congregations can worship the Lord at all. Subsequent to that, the difficulty has been to find properties large enough to accommodate the swelling numbers. It is awesome to begin to see what God has done in these few years – specially built premises, industrial premises, borrowed premises, open-air sites, endured-under-sufferance sites, and so on. Expansion of numbers and spiritual growth usually go hand in hand within the whole Land.

One long-overcrowded meeting on the shores of the Kinneret, made up at present of folk from Russia, Algeria, France, Argentina, the USA,

England, Israel, Holland, Germany, etc., perceives a coming move of the Holy Spirit. They discern from the word that whatever Jesus did in His original ministry in Galilee is going to fade into insignificance when 'in the future he will honour Galilee of the Gentiles, by the way of the sea, along the Jordan' (Is 9:1–2).

'You have enlarged the nation and increased their joy . . . as people rejoice at the harvest' (Is 9:3).

Shall we not be thankful that God is watching over this, His word, to perform it?

SECTION IV

This fourth section examines the role of the Palestinian people, opening with an important and deeply insightful essay by Gershon Nerel examining the relations between Palestinians, Christians and Jewish believers in Yeshua, with attention to the spiritual *intifada* underpinning the most difficult areas for dialogue. The issue confronted is one that has had little attention paid to it and it is essential for the future that the subject should emerge from the shadows.

Nick Gray examines the plight of the Palestinian refugees, giving a wide-ranging overview of the matter, an issue that is usually badly misrepresented in the media. The section closes with a consideration of aspects of the spectre of international terrorism and the role of the Palestinian violence within its development. It is important to consider this aspect among the contours of the Land, as it has left a stain on the history of the Middle East that has been politically laundered.

SPIRITUAL *INTIFADA* OF PALESTINIAN CHRISTIANS AND MESSIANIC JEWS

Gershon Nerel

I owe special thanks to Rose Jenks and Ken Burnett for their kind linguistic assistance.

I would like to share with you a sensitive topic that I also call end-time thinking between Messianic Jews and Palestinian Christians. But first I would like to quote one verse from the epistle to the Romans: 'For if their being cast away is the reconciling of the world, what will their acceptance be but life from the dead?' (11:15 NKJV). In my Hebrew Bible there is no question mark as there is at the end of some of the English texts. I think that there should be an exclamation mark instead of a question mark at the end of this unique verse.

In recent generations we have seen miraculous life from the dead among messianic believers, the first-fruits. This is the beginning of a large reformation. However, this does not mean that it is happening in a vacuum. In reality, Jewish believers in Yeshua (JBY) face serious problems in various arenas, especially in the field of theology. One salient example relates to the current theology of Palestinian Christianity. During the years 2000–04, the Palestinian *intifada* did not merely introduce armed hostilities that brought bloody suffering for both sides. It also unveiled and spearheaded an undeclared spiritual war against Israel.

Physical and spiritual warfare

The current *intifada*, which is a military and terrorist warfare, was recommended by the Palestinians. However, it is far more than an armed

205

aggression. In fact, it also has the dimension of a massive spiritual battle. Palestinian warfare is taking place not only against Zionist Israel. We observe a spiritual *intifada* of Palestinian Christians against both Israel and her Christian friends around the world. This is *de facto* an attack against biblical end-time teaching and against Western Christianity. I believe that we need to have a special gift of discernment to see and to understand the times in which we live.

The present spiritual *intifada* is taking place among the historical churches of the Palestinians. It does not mean that it includes all Palestinian Christians. I do not want to generalise about all Palestinian Christians, but I do wish to mention the established churches in the Land, a tiny piece of land from the Jordan River west to the sea, where we see three major Palestinian blocs that have developed and maintain this spiritual *intifada* against Israel and against the Christian supporters of Israel: Palestinian Catholics, Palestinian Anglicans and Palestinian Lutherans. Each of these three denominations has a local Palestinian bishop: the Catholic (Latin) Patriarch Michel Sabbah, the Anglican bishop in Jerusalem Riah Abu El-Assal and the Lutheran bishop Munib Younan. They are involved in a comprehensive and sophisticated warfare on the theological level.

They have introduced into the churches a new Palestinian replacement theology. The Eastern Palestinian replacement theology, as it was in the early centuries, says that God actually has finished with Israel's election, and that the promises and the covenants with Israel are finished. Moreover, that there is no continuum between biblical and modern Israel; namely, that modern Israel is no longer the natural and legitimate continuation of biblical Israel. Such an approach has many consequences. When Palestinian prelates teach that the people and state of modern Israel are not the continuation of ancient Israel, one gets a 'cut' with the Bible, and almost automatically there is a 'cut' between the New Testament and the Old Testament – a denial of the oneness and completeness of the word of God.

The teaching of this theology is developed systematically, and is disseminated through the modern media, particularly through the Internet, and reaching from this tiny Land of Israel to the entire world. One must be aware of it and face the dangers of this teaching. People must be warned of what is happening and encouraged to follow the biblical way of thinking. What is happening with Israel affects the end-time reality of our times, and the end-time reality of our faith. If this is not clear, then theologically and prophetically there is a total blackout.

Who represents the genuine mother church?

While Messianic Jews claim that they are the historical and authentic continuation of the first *Kehila*, i.e. the first entity/congregation of Jewish Yeshua-believers in the early centuries as it is described in the New Testament, one also finds the Palestinian claim that 'the Arab Christians are *the* inheritors of the mother church in the Land'. These parallel identifications develop more and more within dissenting theological frameworks.

The pleading of Palestinian Christians to represent the genuine mother church automatically undermines the coherent identity of Messianic Jews about themselves being the undistorted succession of the early Jewish Yeshua-believers. If, on that basis, there is truth in the claim of Palestinian Christians that they represent the genuine teaching of the mother church in the Land, then actually the Hebraic message of Messianic Jews is not a novelty, to say the least. Then, in fact, there is no prophetic 'new life from the dead' among modern JBY – making the word of God irrelevant.

One could therefore ask the question: 'If Israel has been displaced or replaced, then since in Romans 11:15 "the casting away of them" clearly refers to Israel (see also Romans 10:21), to whom could the accompanying declaration apply ("what shall the receiving of them be but life from the dead!") other than to Israel?' It would be a grammatical absurdity to try and apply it to Palestinian and Gentile believers.

Palestinian Christians 'become the inheritors of the Jewish mother church' by manipulative exegesis. For example, they take the biblical text of Acts 2:11, where it mentions 'Arabians' and apply it to themselves. However, the whole passage there speaks about *Jewish* pilgrims who come to the Land for the Feast of Pentecost (and Passover) to celebrate with their Jewish brethren at the Temple, and there they were heard '. . . speaking in our own tongues the wonderful works of God'.

Thus, the context of this scene involves devout *Jews* 'from every nation under heaven' (Acts 2:5) – Jewish pilgrims from the diaspora who had come to Jerusalem for the Feasts of *Shavuot* (Pentecost) and *Pesach*, in order to fulfil the biblical commandment to come to the Temple of the Lord (Exod 23:14–17; Lev 23:15–17); namely, from Crete and Arabia, etc., not Gentile Cretans and Arabians. Therefore when modern Palestinian Christians say, 'Those people are our ancestors,' they simply misuse the text. There are other examples too. One of the Palestinian priests, Elias Chacour, a Greek Catholic Melkite, wrote in his books: 'They, my ancestors, were the first to hear the Sermon on the Mount and to accompany the Lord from one peak to another during His life. The Christianity of the Holy Land is Palestinian . . .'

Palestinian churches, alongside historical churches, question the theological legitimacy of contemporary Messianic Jews. Palestinian Christians find no justification for a distinct Messianic Jewish entity outside of the traditional churches – churches which also claim that Messianic Jews have no apostolic succession. In other words, that JBY have no apostolic continuity, no apostolic authority, because their history was disconnected for centuries. In fact, it should be stressed that throughout history, the different churches did not allow the existence of corporate and free entities of Jewish believers in Yeshua.

However, New Testament Scripture explodes this false doctrine by the single statement in Romans 15:8: 'Now I say that Jesus Christ has become a servant to the circumcision for the truth of God, to confirm the promises made to the fathers [patriarchs – Abraham, Isaac and Jacob]' (NKJV).

De-Judaisation of the Bible

Canon Naim Ateek, the Jerusalemite Anglican Palestinian minister, openly declares that he does not accept the entire Bible from Genesis to Revelation. He puts it as follows: As a Christian, I cannot begin my study of the Bible from Genesis. What God did for the world in Christ far exceeded the best that the prophets predicted and anticipated.'

In a similar line, Palestinian Christians also talk about 'Jesus the first Palestinian', and write about 'Mary the Palestinian' or the 'Palestinian apostles'. This kind of exposition replaces the Jewish foundations of Holy Scripture. Actually, there is a growing tendency among Palestinian Christians towards the de-Judaisation of the Bible. At the same time, however, Jewish Yeshua-believers emphasise the point that Israel's role in the last stages of the end-times is focal in the Bible. For example, the biblical concepts of 'the last days', 'the last year' and 'the day of the

Lord' appear clearly within the context of Israel's return to the Land. Ezekiel's eschatological prophecy (ch. 37) about taking Israel to the 'valley', i.e. the Land of their forefathers, refers to taking them out of their graves in the diaspora, and restoring them to life, in a full reality. To deny this is to deny the validity of the Bible, to call the Almighty a liar.

While a partial regathering from north, south and east occurred in 536 BCE, at no point until the twentieth century CE did any regathering take place from the West to fulfil the prophetic word in Zechariah 8:7–8 and Isaiah 49:12. If one does not acknowledge that this regathering is happening now with Israel, in the Land of Israel, one must be deliberately spiritually blind. Yet the leaders of Palestinian Christianity within the historic churches reject this kind of interpretation. For them, the Zionist movement altogether is a disaster, not only nationally but theologically as well.

On the other hand, within the eyes of Messianic Jews, the entire Zionist movement is a tool in the hands of the Lord, just as the Babylonian Nebuchadnezzar was a tool in His hands, and the Persian King Cyrus, and the Roman Titus and other historical forces. At the same time, one must also acknowledge that even the first-century JBY strongly believed that they were already living in the end times. They expressed this notion very clearly in the New Testament. They expected that the return of Yeshua would be very soon. The apostles Peter and Paul, for example, both expected that the Second Coming would happen in their lifetime. But they did not or could not know that 2,000 years would have to pass.

Jewish Jerusalem

Indeed, in the meantime Israel had to go into exile, and Israel had to return from exile. Additionally, Yeshua's prophecy about Jerusalem being liberated from the rule of the Gentiles had to take place literally (Luke 21:24). It is well known that Jerusalem was not fully under Jewish rule for more than 2,000 years – from the times of the Greeks, the Romans, the Byzantines, the Muslims, the Crusaders, the Mamlukes, the Turkish Ottomans and the British, until June 1967. Only after the Six-Day War in 1967 was Jerusalem reunified and became completely under Jewish control. This is a unique sign of the times.

Also logically, one cannot underestimate or ignore such an historical event. It is obvious that Israel's physical restoration is happening while the Jews are definitely not a perfect nation. Israel is far from being a blameless nation. But God miraculously brings together the 'dry bones' out of their 'grave'. The Nazi films indeed visualised the Jewish bones placed in collective graves. The survivors of those 'dry and dead bones', and others too, were taken into the Promised Land. This is being done by God Himself for a purpose, for a spiritual purpose.

We should take into account that there are many passages within both Old and New Testaments that prophesy worldwide contention over this very issue of Jerusalem in the end-days. Chapters 12 and 14 in the book of Zechariah and a greater fulfilment yet of Luke 21:24 are but two examples.

Gradual process

God's plan for Israel is not fulfilled within 24 hours. It takes an historical process, and we know that God often works through a process. Sometimes, however, it takes a one-time event, such as that which happened with the apostle Paul on his way to Damascus. Paul had an instant personal revelation of Yeshua Himself. But I know from my own personal experience and from that of many other JBY that it often takes a longer time to become a believer in Yeshua. Very often it is an inner struggle, a mental and heartfelt struggle, until we accept Yeshua. Not all of us receive a personal Damascus experience. It may require months or years for this to take place.

I well remember from my own personal history that I first had to struggle intellectually in order to understand that Yeshua is the Messiah; that the New Testament is the continuation of the Old Testament. I needed to understand that I would not lose my Jewish identity when I acknowledged that Yeshua is Messiah; that I would not become an apostate or a traitor to my people. It took time to realise that I would not become a part of the historic Inquisition and the Crusaders, and of the other persecutions of the Jews by the church. Only then, after several years, was I ready to accept Yeshua also in my heart.

And today, Israel is accepting Yeshua step by step, but only intellectually. He is accepted as a Jew, as a great moral luminary, a great teacher and prophet, but not yet the Messiah, Son of God. Not yet! But even coming this far, accepting Yeshua as a Jew, is a colossal step forward from the international Jewish attitude prior to 1948 and 1967. Almost universally the name of Yeshua in those earlier days would provoke hostility or a curse. Attitudes have been in the process of change now for several decades.

The deep spiritual revelation will happen only after much suffering. That is how I understand it. So in our generation JBY have a broader spiritual perspective than the early believers 2,000 years ago. While today JBY have wider perspectives than the great apostles of the New Testament, they also hold a larger responsibility.

It is interesting to reflect that the Lord used World War I to release the *Land* (then 'Palestine') for the Jewish people; but through World War II came the release of the *people* for the Land. After 2,000 years of dispersion, how is it that these two unique events coincide?

Several messianic movements

Within the Jewish commonwealth there are several modern messianic movements. It is not enough to use the term 'Messianic Jew'. I prefer to say 'Jewish believers in Yeshua', or 'JBY', because it is more accurate. It is problematic to use merely the appellation 'Messianic Jews', because the followers of the late *Lubavitcher*, Rabbi Menachem Mendel Schneerson, are also Messianic Jews by definition. One must admit that those who follow the *Lubavitcher*, who died in Brooklyn, New York City a decade ago, and attribute to him divinity, etc., are also Messianic Jews. It is a fact that all Jews who believe in the biblical promise of a Messiah are Messianic Jews.

And in the Land one also finds political Messianic Jews – those like *Gush Emunim* (Block of the Faithful), who seek territorial restoration through settlements in Judea and Samaria. Additionally, there are also those Messianic Jews who follow certain rabbis in Israel; false rabbis who claim to be full messiahs, or half messiahs, or three-quarters messiahs, like Uzi Meshulam, Mordechai Eliyahu and the late Bratslaver Rebbe, Nachman of Bratslav, who led the Chasidic movement in Uman (modern-day Ukraine). Moreover, some Israelis even view Ben Gurion as a secular messiah of Israel. They all are by definition Messianic Jews.

Therefore, people always need to clarify precisely in which Messiah they believe. In Hebrew we often say *Yehudim Talmidei Yeshua* (Jewish disciples of Yeshua) or *Yehudim Hassidei Yeshua* (Jewish followers of Yeshua). In fact this is the scriptural nomenclature. In the New Testament, the term 'disciple(s)' appears about 200 times. Indeed, we are the disciples of Yeshua, because we have only one Teacher and Master.

Spiritual authority of Messianic Jews

Messianic Jews firmly declare that they do not need the formal approval of the historic churches for their legitimacy in these end times. JBY receive their authority directly through the Holy Spirit, just as some believers do today in, say, China. JBY receive their ordination by the Holy Spirit in these prophetic times, in a prophetic way. Occasionally, such a reality may also cause difficulties. Sometimes there are problems because there exist self-appointed teachers, and self-appointed leaders and prophets. But there have always been problems. Even when the Israelites came out from Egypt, there was Korah, and others. Wherever one finds human beings, there are problems! This is true everywhere, in every time. That is reality. However, JBY do assume full spiritual and prophetic authority. I mean, real believers, real servants of the Lord as revealed in the Bible, do have full prophetic, divine authority, to teach and to interpret Scripture – and we talk within a framework of the canonical texts.

Messianic Jewish Yeshua-believers stand on a solid scriptural basis, and for this they definitely must credit the churches. Much credit goes to the churches of the nations that shaped and preserved the canon. The Old Testament was already canonised within the Jewish world, but the New Testament was canonised within the churches, and Messianic Jews accept it without question. The canonical text, together with the guidance of the Holy Spirit, is the real life framework of JBY. In that connection there is a sense of indebtedness to the wider (Gentile) church from the JBY for the preservation of the Scriptures and the gospel through the centuries to this present day. Additionally, it is the daily guidance and wisdom of the Holy Spirit that elevates the remnant of JBY.

So, Messianic Yeshua-Jews do come with a prophetic authority in a way that emphasises the Scripture and its fundamentality – not as fundamentalists, but fundamental; not as radical extremists who want to explode the mosques on the Temple Mount. Obviously such ideas are not on their agenda. The agenda is primarily to understand and to follow the divine words of Yeshua, Son of God and Lord. His teaching is the foundation for everything: in personal life, as well as in national affairs and in universal spirituality. This fundamental approach of JBY poses a theological headache for Palestinian Christians.

Liberation theology of Palestinian Christians

Alongside their theology of replacement of Israel, Palestinian Christians also introduce a liberation theology. This so-called liberation theology is very much based on social and political views taken from Latin America and the Third World. Palestinian Christians justify their liberation theology with isolated concepts like 'justice and only justice', 'love' and 'mercy' in a one-dimensional manner while totally ignoring other dimensions of God, like a God of faithfulness, a sovereign God who keeps His promises, the Lord of judgement, and the King of history. No doubt God is the Lord of love and mercy and justice! No question about it. Nobody denies that.

But God is not simply and solely a God of 'justice and only justice', or merely a God of mercy and love. There are also other attributes of God that are clearly manifest in the Bible. He is also a God of the eternal covenants and of judgement. Indeed, Israel was punished seriously with God's judgement. Israel was not spared. Nobody can say that God is partial, and that He is only the God of the Zionists. So when Palestinian Christians spread made-up slogans such as 'the God of the Old Testament is the God of the Zionists only', should Messianic Jews feel ashamed to call themselves Zionists? Absolutely not! I am not ashamed to call myself a biblical Zionist, because I see that even God is a Zionist, as I understand it from my own Bible.

The prophets of the Bible are Zionists too, because they speak about Zion and the Land of Zion and the return of the Jews to Zion. A key teaching in the New Testament is that the word of the prophets, i.e. Old Testament prophetic teaching, is as a light in a dark place (2 Pet 1:19) – an apt illustration of the present spiritual morass in the whole world. In other words, spiritual light for today is given through understanding and accepting Old Testament prophecy. But the converse is also true: denying the validity of Old Testament prophecy inevitably brings spiritual darkness and confusion. (When 1 and 2 Peter were written, the New Testament had not been brought together, so Peter had the Old Testament in mind when he, via the Holy Spirit, wrote this passage.)

The whole Land of Zion was promised to Israel, not to the Palestinians. There is no biblical promise for a Palestinian state. And history never witnessed the existence of a Palestinian state. However, as individuals, Arabs should have full human rights. There is no question about that, and this principle was already quite clear in the Old Testament. According to the Torah, the *Ger* (local inhabitant) is the resident in the Land, and he should be treated with full respect and with rights and with all that goes with biblical principles. Just as a reminder, before the current terrorist *intifada*, the Israeli military had left the Palestinian cities and villages, and they enjoyed domestic autonomy. Then they started with suicidal massacres.

Israel never developed an ideology of oppression for the sake of persecution and exploitation of other nations. However, when there are exceptional cases of injustice, they are systematically brought to court. I myself served in the Israeli army for many years, and now my children serve in the IDF, and I know personally that it is an army with the highest standards of morality, even when deviations do occur. The Americans and their allies in Iraq treat no less seriously the wrongdoings of some of their military. In fact, American forces and other 'enlightened armies' around the world, not to mention Muslim troops, would not be as scrupulous as the Israelis.

Palestinian 'martyrdom'

Israeli Messianic Jews completely disagree with Palestinian Christians when they misuse the concept of martyrdom, taken from Scripture and from history, and link it with Arab suicide activities. From both the Bible and church history it is well known what it means to be a martyr. Stephen, the proto-martyr from the book of Acts who gave his life for his faith and witness, was a real martyr. But how can Palestinian Christians say that terrorists are martyrs? How can they employ this terminology in Palestinian Christian writings?

Palestinian Christians even mention Samson from the book of Judges, placing him as a model to justify suicide activities indirectly. Samson, in their reasoning, is a model because he 'committed martyrdom as a Jewish freedom fighter . . .'. Thus, if Samson is the heroic freedom fighter, then Palestinians can justify their own suicide . . . and, instead of calling their martyrs Samson, they may name them Mohammed, or Ahmed, or Mustafa. This way of thinking is paradoxical indeed when one remembers that Palestinian Christians wish to disregard the Old Testament. Yet in many churches nowadays, people hardly read their Bibles, so they are easily deceived by this kind of propaganda.

Palestinian crusade against Jewish and Christian Zionists

Recently, Palestinian Christians have been waging a massive verbal crusade against Christian Zionists. It is a war of words, a 'terminological' warfare. It is not a virtual game. Words can kill. On 1 April 2004 I attended a conference in Jerusalem, organised by Sabeel, a Palestinian Christian organisation led by the Anglican minister Naim Ateek, already mentioned above as an Arab church leader who does not acknowledge the literal truth of the Bible. Before the conference started, the planners projected only one word on a large screen as an introductory logo. The word was 'Truth', and it appeared in different languages – English, French, German and I think even Hebrew. Thus the word 'Truth' was rotating on the screen, raising the question 'What is truth?' Indeed, what is truth? And where is truth?

The 'truth' of Palestinian Christians condemns Christian Zionists as heretical extremists. Palestinian Christians sharply attack Christian Zionism as if it is one of the biggest sins in these days. According to Palestinian teaching, the Christian supporters of Israel in the West deserve excommunication. An example for this is found in a pastoral letter which was officially published by Munib Younan, the Palestinian Lutheran Bishop in Jerusalem, on 6 January 2003. In his greetings for the New Year, Younan wrote a whole document against Christian Zionism, as follows:

> I hereby declare that Christian Zionism is not only a sick theology, but it is a heresy, right along with Arianism and Nestorianism. I believe it is time we named this misinterpretation of Christ and the gospel for what it is. Christian Zionism is anti-justice, anti-peace, anti-reconciliation and the enemy of peace in the Middle East.

This letter is signed with the impressive title of 'Bishop in Jerusalem'. By using the title of 'Bishop of [or in] Jerusalem' he assumes the full spiritual authority of the Bishop in the Holy City. In other words, Younan claims *de facto* to sit on the See of the first Jewish bishop in Jerusalem. In fact, today there are at least seven Gentile bishops in Jerusalem who claim to sit on the Seat of Yaakov (James), the first Messianic Jewish leader in Jerusalem 2,000 years ago. Furthermore, all the denominational bishops in Jerusalem expect modern Messianic Yeshua-Jews to dwell under their wings and accept their authority.

British clergy support Palestinian theology

Palestinian propaganda against biblical Zionism, both Jewish and Christian, is promulgated via the Internet worldwide, aiming to repeat and diffuse the libel that Zionism is nothing but a dangerous heresy. Consequently, some superficial believers already feel guilty and even apologise for being Zionists. That is an absurdity. This is a real spiritual battlefield, where end-time thinking is ridiculed and delegitimised. Within the Palestinian Christian teaching, which 'comes out from Jerusalem', there is no room for end-time thinking, or for end-time warning and end-time education.

In actual fact, from within Scripture, the greatest Zionist of all appears to be none other than the Lord Himself! One clear example of this is that in Isaiah 62, we find in effect that it is the Lord speaking; even though it is through the mouth of the prophet Isaiah, it can *only* be the Lord who says, '*I* have set watchmen on thy walls, O Jerusalem [Zion], which shall never hold their peace . . .'

And the same Lord states: 'For Zion's sake I will not hold My peace, and for Jerusalem's sake I will not rest . . .' (Is 62:1, NKJV). While this has a spiritual connotation (i.e. for the church), it has a distinct earthly application. The Lord goes on to declare: 'Thou shalt no more be termed Forsaken, neither shall thy *Land* any more be termed Desolate . . . thy *Land* (shall be called) Beulah, for the Lord delighteth in thee' (Is 62:4 KJV). Zionism, while in fact a divine concept, conceived in the mind of God, has been reduced to a political level by many within the church.

In the UK particularly there are numerous supporters of Palestinian Christian theology. Stephen Sizer, for example, introduces a variety of devastating misteachings. He rewrites and manipulates history. Sizer even manipulates Holy Scripture. He benefits greatly from the general ignorance of people, particularly ignorance about the Bible. Stephen Sizer regularly distorts biblical Zionism and aims to undermine the unique linkage between Jewish and Christian Zionists. Thus, for example, in his writings he attacks Jews for Jesus, the Messianic Jewish Alliance of America (MJAA) and the British Church's Ministry Among the Jewish People (CMJ), because they are committed to biblical prophecies about Israel and the restoration of Israel. Sizer not only fights against end-time thinking, but fuels the Palestinian spiritual *intifada* against Zionism, against Messianic Jews and against Christian supporters of Israel. I do want to clarify and emphasise that situation as much as possible. We must be aware of and warn against this.

Co-operation between Palestinian Christianity and Islam

I wish to highlight a significant development within Palestinian churches: the specific collaboration between Palestinian Christians and Palestinian Muslims. Substantially, both Palestinian Christians and Palestinian Muslims find a common enemy: Zionism and Israel. Thus, the replacement theology of Palestinian Christians, as it is spread in the Land, now finds a common language with a Muslim replacement theology. Yes, there is also a Muslim replacement theology against Israel, which must be recognised – a Muslim replacement theology which declares that it wishes to replace *all* infidels. First, to substitute the infidels of the *Shabbat*, and then the infidels of the Sunday; and we know who are the 'infidels of the *Shabbat*' and who are the 'infidels of the Sunday'.

There is a pan-Arabist theology against Israel. A large number of Muslim leaders are united by such theological attacks against Israel and Zionism; namely, against the prophetic restoration of Israel. There is, in fact, even a kind of symbiotic relationship between Palestinian Christians and Muslim Arabs. A quote from Mitri Raheb, a Palestinian Lutheran pastor from Bethlehem, shows this: 'I think we have to go further and recognise that Islam too is included in this Jewish–Christian context, theologically and historically. We have things in common with Muslims too, just as Judaism is part of the Christian history, so Islam is part of the history of the effects of Christianity.' This is an example of the kind of teaching that is coming out of Bethlehem, Christian Bethlehem, today.

Refugees from the Bible

One has to acknowledge that currently we see a creation of a new Palestinian Christian theology based on a new Palestinian Bible, detached very much from the original Scriptures (Jewish Bible). Practically, the interpretation of the Bible by Palestinian Christians is detached from the canonical text, which is interpreted literally by Messianic Jews. Consequently, one observes two polarised groups, i.e. Palestinian Christians and Messianic Jews, who, while living in the same Land and quoting the 'same' Bible, shape very differently their end-time thinking.

Just as not a few Palestinians, including Palestinian Christians, have suffered physically as displaced refugees in the Land (and this isn't the place to deal with the reasons for that), nowadays we also see a new phenomenon: their choice of displacement in the spiritual sphere. In other words, by shaping their own theology, Palestinian Christians push themselves into a new status of refugee – refugees from the Bible. In 1947, all Palestinians, supported by the Arab countries, rejected the UN partition plan and attacked Israel. It could be said that they created the physical problem of the refugees. Nowadays, in fact, Palestinian Christians freely choose to become refugees from Scripture. Obviously, they will not be able to blame anyone else for that. They themselves wish to become refugees from the Bible, because they deliberately and systematically distance themselves from the Jewishness of Scripture.

Evangelical Arab Christians

In order to present a balanced picture, it is also important to underline that not all Arab Christians hold an anti-Israel theology. Praise God, we do know personally some Arab Christians in Israel who are faithful believers in the Bible, and they have had to suffer repeatedly for their stand. But they are not afraid to read and interpret Scripture as small children (as Yeshua demands that every person comes to Him like a child). Indeed, each and every person, Jew and Arab, should come to the Lord as a small child. I can testify personally about Arab Christians in the Land who believe wholeheartedly in Israel's restoration according to prophecy.

For many years I have been involved in the work of the Ebenezer Home in Haifa, Israel, a home for elderly Jewish believers in Yeshua and Arab Christians. I had the privilege of involvement in the appointment of Johnny Khoury, a young Arab believer, who is the current manager of the home. He and I are very good friends, and we have excellent working relations. This mutual respect is based on our relationship to the Bible and our relationship to Yeshua. I can also mention other people, dear Arab Christians who faithfully support the Ebenezer Home, like Samuel Sabbah, who once a week leads the morning devotions at the home, and Rev. Samuel Aweida, the pastor of *Beit Eliyahu* congregation, which is very close to the Ebenezer Home. Rev. Aweida is a young Arab Christian who supports the home and shares the belief in Israel's physical and spiritual restoration. I feel that we are real brothers in the Lord, and this is possible through our belief in Yeshua and in Scripture – without distorting, without rewriting, without manipulating the holy text.

The imminent return of Yeshua

I believe that great times and great events are ahead of us. The contention over the city of Jerusalem, for example, is a thin screen over the battle against the Lord's return. The Lord Himself is behind the declaration in Psalm 132:13–14: This is My rest forever; here will I dwell. *For the Lord has chosen Zion. He* has desired it for *His* habitation.

We have great responsibilities and may our Lord help us and strengthen us to be ready to fulfil our call for that, because Yeshua is returning soon. Anyone who teaches a different interpretation, that the Second Coming will take place centuries from now, is a false teacher. It is a false teaching to say, 'Yes, He can come in 300, 500 years from now.' The Lord Himself never taught so. On the contrary, even though we are not allowed to set the exact year, day and hour of His return, yet we must all get ready and prepare ourselves day by day, as our Lord and Saviour taught us. He is our Master. We don't know the day. Only the Father knows that. Our responsibility is to be wise, according to the parable of the Lord (Mt 25), like the five clever virgins who had extra oil, and not like the five foolish ones. May Yeshua help us to be ready when He comes. Maranatha! O Lord, come!

GENERATIONS OF POVERTY
The Question of Palestinian Refugees

Nick Gray

To travel from Jerusalem to Bethlehem is to travel between cultures, values, religions and standards of living. Despite the millions of dollars in aid that have been pumped into the Palestinian Authority in the last ten years, the living standards and prosperity of the majority of its citizens have seen little improvement. To take the few steps from a Bethlehem street into one of its Palestinian refugee camps, however, is to enter another world! If many are still searching for Arafat's stolen millions of diverted aid, then one can immediately see where most of it would have been best spent.

'Camp' is a misnomer, for the refugee camps are in reality areas of housing within or adjoining Arab communities. Many are named after the original villages of the majority of their inhabitants and all are crowded and poverty-ridden. The refugee children are segregated into camp schools and not allowed to learn alongside those in the rest of the village or town. The men are in many cases not allowed to take employment outside of the camp and live lives that are totally dependent on UN handouts of food and essentials. The families are not even allowed to participate in local politics and elections. In short, those living in the refugee camps are as isolated as they can be without a wire fence being built around their substandard dwellings. The camps created following the illegal occupation of parts of the new sovereign State of Israel by the invading Arab armies are still scattered across Jordan, Syria, Lebanon and the so-called West Bank, where the residents live in slum dwellings of the worst kind.

It is no surprise that these camps have become breeding grounds for

Hamas, Islamic Jihad and the other terror groups. Economically and socially isolated from their 'brethren' just a street away, the refugees are fed an unremitting diet of hatred against Israel that diverts their anger and frustration away from the real perpetrators of their misery: their own leadership! What follows will hopefully lift the veil of 'received wisdom' that somehow Israel is responsible for the present condition of the refugees and should be made to allow all of them back to their original homes in Israeli population centres. Propaganda, lies and clever manipulation of the media have insidiously cloaked what must rank as one of the greatest twentieth-century miscarriages of justice by a people against their own kind.

Why are Palestinian refugees unlike all other refugees?

> Palestine refugees were specifically and intentionally excluded from the international law regime established by the 1951 Convention . . . as long as the Palestine refugees receive assistance from UNRWA.[1]

In 1947, frustrated at its failure to reconcile Jewish and Arab interests in the region, Britain surrendered its Mandate to rule Palestine and handed the whole situation over to the newly inaugurated United Nations. The UN sent an investigating committee to the area, following which the General Assembly proposed a solution of 'partition with economic union', dividing Palestine west of the Jordan River into independent Arab and Jewish states, existing side by side in economic partnership. The area to be partitioned under this plan extended from the Huleh lake in the north to Eilat in the south and bordered the Mediterranean Sea and Egypt to the east and Jordan on the west. Under the terms of the resolution, Jerusalem would come under an 'international regime' (whatever that meant!). The Jews reluctantly accepted the plan, understanding that at least they were being offered a state of some kind and, even more importantly, international recognition of a hard-won foothold in their historical and biblical homeland.

The Arabs rejected the partition plan out of hand. Nevertheless, on 14 May 1948, the Union flag was removed from Government House in Jerusalem after 26 years of rule. On that day, David Ben Gurion stood before a Jewish assembly in Tel Aviv and solemnly declared the inauguration of '. . . a Jewish state in Palestine, to be known as Israel'. Even as he spoke, the armies of six surrounding Arab states were rolling towards him and the fierce War of Independence had begun.

Even before Britain handed over the reins of power, many Arab families had left Palestine for surrounding nations (particularly Jordan). These were predominantly the wealthier Arabs: businessmen, professionals and the like. With their available funds and contacts they soon established themselves and assimilated into the life of whichever state they had fled to. These more fortunate men and women (totalling around 30,000) quickly ceased to be refugees, although as we will see they were added to the totals of genuine refugees in each country.

As British withdrawal drew nearer, the situation in Palestine grew increasingly tense and violent. Jewish settlers were accused of driving out whole villages of Arabs while Arabs carried out terrorist attacks against Jewish settlements and towns. Arab families began to flee the inevitable war that was brewing in ever increasing numbers. They were driven basically by the fear of war and death, but there were other factors that increased the flow away from Palestine.

The fear was compounded by calls from Arab leaders, both within and beyond Palestine, urging Arabs to leave temporarily while the invading armies dealt with the Jewish population. In a few weeks, these folk were assured, they would be able to return as conquerors to their homes, farms and businesses. The Jews, they were told, would all have been driven into the sea by the combined victorious armies. In Haifa, which was a good example of Jewish–Arab coexistence, the Jewish Haifa Workers' Council issued this appeal to the Arab population of the town:

> For years we have lived together in our city, Haifa . . . Do not fear: Do not destroy your homes with your own hands . . . do not bring upon yourself tragedy by unnecessary evacuation and self-imposed burdens . . . in this city, yours and ours, Haifa, the gates are open for work, for life, and for peace for you and your families.

Counter-appeals in the form of strident messages were broadcast over Arab radio stations. The Arab High Committee in Jerusalem encouraged all Arabs to flee Jaffa, Haifa and Jerusalem and take temporary refuge in neighbouring states until the approaching war was over and they could return as victors to their homes.

The fact that the leaderships of both sides in the conflict made appeals to the Arab population is significant for the subsequent refugee crisis. Contrary to the common perception that Arabs were driven out of Palestine by the Jews, it is a matter of recorded history that they were encouraged to leave by their own people before large-scale fighting began, and that the Jews in their home towns did their best to persuade them to stay and live in peace. Had the Arab leadership not made the radio appeals they did, there would have been only a fraction of the final number of refugees and it would have been very hard to make political capital out of their situation.

In the pre-World War II days of British rule, many Zionist settlers and immigrants, intent on the re-establishment of Israel as a Jewish state, had intimated that one solution was to evacuate the entire Arab population of Palestine. Even Theodor Herzl, the father of modern Zionism, tentatively suggested this and it was picked up by such groups as the Revisionists, led by Ze'ev Jabotinsky. Although Ben Gurion and the Labour movement played down these ideas, concern that such a policy would be adopted as the British departed fuelled the fears of the nervous Arabs.

This fear was especially increased by one notorious incident: the massacre at Deir Yassin. This Arab village is strategically placed near the old Jerusalem to Tel Aviv road as it winds down through the Judean hills. In 1948 it was an Arab strong-point, preventing supplies reaching the besieged Jewish remnant in Jerusalem. Since the British had refused to safeguard this route, the Irgun, an unofficial armed Jewish group, attacked Deir Yassin with the approval of the Palmach command. But the attack went badly wrong and around 40 Arabs were killed (not the 240 reported by the Arab media of the time). The Arab leaders in Jerusalem made the most of this as a PR gift from the Jews, and to this day Deir Yassin is held up as an example of an (imagined) official policy of brutally slaughtering innocent Arabs. Whatever the truth of Deir Yassin, it caused many more Arabs all over Palestine to flee, adding to the mounting refugee problem.

A combination of incidents like Deir Yassin, the encouragement of Arab leaders to leave and a natural fear of war and death all contributed to the final total of some 600,000 Arab refugees leaving Palestine for squalid camps in surrounding Arab nations and the West Bank and Gaza Strip (illegally seized respectively by Jordan and Egypt in 1948). As they do today, the UN swung into action and provided a degree of shelter, food and medical aid, assuming that the refugees would soon be resettled in their host nations or allowed to return home to what was now Israel.

It was at this point, during the three years or so following Israel's establishment, that things went badly wrong for the refugees.

In retrospect – the other refugees

Two large refugee problems were created as a result of the [1948] conflict, each encompassing approximately 800,000 persons: a Palestinian refugee problem and a Jewish refugee problem . . . (Chaim Herzog, 'The Arab-Israeli Wars')[2]

Something frequently overlooked is that not one but *two* refugee situations were created by Israel's War of Independence. Since their expulsion from a defeated Israel by the Roman army in 70 CE and 135, many Jewish families had lived in the surrounding regions of the Middle East and along the North African coast. Before the birth of Islam, many of these groups lived in peace with the various cultures they settled among. They built strong communities, which lasted hundreds of years, becoming known as the Sephardic Jews and now an important part of modern Israel. The aggressive expansion of Islam in the 600s CE brought with it a doctrine of theological superiority that reduced all non-Muslim cultures to inferior status (Q. Sura 9:29).

The centuries of persecution came to a head with a rise in anti-semitism across the Arab world in the lead-up to the formation of the Israeli state. The totally unplanned and unforeseen result was the beginnings of what was effectively a population exchange. Astoundingly, even the relative numbers of Jews and Arabs on the move in 1948 were similar. As already stated, some 600,000 Arabs left Mandated Palestine, most of whom, it has to be said, without ever seeing a Jewish soldier or coming under fire (Chaim Herzog's total above is not in accord with most estimates). At the same time, an almost identical number of Jews were uprooted from towns and cities they had lived in for centuries, often leaving valuable property and assets that the local people in their host countries would not buy or redeem, knowing that they would shortly be able to plunder and steal whatever they wanted.

From Iraq in the east to Morocco in the west, the Arab world's Jewish population haemorrhaged in the space of two or three years, most of them heading for their ancient biblical homeland, now about to become Israel again. Every one of them was resettled or absorbed by Israel and swiftly settled on vacant land, some vacated by the fleeing Arabs. At the time, Israel was able to point to her own handling of the Jewish refugees and argue that the Palestinian Arab refugees should be similarly settled in Arab lands. Had this happened, which would have brought great benefit to the economic and social stratum of the receiving Arab states, there would be no Palestinian refugee population today.

There have been several major population exchanges in recent history that have taken place to relieve demographic tensions that would otherwise have exploded into large-scale cross-cultural violence. Probably the best known of these, involving the reluctant migration of millions of Hindus and Muslims, took place in 1948 (coincidentally) between India and newly partitioned Pakistan. Those who foresaw a similar demographic flashpoint coming in Palestine as the British Mandate drew to a close, even suggested an arranged exchange between the Arab population of Palestine and the Jews living in Arab countries. In 1939 a member of the Arab Defence Committee for Palestine, Mojli Amin, proposed that '. . . all the Arabs of Palestine shall leave and be divided up among the neighbouring Arab countries. In exchange for this, all the Jews living in Arab countries will go to Palestine.' It is important to understand why this did not happen.

The rise of Arab nationalism following the end of the Ottoman Empire in 1917 gave birth to the concept of 'Pan-Arabism' – the dream of a unified and coherent Arab entity in the Middle East. In 1948 an overwhelming expression of this potential would have been a warm welcome for the brothers and sisters so suddenly bereft of homes and livelihoods in the area now legally held by the State of Israel. With little effort, the surrounding Arab nations could have absorbed every single family and given them citizenship and a home. Such a move would have strengthened their own economies and bolstered their armies for subsequent struggles against Israel. This one thing they almost all resolutely refused to do, since this would have implied recognition of the new political reality and an acknowledgement of defeat in the war of 1948–49. The population exchange was never completed.

So it was that a tiny slip of a state, struggling to recover from its first major war, absorbed not only Jewish refugees from the Holocaust but those fleeing their enemies in the Middle East also. This ethos of a 'right of return' was enshrined in one of Israel's first basic laws, and today still allows for anyone who can prove their Jewish identity to enter and become a citizen in their ancient homeland. In contrast, the states surrounding Israel closed their hearts to fellow Arabs and to this day will not tolerate efforts to have the refugees resettled in their host countries. Even the children and grandchildren of the original refugees, who have never known a life outside of their host state, are forced to remain in impoverished statelessness. For approaching 60 years, blind hatred of Israel has taken priority over the needs and well-being of fellow Arabs in the camps. What price the unity of the 'Arab nation'?

An 'inalienable right of return'?

> . . . Palestinian refugees are persons whose normal place of residence was Palestine between June 1946 and May 1948, who lost both their homes and means of livelihood as a result of the 1948 Arab–Israeli conflict. (UNRWA operational definition of a Palestinian refugee)[3]

Today, the United Nations High Commission for Refugees (UNHCR) is the UN body primarily responsible for helping refugees in time of war or catastrophe. Their aims are to achieve for their 'clients' one of three solutions: (a) to return home to their native country, (b) to settle in the state within which they have taken refuge (the host state) or (c) to find a home in another country (perhaps with family or other personal contacts).[4] A survey of refugee situations that have arisen throughout the world since the early twentieth century shows that almost every single case has been resolved in one of these three ways.[5] Almost the only exception to this is the case of the Palestinian Arab refugees from the wars of 1948 and 1967. Turkish and Greek refugees from the Turkish invasion of Cyprus in 1973 are in a similar political limbo, but the numbers are smaller and the respective governments have helped the affected families to resettle, or at least live and work in reasonable housing and jobs.

The Palestinian Arab refugee situation was created in 1948. At that time, there was no single UN agency to handle such crises (UNHCR was created in 1951). To enable the provision of temporary aid and shelter until the situation could be resolved, the UN Relief and Works Agency (UNRWA) was established in 1949. It was envisaged at the time that the refugees' host nations would absorb them or (under some circumstances) a return to what was now the sovereign State of Israel might be possible.

Alongside aid provision, UNRWA began to initiate resettlement and assimilation programmes for the stateless refugees in the countries to which they had fled. With the sole exception of Jordan, herself a Palestinian state, not one of the surrounding governments would co-operate with any resettlement plans put forward. Only Jordan granted citizenship to refugees within her borders. About half of these found jobs in Jordan and the remainder lived on in the camps maintained by UNRWA.

UNRWA was given a mandate, based on UN Resolution 194, to provide *only* humanitarian aid (education, health care, welfare assistance, social services[6]); again because its life as an agency was not initially foreseen as extending beyond the few years following its birth. Paragraph 11 of UN Resolution 194 says that '. . . the refugees wishing to return to their homes and live at peace with their neighbours should be permitted to do so at the earliest date'.[7] Although the Arab states initially rejected the resolution for its implicit recognition of Israel as a state, they were later happy to seize on the wording of this one paragraph. It has subsequently been used to claim an 'inalienable right of return' for all Palestinian refugees to their former homes in pre-1948 Palestine.

The hatred held by the Arab nations for Israel is such that under no circumstances will any of them acknowledge Israel's right to exist as a state in the Middle East. This extends to a falsification of 'facts on the ground' in school books, atlases and many other publications, where any graphic representation of Israel is shown as belonging to the Palestinian Arabs in its entirety. Jewish towns are shown as Arab towns, Jerusalem as a Palestinian Arab capital and the *de facto* borders of the West Bank and Gaza Strip are ignored. To allow thousands of refugees to settle within the 1948 ceasefire lines would be to acknowledge the existence of Israel on land that 'should' belong to Arabs. It would also be an acknowledgement that, after four wars, none of these large and well-armed states can defeat the tiny 'Zionist entity' in their midst.

For these reasons, the only solution acceptable to the Arab states is for the refugees to return to their original homes in what is now Israel, despite the fact that most of these no longer exist. Conversely, this situation is unacceptable to Israel, for whom a deluge of Arab immigrants would destroy her identity as a Jewish state.

Over the years, Arab leaders have seized on the phrasing of several UN resolutions to support their case for the repatriation of the refugees.[8] Despite the fact that all these resolutions were initially rejected by the Arabs, they later relied heavily on specific wording from them to bolster their case. But neither these nor the periodic Arab–Israeli agreements have ever allowed for a 'right of return'. A survey of legal aspects of the Palestinian refugee situation in 2002 concluded that '. . . neither under the general international conventions, nor under the major UN resolutions, nor under the relevant agreements between the parties, do the Palestinian refugees have a right to return to Israel'.[9]

It is important to note that the UNRWA definition of a refugee (see head of section) differs significantly from the normal UN worldwide one. According to the UN Refugee Convention, the refugee must have been driven '. . . outside the country of his nationality . . .'.[10] Since Palestine was not a sovereign state, and the original 'country of nationality' for most of the refugees was one of the neighbouring Arab nations, some other definition was needed to allow 600,000 people to be termed as refugees from the 1948 war.[11] Had a more generally accepted international definition been used, the current numbers of refugees would not be the millions claimed by UNRWA.[12]

In addition, restriction of an acceptable period of residence in the war zone to a mere two years was an acknowledgement that most of the Arab population of Palestine had not lived there for the centuries often claimed. They had in fact immigrated to the area within the past 70 years in response to the increased economic prospects offered by Jewish immigrants' improvement to the agriculture and general economy of Palestine. Thus, from its foundation UNRWA was a willing accessory to the aggressively anti-Zionist political agenda of the Arab leadership of the region.

The exploitation of misery

[after 1948] . . . neither Egypt nor Jordan ever allowed Palestinian self-determination. Their purposes were better served by forcing the Palestinian
refugees to remain in squalid, harshly-supervised camps, where they could
serve as a rallying point for anti-Israel sentiment. (Ephraim Karsh, 'Arafat's
War'[13])

A vital part of the jigsaw puzzle that is the Middle East conflict is the
total rejection by the Arab nations (and indeed the whole worldwide
Islamic community) of the very existence of a Jewish state on land that
once belonged to Islam.

Mohammed died in 632 CE. One hundred years after his death, Islam
had conquered a swathe of territory that included the south and east
coasts of the Mediterranean Sea, within which was the vague area
known as Palestine. According to Islamic theology, no land that has once
been conquered by Islam can be allowed to belong to any other religion
– especially not to Jews! Thus, the area from which the Arab refugees
fled can never be acknowledged as anything other than Islamic territory.
For the refugee situation, this means that formally allowing the
Palestinian refugees to settle where they fled to would be an acknowledgement of both the existence of the Jewish state and the Arabs'
inability to cause it to cease to exist (something they have tried to do several times!). Thus, the refugees must be permitted to return to their
previous homes (even though most of these no longer exist) in order to
reinstate the area within an Islamic framework.

This obsessive refusal to accept the very existence of Israel has led to
the assassination of two heads of state who dared even to talk to Israel:
King Abdullah I of Jordan and President Sadat of Egypt.

The fabrication of the 'Palestinian right of return' has therefore
turned several generations of impoverished and stateless Arab refugees
into political pawns. Not only have their host countries refused them
citizenship, but they will not even allow them reasonable accommodation, since this might entice them to settle and no longer desire to return
to their previous homes. Thus, poverty and statelessness as a *deliberate
policy* keep the consciousness of several million men, women and children focused on the one place on earth they can never relocate to (since

for Israel to allow this would lead to her own loss of Jewish identity and the admission of a 'fifth column' of potentially destructive proportions). This 'red line' drawn by Israel has been seized on repeatedly as the real reason for the refugees' poverty, but in accepting this the world has acquiesced in a fiction, for no other refugee population has been subjected to this kind of political kidnapping for such an extended length of time. No other state has been as pressured as Israel has been to yield to an influx of people that would destroy her cultural identity and lead to her ultimate 'destruction by demographics'.

The UN has itself, through the unrestricted activities and policies of UNRWA, promoted the politicisation of the refugees and has kept them permanently dependent on handouts and free housing and services. On a number of occasions, Israel has offered to better the condition of the refugee camps that have come under her jurisdiction. Following the Six-Day War of 1967, the Israeli armed forces entered a number of refugee camps in the West Bank and Gaza Strip as they took these areas from Jordan and Egypt respectively. The Israeli government was horrified at the plight of the inhabitants of the camps (in Gaza, Egypt had allowed no running water or electricity and had prevented refugees from seeking work outside the camps).[14] As 'the territories' came under Israeli civil administration, a special government department was created to help resettle the refugees. It is a measure of who actually had the refugees' well-being at heart that UNRWA did everything in its power to *prevent* Israel from helping the refugees, while those who were supposed to be the refugees' enemies were offering them such help as their own people had repeatedly refused them (sounds like the story of the Good Samaritan!).

The manipulation of demographics

> The facts – that many of those originally registered were not truly refugees, . . . and that some refugees have a predilection for falsifying . . . births and deaths – make it eminently clear that the number of legitimate registrants is considerably smaller than the current 'operational number' . . . (UNRWA, A Report)[15]

Each summer, the Commissioner-General of UNRWA submits his annual report to the United Nations. In his report for the year July 2003 to June

2004, he recounted that UNRWA began its work in 1950, helping some 880,000 Palestinian refugees living in four of the region's states (Egypt, Jordan, Syria and Lebanon).[16] He also reported that this original population had now grown to more than 4 million people.

The picture usually conjured up by the word 'refugee' is of an impoverished family escaping from persecution or war with only the clothes they stand up in and a few meagre possessions carried as best they can. They are housed in temporary, usually tented camps and are resettled as quickly as possible, frequently outside their country of origin. Once resettled and beginning to regain some semblance of a normal and productive lifestyle, their classification as refugees is removed.

So how can so many people, having lived long enough in one place for three further generations to be born, still be classed as refugees? Yet this is precisely what has happened to the descendants of the original Palestinian refugees from 1948. The Commissioner-General of UNRWA admits in his report that only about a third live in the established camps.[17] In fact, describing those living in Jordan he says, 'The majority enjoy full Jordanian citizenship, are able to work in government offices and throughout the local economy and have access to governmental institutions and developmental and other assistance.' Many of these are also among the families who escaped western Palestine before the 1948 war began and resettled themselves in Jordan; yet UNRWA continues to classify them as refugees nearly 60 years after they resettled themselves. In any other refugee situation, these families would long ago have been removed from any classification as refugees and accepted as successfully resettled.

A similar situation was discovered after Israel invaded Lebanon in 1982. A substantial proportion of the registered refugee population did not live in camps and many held good jobs and owned their own houses. In spite of this *de facto* resettlement, UNRWA continued to maintain them on their register as having refugee status.

These are two examples of the deliberate manipulation of refugee statistics by UNRWA to bolster a political agenda. UNRWA's mandate will end when a '. . . just and durable settlement of the refugee problem is achieved'.[18] Since the organisation employs some 25,000 people, over 90 per cent of whom are Palestinians, one could cynically argue that they are simply seeking to prolong the journey of their particular 'gravy train'. Principally, though, the standard (Palestinian) definition of a 'just and durable settlement' means the return of all or most of the current 4 million refugees to their original home locations in what is now Israel – *not* to the confines of any future Palestinian state in the West Bank and Gaza. This is just one of several intractable 'Final Status' issues to be resolved between Israel and the Palestinian Arabs. The existence of UNRWA looks secure for the foreseeable future!

One way to ensure that generations of refugees stay 'unsettled' is to encourage a culture that for ever looks back to the people's past in a land they can never return to. Many refugee camps are named after the original village of most of the inhabitants. Coach trips have been arranged for refugees to return and view their previous home areas. Of course, this linkage has been promoted for decades by the PLO and most (certainly older) refugees can tell you their pre-1948 address in what is now the State of Israel. Some even have the keys to houses that no longer exist, in villages that have long been renamed and legitimately resettled by Jewish immigrants.

The generational continuum of memory and refugee status is further enforced by the PA in a number of cruel ways. Refugee children can only go to UNRWA schools in the camps, thus isolating them from the rest of their own people from an early age. Refugee adults are, in many cases, not permitted to seek work outside their camp or immediate residential area. This deprives them of the dignity of supporting their own families and ensures they are continually dependent on UN handouts and kept as isolated as possible in the camp areas. Adults are not even allowed to participate in local politics. In PA local elections in Summer 2004, refugees were not allowed to vote, reinforcing the culture of impermanence and statelessness.

In surrounding non-Palestinian states, where governments do not want to upset fragile economies and social structures, one can understand such a policy of separation and isolation (much as asylum seekers and refugees everywhere cannot vote and are restricted in their permitted range of activities and jobs). What is repulsive is that the Palestinian authorities in the West Bank and Gaza apply the same instruments of impoverishment and oppression *to their own people* in territory over which they have full jurisdiction. Every refugee camp in the West Bank and Gaza could have been emptied during the 1990s and the inhabitants resettled among the Arab towns and villages of the 'territories'. The PA could have established 'facts on the ground' in support of having their own sovereign state, instead of which they have maintained thousands in poverty and isolation for the sake of an impossible dream of return. Can you imagine Welsh 'immigrants' to England being kept in sub-human impoverished camps on the outskirts of Birmingham or London for three generations, for purely political reasons? Britain would long ago have been called to account by the international community. As we have seen, this isolation and impoverishment of their own brothers and sisters is simply part of the overall policy of ensuring that the people only ever see themselves as refugees and are 'programmed' to keep in their hearts an impossible dream of return to non-existent homes and villages. The manipulation of Palestinian refugee numbers over the generations by both fellow Palestinians and a major UN agency is tacitly maintained by the international community's refusal to intervene, held to ransom by anti-semitic Arab regimes controlling the West's oil!

The future? (Possible and impossible resolutions to the refugee situation)

The two most recent attempts to bring about a lasting peace between Israel and the Palestinian Arabs have been the Oslo Accords in the 1990s and the 'Roadmap' plan, which failed to bring an end to the *intifada*. In both these projects, the refugee problem was made one of the so-called 'Final Status' issues to be resolved. In other words, along with the status of Jerusalem and firming up new borders, a resolution of the refugee situation is such a thorny problem that it will be left to the very end! This is yet another reason why these several million souls languish still in poverty and statelessness. For humanitarian reasons, their 'Final Status' should have been at the top of the negotiating agenda, not in the final paragraphs!

The world's media (and not a few statesmen as well) claimed that the death of Yasser Arafat in November 2004 opened a new window of opportunity for peace. But the word 'peace' is open to multiple inter-pretations, depending on which side of the negotiating table you sit. The new Palestinian leadership of Chairman (*not* President!) Abbas may appear to have turned a new page in the relationship with Israel. The PA's official police appeared on the streets of Gaza and the West Bank and terror leaders agreed to a truce of some kind, but yesterday

Mahmoud Abbas and his team were close supporters of the diehard Arafat. This included a 'red line' position on the mythical right of return and the maintenance of the status quo in the camps until it is achieved. Today, have they so quickly changed some of the most sacred elements of their decades-old ideology?

Events in the Middle East have a habit of moving so fast that any analysis of the possible future for the refugees stands a very good chance of being obsolete before its publication. Nevertheless, acknowledging the likelihood of history recording these next paragraphs as being simply wrong, an analysis must be attempted – if only to look back and see what *might* have been possible. A number of options are open to the Israeli and Palestinian Arab negotiators. Some are desirable but unthinkable in the volatile climate of Arab politics; others are unthinkable in human terms, though possibly politically acceptable. Somewhere in the middle lies a compromise that will determine the future conditions of thousands of ordinary families, with their hopes and dreams for happiness and perhaps just a little less poverty in their lives.

Option 1: complete ex-patriate resettlement

In this scenario, the camp gates in Lebanon, Syria, Jordan, Gaza and the West Bank are flung open, the inhabitants are granted citizenship of their host countries and given incentives to settle there and contribute to the economy and social life of their adoptive states. Some resettle to a new Palestinian state and a controlled number are permitted to resettle within Israel's borders. For this to happen, immense pressure would have to be placed on the Arab states concerned, since Palestinian refugees have never been welcomed with open arms by their respective hosts. Furthermore, for the Arab governments to accept this option (or a version of it), they would have to admit that the 'Zionist entity' that is Israel had won the decades-long struggle for territory and to recant on the concept of a Palestinian Arab right of return. This humiliation, coupled with the theological rejection of the Jewish occupation of Islamic territory, makes this option one of the most unlikely.

Option 2: return to original homes

In this scenario, the Israeli government opens its borders to some 3 million Palestinian Arabs wishing to return to their original homes and towns (assuming many stay where they are already effectively resettled, particularly in Jordan as we have seen). Under this scenario, the demographic balance within Israel changes suddenly and dramatically. Within 10 to 15 years she is no longer a Jewish state, since Arab population growth is much faster than Jewish![19] In addition, an unknown number of terrorists enter Israel freely with their returning families and commence a campaign of terror against Israeli society from within. Now pressure cannot be brought against any governments playing host to restrain the terror groups, since all these groups have been permitted to take up Israeli citizenship. In the subsequent bloodbath, the strong and vibrant State of Israel would likely be brought to her knees – something decades of external threats failed to achieve. If resettlement in host states is unacceptable to the Palestinian leadership, then this option is certainly unacceptable to Israel.

Option 3: resettlement in a Palestinian state

The aim of both the Oslo and Roadmap plans mentioned above is a 'two-state solution'; i.e. the territory from the Mediterranean Sea to the River Jordan is split between Israel and a new Palestinian state. As a sovereign nation, Palestine could open its borders to its diaspora, just as Israel did in 1948. The hills of biblical Judea and Samaria, so far mostly undeveloped by the Palestinian Arabs, would be populated with the above 3 million ex-refugees. Aided by millions of dollars of aid, new towns, villages and industries spring up. The prosperity of Palestine is enhanced by the immigration of its own people and the state becomes a stable and vaguely democratic nation. In many political eyes, this scenario ranks as a highly desirable one. The Arab states are relieved of their eyesore camps and UN-dependent Palestinian families; Israel is spared a 'death by demographics' and the economy of the infant state of Palestine is strengthened, as each refugee is accompanied by a handsome handout from the international community. Against such a move being readily accepted is, once again, the humility of having to accept that Israel has 'won'. Additionally, there is the probability that the terror groups would be re-affirmed in their determination to go the whole way – not to stop at Ramallah but to press on to Tel Aviv. Again, the terror groups would be conveniently regrouped within their own state, within easy missile range of many of Israel's population centres. Despite this, however, this option would indeed be desirable from many points of view and might possibly be acquiesced to by a war-weary Israel.

Option 4: the Elon peace plan

Based on the assumption that the 'Final Status' issues of refugees, borders and Jerusalem will never reach a satisfactory solution, ex-tourism minister Benny Elon suggested a paradigm shift in thinking and proposed that Jordan re-assume its natural role as a Palestinian state and the only effective representative of the Palestinian Arabs of Gaza and the West Bank. He points out that, following its conquest of Judea and Samaria in 1948, Jordan offered full citizenship to all inhabitants of that region – both local residents and refugees. In other words, there is already a Palestinian state in existence that could easily absorb all the Palestinian diaspora and every refugee in the Gaza Strip and West Bank, thus solving the refugee problem with one easy stroke. At the same time, the Palestinian Arabs would be part of, and represented by, a stable and sympathetic government and a genuine peace would exist between Israel and her Palestinian neighbours.[20]

Sadly, Elon's paradigm shift is beyond the imagination of just about every major player in the drama, for reasons ranging from the theological objections already mentioned, to simple pride and desire for power. It is mentioned here because it has been tabled as a possible solution, but it is idealistic in the extreme to believe that it would overcome the realities of Middle Eastern religion and politics to become a reality.

Conclusion

The Palestinian Arabs have been offered 'land for peace' four times: by the UN in 1947, by Israel following the 1967 war and in the Oslo and Roadmap negotiations in 1993 and 2003. They rejected the first three, and the outcome of the Roadmap plan is still uncertain. Since 1948, each of these points in history presented an opportunity to end the misery and statelessness of the growing numbers of Palestinian refugees scattered around the Middle East. Israel can in no degree be accused of refusing to consider the plight of the refugees; it is only the intransigence and incredible cynicism of their own leaders down the years that has prolonged their suffering in the camps.

Inevitably, however long it takes, pragmatism will have to prevail and a compromise solution found. It is likely to comprise the ingathering of most of the Palestinian diaspora to a future state of Palestine, based approximately on the 1948 'green line' and the Gaza Strip. Some will remain where they have succeeded in carving out a living for themselves in their host countries (particularly Jordan) and a strictly controlled number will be permitted to return to their original home areas within Israel. Because of the ideological and theological pit the Palestinian Arab leadership have dug for themselves over the years, it is they who will have to bite the bullet the hardest in order to agree to such a compromise. To achieve statehood, they will have to recognise Israel's right to her own secure borders. If Israel continues to resist the Palestinian claim to a right of return, but yields to the establishment of a Palestinian state in the disputed territories, ideology will eventually have to give way to reality and the refugees will be permitted real homes in a real state of their own. International recognition of this reality appeared in the Bush/Sharon exchange of letters in June 2004, in which Bush said that 'a solution . . . would require the settling of Palestinian refugees in a Palestinian state, rather than in Israel'.

In the meantime, what of the young men and women of the Bethlehem refugee camp described at the start? Will they be permitted the dignity of a job, so as to be able to support their own families? Or will their sons and daughters also grow up as political pawns in the grand plan of Israel's destruction? Will they be living statistics, existing in the same atmosphere of despair, poverty and hopelessness that has produced only anger and violence – raw emotions channelled against Israel by hard men bent on sacrificing their own people on the altar of ideology?

Notes

1. UNRWA website (www.un.org/unrwa), refugee section, 'Why do Palestinian refugees not come under the mandate of UNHCR?'
2. Vintage Books, 1984, pp. 105, 106.
3. From (www.un.org/unrwa), the official UNRWA website, refugee section.
4. UNHCR web site, 'Basic Facts' page (http://www.unhcr.ch/cgi-

bin/texis/vtx/basics).

5. From 'UNRWA, A Report', Israel Resource News Agency 2003, Appendix B.

6. *Ibid*, p. 11.

7. From copy of Res 194 on MidEast Web site (http://www.mideast-web.org/194.htm).

8. Specifically, General Assembly resolution 194 (1948) and Security Council resolutions 237 and 242 (1967).

9. Jerusalem Viewpoints paper No. 485, 1 September 2002, 'Some Legal Aspects of the Palestinian Refugee Question', by Ruth Lapidoth. Published by the Jerusalem Center for Public Affairs (www.jcpa.org).

10. UN Convention Relating To The Status of Refugees 1951, Article 1, A(2) (www.unhcr.ch).

11. Although the UN Convention was accepted after the formation of UNRWA, it incorporated definitions of refugee status going back to 1926. UNRWA therefore had access to internationally accepted criteria for its own refugee definition, but chose not to include them.

12. Alan Dershowitz, in his excellent book *The Case For Israel* (Wiley, 2003) calls the UNRWA definition (p. 86) '. . . a remarkable decision to change the definition of refugee – *only* for purposes of defining who is an *Arab* refugee *from Israel* – to include any Arab who had lived in Israel for two *years* before leaving [author's emphasis].

13. Published by Grove Press, New York, 2003, p. 34.

14. From 'UNRWA, A Report', Israel Resource News Agency 2003, p. 14.

15. Pearl Herman, Israel Resources News Agency, 2003, p. 9.

16. From its inception, UNRWA admitted that many people it supported were claiming refugee status fraudulently and that births were exaggerated and deaths concealed (UNRWA website, refugees section).

17. Report of the Commissioner-General of UNRWA, 1 July 2003–30 June 2004, Chp. 1, para 1.

18. *Ibid*, para 41.

19. According to the CIA World Handbook 2004. (www.cia.gov/cia/publications/factbook), the birth rates in both the Gaza Strip and the West Bank are approximately twice those in

Israel and overall population growth in the Gaza Strip is three times that in Israel (in the West Bank it is two and a half times that in Israel).

20. Published on the internet as 'The Right Road to Peace', (www.therightroadtopeace.com).

ASPECTS OF INTERNATIONAL TERRORISM

Fred Wright

'One man's terrorist is another man's freedom fighter.' There is no basis in law for this facile and shallow expression. The issue here is not one of subjective interpretation. On the contrary, there exist precise and settled criteria that are readily available to distinguish one from the other. Any insurgent who intentionally causes the explosion and burning of women and children at lunch or at prayer or at a wedding ceremony or in a shopping mall is a terrorist – Period! (Louis Rene Beres)

The above comment by Professor Beres sets the scene for the following discussion of the Palestinian contour within international terrorism. Palestinian terrorism has become legitimised in a most alarming manner. The Palestinian cause, aside from being unhistorical and spurious in origin (that is not to say that the Palestinians are not entitled to just treatment), has gained support of unprecedented proportions, within society and the church, at odds with international law and justice. Deliberate attacks upon non-combatants are always indefensible and illegal. For an insurgent movement to be recognised as having any legality it must, according to the Geneva Conventions of 1949 and by the two protocols to these Conventions of 1977, operate broadly within the rules of just warfare (Common Article III). The Palestinians have never taken heed of such protocols.

As Joseph Stalin remarked: 'One death is a tragedy; one million deaths are a statistic.' The truth of this comment is illustrated in the deaths of Israelis at the hands of Palestinian terrorists. There are so many terrorist incidents in Israel causing death and mutilation that few, except for major incidents, reach the Western press. On the other hand Israeli retaliation which results in death, usually by collateral damage or by human shield, is given a high profile. It is important to better understand the profound moral and legal differences between Palestinian terrorism, which is always deliberately barbarous, cruel in intention, indiscriminate and gratuitous, and, on the other hand, Israeli retaliations, which are always consciously designed to *avoid* civilian casualties. Prior to Israeli troops targeting an area, it is custom and practice to give notice. The notice to civilians to get out of the area is often met by a movement of people into the area, and in particular children and youth. With regard to international law, Palestinian terrorism is a blatant violation of the rules of armed conflict as understood by international conventions and authorities.

Terrorism in one form or another is as old as time, and was a practice that generally did not succeed as a tactic, and those engaging in it were pursued and severely punished. A discernible shift began in the 1960s with the birth of the Palestinian contour. Before commencing, it is important to point out that *Palestinian terrorism against Israelis began while the West Bank and Gaza were occupied not by Israel, but by Jordan and Egypt*. Although there had been terror attacks against Jewish people in Israel before 1967, the scale of terrorism intensified, with the PLO increasingly choosing to attack Israeli targets, or targets that simply were Jewish, outside of the Middle East. The decision was similar to that of Adolf Hitler: a desire to destroy the Jewish people wherever they were to be found.

Throughout the late 1960s, a cycle of Palestinian terrorist attacks was invariably followed by Israeli retaliatory raids against Jordan from whence they were launched, putting major strains on Jordan's relationship with the US and other Western nations. The Six-Day War of 1967 ended with a crushing and humiliating defeat of the Arab nations, which resulted in the Israeli takeover of the West Bank, Gaza Strip, Golan Heights and Sinai. The Israelis, in an outstandingly generous move, offered to return what in reality was regained territory in return for recognition, negotiation and peace. The Arab nations, meeting in Khartoum in August 1967, rejected the three points outright. The blind refusal of the Arab nations can be considered a major causation of the bloodshed that was to be the defining mark of the region in the years to follow. Seven groups, whose goal was a Palestinian nation (who were in reality state-sponsored tools of Arab nations to undermine and destroy Israel) began to become more defined. The common denominator was that they decided that terror campaigns were the tools to be employed.

In February 1969, Yasser Arafat (born Rahman Abdul Rauf Arafat al-Qudwa al-Husseini), who had fled Egypt in the late 1950s due to subversive activities, and was expelled from Syria in 1966 after murdering Syrian military officers, while remaining the leader of the Al Fatah group, became the head of the PLO. Although the PLO ostensibly united the various groups, the Popular Front for the Liberation of Palestine (PFLP), led by George Habash, maintained a strong identity. The PLO established itself in Jordan where King Hussein, in part from support and in part from political constraint, provided training sites and assistance. Hussein soon realised that it had not been a good move, as the next four years witnessed a struggle for political control of the country between the government and the PLO, who rode roughshod over the legal apparatus of the country while receiving funding and weaponry from other Arab states. By the late 1960s, the PLO openly regarded themselves as a nation within a nation, controlling their own camps, and had a strong enough army, estimated at various times to number between 15,000 and 20,000, to overthrow the Hashemite regime of King Hussein, and at more than one point seemed inclined to so.

Concerned by their activities King Hussein made an agreement in July 1970 with Yasser Arafat. The government allowed the PLO freedom of movement within Jordan, agreed to refrain from action against them, and expressed its support for them in their battle against Israel. In return, the PLO pledged to remove their bases and armed personnel from Amman and other major cities, and to show respect for law and order. The meaninglessness of the agreement to the PLO is illustrated in that almost immediately the Palestinians embarked upon a hijacking campaign. On 6 September 1970, three planes from TWA, Swissair and BOAC carrying more than 400 hostages were hijacked and ordered to fly to the Jordanian airport by the PFLP, in what is known as 'Skyjack Sunday'. Another terrorist team tried to hijack an El Al Boeing over London, but security staff foiled the attempt by killing one of the hijackers, a Latin American named Patrick Arguello, and capturing the second, Leila Khaled, alive. Khaled had previously been involved with one other person in the successful hijacking of a TWA aircraft on 29 August 1969. The aircraft landed in Damascus and the two hijackers were taken by the Syrian authorities, put under house arrest and later set free quietly. Khaled's name and face became internationally known, and to avoid detection, she had undergone six plastic surgery operations on her face.

The German, Swiss and British governments all agreed to the PFLP's demands to release imprisoned Fedayeen (members of the Palestinian movement) held in jails in Germany, Switzerland and Israel, and released a number of terrorists, including Khaled. To 'up the ante', the next day the group hijacked a BOAC VC-10 on course from Bombay to Beirut. The guerrillas, after releasing some women and children, then held over 300 hostages, 65 of them British. The pressure increased with a 72-hour deadline for the release. Two of the planes were taken to a former RAF airstrip in the middle of the Jordanian desert, known as Dawson's Field. A third was blown up in Cairo after the passengers and crew were released on 12 September. The destruction of the aircraft was watched by a worldwide television audience. Leila Khaled and the other terrorists held in Switzerland and Germany were released two weeks later on 30 September. Reflecting upon the incident some 30 years later Khaled said in a BBC interview on 1 January 2001: 'It was a good step for us that we saw governments could be negotiated with. We could impose our demands . . . The success in the tactics of the hijacking and imposing our demands and succeeding in having our demands implemented gave us the courage and the confidence to go ahead with our struggle.'

The hijacking incident served to cause high tension between the King of Jordan and the PLO, resulting in incidents of violence. On 19 September around 200 Syrian tanks crossed the Jordanian border with the intention of supporting the PLO against their Jordanian hosts. A bitterly fought ten-day civil war followed, primarily between the PLO and the Jordanian Arab Army.

King Hussein, alarmed at the Syrian incursion on 19 September, requested help from the USA and the UK by means of air strikes against the invaders. President Nixon was not in favour of direct US intervention, preferring the action to be taken by the IDF. The Israeli leadership were prepared to support the idea as long as it was agreed to by Jordan. In the event the Jordanian forces defeated the Syrians and then turned their attention to the PLO. The following action, which should be considered defensive, led to the killing and wounding of thousands of Palestinians and forced the leadership, along with thousands of followers, into Syria and Lebanon. The incident came to be known among Palestinians as Black September. The civil war caused great material destruction in Jordan, and the number of fighters killed on all sides was estimated as high as 3,500. Nonetheless, in 1974 Jordan recognised the PLO as the sole representative for the Palestinians and in 1988 Jordan gave up all claims on the West Bank, considering it as Palestinian territory.

Following the expulsion from Jordan, the PLO relocated their operations to Lebanon where the Cairo Agreement of 1969, masterminded by Egyptian President Gamal Abdel Nasser, allowed them special military and political privileges. In Lebanon they once again attempted to establish a kingdom within a kingdom, the PLO insisting on political, police and economic control of the refugee camps, as well as access to large areas of south Lebanon and the Beqaa Valley, which were employed for training. The PLO seized villages along with property near the borders they brutally occupied, and the area became known as Fatah Land. From their new theatre of operations they staged infiltrations into northern Israel to murder Israeli civilians. Witnesses report a nauseating trail of rape, torture, mutilation, gratuitously inflicted slow death and murder. This seemed to be the 'normal' behaviour of the PLO in Lebanon, in addition to extortion, drug trading and running prostitution and protection rackets.

During their time in Lebanon, international terror operations continued. The year 1972 witnessed PLO groups blowing up a West German electricity plant, a Dutch gas plant and an oil refinery in Trieste, Italy; the killing in conjunction with the Japanese Red Army of 24 at Israel's Lod (Tel Aviv) airport; and the infamous massacre of eleven Israeli athletes at the Munich Olympics. In early 1973, Black September took the American ambassador and his deputy (along with one Belgian diplomat) hostage in Sudan's capital, Khartoum, and, after President Nixon refused to negotiate, murdered them. By 1975 Arafat had 15,000 troops under his command, with many more associated paramilitaries (of whom 5,000–6,000 were foreign mercenaries, coming from such countries as Libya, Iraq, India, Sri Lanka, Chad and Mozambique). Bases in Lebanon provided training for other international terrorists such as the Italian Red Brigade, the Irish Republican Army and the Baader-Meinhof gang.

Arafat was also acquiring more sophisticated weapons such as tanks and anti-aircraft guns.

The PLO's ravaging of Lebanon was brought to the attention of the UN in 1976 by the Lebanese ambassador Edward Ghorra, who informed the UN General Assembly: 'Palestinian elements belonging to various . . . organizations resorted to kidnapping Lebanese – and sometimes foreigners – holding them prisoner, questioning them, torturing them and sometimes killing them' (*New York Times*, 15 October 1976). Bashir Jemayel, Lebanon's president-elect, stated in 1982: 'In eight years of fighting we have, out of a population of three million inhabitants, more than 100,000 killed, more than 300,000 wounded and almost half of the population uprooted from its homes.'

On 11 March 1978, a group of PLO terrorists using Zodiac rubber commando dinghies landed at the beach of Kibbutz Ma'agan Michael. After first murdering an American tourist who was walking near an Israeli beach and a taxi driver, they hijacked a civilian bus. Among the passengers were a number of schoolchildren on a day trip. The terrorists began shooting through the windows as the bus drove down the road. Israeli troops were sent to intercept the bus, and a gunfight with the terrorists ensued. The terrorists left the bus and began to fire missiles. The bus caught fire and resulted in many of the passengers being burned alive; others were killed by the terrorists' gunfire. The death toll was 37 and around another 100 were injured. The terrorists were identified as belonging to Fatah, of whom nine were killed and two captured. The IDF entered Lebanon on 15 March and attacked terrorist bases in the southern part of that country, withdrawing after two months in favour of the UNIFIL troops, who subsequently were unable to prevent terrorists from returning to the region and introducing new, more dangerous arms. The limited action became known as the Litani River Operation.

The cycle of violence continued and despite a ceasefire in July 1980 the PLO, as is their constant practice, repeatedly violated the ceasefire. In the ensuing eleven months, the PLO staged 270 terrorist acts in Israel, the West Bank and Gaza. Twenty-nine Israelis died and more than 300 were injured in the attacks.

In June 1982, following the attempt by a Palestinian terrorist group led by Abu Nidal to assassinate Israel's ambassador to Great Britain, Shlomo Argov, 'Operation Peace for Galilee' was launched by Israel. The

IDF invaded and occupied Lebanon with the sole intention of destroying the PLO and preventing attacks against northern Israel. Henry
Kissinger, the former US Secretary of State, remarked at the time: 'No
sovereign state can tolerate indefinitely the build up along its borders of
a military force dedicated to its destruction and implementing its objectives by periodic shelling and raids' (*Washington Post*, 16 June 1982).

The IDF penetrated all the way to Beirut, putting both the PLO and
the Lebanese civilian population of that city under siege. After a typical
round of making agreements and then either ignoring or deliberately
breaking them, Arafat and the PLO leadership and forces fled from
Lebanon in August 1982. This was mainly the result of negotiations by
US ambassador Philip Habib. They relocated their headquarters in
Tunis, Tunisia (which served as the headquarters of the Arab League
from 1979 to 1990), leaving many thousands of dead Lebanese and
Palestinians in their wake. *Once again terrorism and atrocities went
unpunished.*

Despite the removal of the PLO from Lebanon it has remained a loca-
tion for major attacks against Israel, in particular by Iranian-backed
Hizbullah, who rain rocket attacks on the north of Israel on a regular
basis. US forces in Lebanon were also the subject of terrorism when in
October 1983 a suicide bomb attack killed 241 US marines.

The 'critical mass' year for international terrorism is, as Alan
Dershowitz correctly affirms, 1968, when the Palestinians used terrorism as the first resort, not the last resort. They perfected it, refused to
desist from it and benefited from it. By their obduracy and refusal to take
a diplomatic path, they illustrated to the world the rising value of terrorist activity, how to deploy it and gave assurance to others of its great
potential for success. So when Ehud Barak and Bill Clinton in 2000
offered the Palestinians 97 per cent of what they had been demanding,
the Palestinians rejected the offer and played the card that had worked
for them in the past: terrorism (*New York Times*, 10 May 2002).

The Palestinians' methods should be a cause for concern to the
church, who have backed them in the wrong way. It is true that the
Palestinians have suffered greatly, but the agents of their sufferings have
been their Arab neighbours and their Islamic co-religionists. The discussion of the history of Arab–Israeli conflict is outside the scope of this
work (the reader is referred to the author's previous works dealing with

the matter: *Words From the Scroll of Fire* [Jerusalem 1994] and *Father Forgive Us* [London 2002]). Sufficient to say, for those unsure or un-familiar with the situation, the Arab–Israeli conflict is possibly the worst example in modern history of biased news reporting and uneven inter-national response. The conflict in itself is artificial, and is not grounded in the usual grounds for uprisings or social deprivations imposed by a tyrannical power. A sovereign state of Palestine has never existed, let alone before 1948 or 1967; neither was it promised by UN Security Council Resolution 242; there was no legal entity of Palestine as a sovereign state while under the British Mandate. Between 1948 and 1949 the so-called West Bank and Gaza came under the illegal control of Jordan and Egypt. The legal right of the Jewish people to the Land of Israel was recognised by the Balfour Declaration following the cessation of World War I, and by the San Remo Peace Conference of April 1920. *Present-day Israel, including the West Bank and Gaza, comprises only 22 per cent of Palestine as defined and ratified at the San Remo Peace Conference of 1920.*

Following escalating acts of terrorism, and in particular the Munich massacres of 1972, more countries began to recognise the Palestinians. The more violent and widespread their terrorism became, the greater the recognition they gained. The year 1968 saw a new strategy in terrorism: the hijacking of an airliner. One year and ten terrorist incidents later, the United Nations gave the Palestinians 'observer status', a measure unique and not repeated towards any other group seeking statehood – a strange reward for an un-elected blood-soaked organisation, who by all stan-dards of international law should have been called to account.

Palestinians have adopted suicide bombing as a strategic choice, not out of desperation. As of 21 November 2002, there had been a total of 15,299 Palestinian terror attacks against Israel since the start of the *intifada* in September 2000. Although this strategy has wrecked their society, they feel a rising sense of empowerment. In no small way the increase of violence has perversely given the Palestinians a sense of moral heroism, strangely accepted by some intellectuals and church leaders. More than this, as a consequence of the quasi-legitimisation they have acquired, they feel that they have gained the strategic advantage not available through negotiation. A second strand is that if violence were to cease, the leading role and rewards of the power elite who eschew violence would evaporate in peacetime.

It should be remembered that the premise and basis for discussion that led to the Oslo Accords was that the Israeli–Palestinian conflict was not an irreconcilable religious war, but one over territorial borders. Palestinians have redefined the conflict from one over borders, in which compromise may be a solution, into a religious war in which compromise is heretical. Anyone monitoring the Arab language press will clearly see that the Palestinian religious leaders, all of whom are appointed by the leadership of the PA, constantly preach publicly on broadcast radio and television that the Israel–Palestinian conflict is part of Islam's eternal religious war against the Jews; killing of Jews is *Allah's* will. Examples are Dr Muhammad Kamal Al-Din Al-Imam, a lecturer on Islamic law at the Alexandria Law Faculty, who proposed that there was no such entity as 'Israeli civilians': 'The [Israeli] society as a whole are a military force raised from various countries in order to occupy someone else's land.' Dr Ali 'Aqleh 'Ursan, the head of the Syrian Arab Writers Union, declared that the march of liberation will take place only by the use of force, through jihad, and martyrdom (Al-Usb'u Al-Adabi [Syria], 9 June 2001 tr. MEMRI 66).

It is sad to report that admiration for terrorists and suicide bombing has almost become legitimised in some wings of the church. The following comment was made by Father 'Atallah Hanna' (also known as Archimandrite Theodosios Hanna) on 19 January 2003 in a sermon marking the Epiphany and the Baptism of Jesus, at a Greek Orthodox cathedral in Jerusalem:

> We encourage our youth to participate in the resistance, to carry out martyrdom attacks, and to participate in removing the occupation. There is a need for resistance to the occupation, and for Islamic–Christian cooperation, so that we will remove the foreign Zionist Jewish intruders and so that the gates of Palestine will open wide and all those who were uprooted or emigrated in 1967 and 1948 will return.

At a reception in Haifa he stated: 'The Fedaiyin are the heroes of this nation. We are proud of them and resolutely refuse any attempt to defame their deeds . . . They are not committing suicide, as some claim, and they are not terrorists, as others claim – they are resisting the occupation. We unreservedly support the martyrdom operations.'

Although Father Hanna was dismissed from his position as representative of the Orthodox Church by the Patriarchate in June 2002 for making this and similar comments, he has chosen to ignore the dismissal and carry on as usual.

A war of symbols

'Palestine-as-symbol' has become a defining factor of many protest movements as diverse as those opposed to globalisation and supporters of the IRA in Northern Ireland. It is almost as if to employ Palestine-as-symbol has become a defining element of authentication for protest movements. An element within Palestine-as-symbol is the wearing of the black and white *khefiyah* that became Yasser Arafat's trademark. At protests held during various economic summits during 2002 a whole sea of such symbolic clothing was evident. What many people do not know or understand is that the distinctive way that Arafat wore the headdress is a piece of theatrical propaganda. The *khefiyah* draped down the side of his head was shaped to represent the Land of Israel, or 'Palestine' in PA terms – that is, the whole sovereign State of Israel as it exists today. The statement is of course consistent with Arafat's clearly, consistently stated aims in the Arabic press and represented in all PA maps, schoolbooks and official documents: the ultimate aim is to take the whole Land with Jerusalem as its capital.

Michael Scott Doran, Assistant Professor of Near Eastern Studies at Princeton University, suggests that Palestine-as-symbol has a protean nature, a capacity for expressing grievances wholly unrelated to the aspirations of the Palestinians themselves. Likewise those employing Palestine-as-symbol, particularly the Arab nations, have little interest in Palestine as a land and a people. Although Palestine is central to the symbolism of Arab politics, it is actually marginal to its substance. Doran remarks that Palestine has acquired this broad meaning because in Arab political discourse the maltreatment of the Palestinians signifies the prejudice of the West towards all Middle Easterners. Palestine is the only Arab land successfully colonised in modern times, a fact that rankles deeply. The irony here is that the author of Palestinian suffering is not the State of Israel but the Arab nations themselves. With the possible exceptions of Jordan and Israel, alleviating the suffering of the Palestinian people is not a primary policy objective of any Middle Eastern state.

Likewise Israel-as-symbol is employed not only by Arab nations but by a variety of causes. 'Zionism' is the symbol of international conspiracy, the power behind globalisation and repressive politics worldwide. A typical comment came from Iran's spiritual leader Ayatollah Ali Khamenei, who described the usurper Zionist regime as a 'symbol of state terrorism' and a 'calamity befalling the world'. 'By gathering together groups of Jews with records of murder, theft, wickedness and hooliganism from throughout the world, the Zionist regime has created an entity under the name of the Israeli nation which only understands the logic of terror and crimes' (Tehran, Irna). Israel as the symbol of the terrorist state is a calumny, as it is widely known that Israel is the only true democracy in the Near and Middle East and that the IDF are anything but the Nazis they are often portrayed to be.

Doran suggests that the Palestinian issue is a game of 'four-dimensional chess'. When an Arab leader announces a policy regarding the Palestinian issue, the move is directed simultaneously at critics at home, Arab rivals abroad, the United States, and the Palestinians and Israelis themselves, with the last being by far the least important audience.

Charles Hill agrees that terrorism's primary targets are virtually all the Middle Eastern regimes – not just Israel's but those of the surrounding Arab countries as well. Fear of being overthrown by terrorists leads those regimes in an effort to divert their people's attention towards external targets, to inundate them with anti-Israel propaganda. Israel's willingness in recent years to abandon its formerly non-negotiable positions and the withdrawal of Israel Defence Forces from southern Lebanon, and the offer to give up the Golan Heights to Syria, have created a conviction among Arabs that terrorism is working and that no accommodation of Israel need be considered.

The employment of death- by -suicide has also emerged as a symbol. The deaths of families at prayer, at weddings, eating in restaurants, at discos, children on their way to school, or individuals tortured to death, numbered in thousands, have no symbolic impact, while the suicide bomber is generally not condemned and their families receive sympathy, along with having financial rewards and social status bestowed upon them. The grieving Palestinian elicits sympathy, while the grieving Israeli elicits little or none. In a newscast on UK television in February 2003 showing various Iraqi military parades and protest marches, a number of individuals marched in rank dressed in the white hooded costume of the *shahidim*. No comment on their inclusion was passed on a single occasion.

It is a gross error to mistake symbol for substance as the USA, Britain and particularly the EC and UN frequently do. The results are never cohesive and they invariably become tied into knots trying to resolve the Palestinian issue rather than tackling more substantive issues. By not paying more attention to other matters, for example Saudi Arabia's support for terrorism both within and outside Israel, and gross abuse of basic human rights in the Arab world, they merely succeed in providing both their own and Israel's enemies with even greater encouragement and incentives to 'up the ante' of violence and bloodshed on an international scale.

Suicide bombing and the cult of martyrdom

> The Palestinian people love suicide more than Israelis love to live. (Hamas Official Rantisi, 8 May 2002)

Suicide as a means of inflicting death on third parties is not a new tactic; it is recorded as a practice of the Islamic Order of Assassins (*hashashin*) during the early Crusader period. However, prior to the Middle East conflict, it was an activity generally directed towards the military apparatus of real or perceived enemies, as was the case with the Japanese suicide mission airmen (kamikaze) and submariners (kaitin). At the start, it is worth pointing out that up until the time of writing there have been no recorded suicide attacks undertaken by Christians or by Jews as 'in kind' retaliation.

The first wave of some 51 suicide bombings was undertaken by the Hezbollah in Lebanon between 1982 and the Israeli withdrawal in 1999. The first such attack took place in November 1982, in the city of Tyre, when a detonation killed 76 Israeli security personnel. The nascent suicide bombers' campaign brought forth an immediate and probably better-than-expected result the following year, when in October 1983 one detonation resulted in the death of 241 American marines plus a few ancillaries, and a second detonation resulted in the death of 58 French paratroopers. The American and the French immediately withdrew, sending the clear message that terror tactics reap the greatest rewards at the lowest cost – effect ratio. The signal that it sent to the Islamic terror movement served to underline the perceived notion that the West caved in to terror tactics, and that the weight of military might and numbers could be manipulated by the use of tactics that were inherently abhorrent to the Western mind.

The Palestinians were quick to realise the value of the suicide attack. At first they had responded to a call to jihad; when this proved to be unattractive they began to major on calls to the glory of martyrdom. The notion of the *shahid* caught the popular imagination and in no time a whole theology of martyrdom began to evolve by co-joining the notions of religious duty with honour, power and revenge. The suicide bomber as martyr soon became iconic and a cult rapidly developed. As the Qur'an appears to decry suicide, all terrorist terminology refers to the operatives as 'martyrs', operations being referred to as *amiliyyat istishadiyye* (martyrdom operations).

Initially Hamas and its military branch, the Izz al-Din al-Qasam Brigade (henceforth Hamas), along with Palestinian Islamic Jihad (henceforth PIJ) took the initiative. In the opening phase the typical suicide bomber was a young, single male. This was to change when the far more cynical Al-Aqsa Martyrs' Brigade, under the tutelage of Yasser Arafat, joined in the initiative. From this point anyone who was willing, along with some believed to be coerced, were considered suitable candidates, no matter what their sex, age or social standing; it appears, however, that they are generally drawn from the middle class.

The *shahid* by the act becomes a sort of phantom celebrity. In schools there has developed a cult of martyrdom, and 'swap cards' of martyrs and martyr medallions are highly prized. In Palestinian homes young people hang images of 'martyrs' on their walls, where in the West there would be images of sporting heroes or pop stars. In a recent poll, 36 per cent of twelve-year-old boys in Gaza said they believed that the best thing in life was to die as a martyr (Dr Eyad Serraj, a psychiatrist in the Gaza Strip, *Christian Science Monitor*, 5 March 2004). It is hardly surprising that school age children of both sexes, fed on a diet of hatred against Israel and idolatry of suicide bombers and 'no escape operatives', should be keen to emulate their heroes. Three examples of adolescent 'no escape actions' involved 14-year-old Ismail abu Nida, who was killed while taking part in an attack, as were Yussuf Zakoot, 14, and Anwar Hamduna, aged 13.

The response of most families of the *shuhada* is presented to the media as one of pride and satisfaction. Those undertaking martyrdom operations are supposed to undertake them only from a purity of motive (*niyya*), but the rewards, both temporal and spiritual, are considered to have at least a modicum of influence. The family of *shahid* are respected and in some quarters revered within the community as it is considered a religious duty to honour the family of a *shahid*. Bounties of thousands of dollars were paid to the families of those who undertook their non-return missions by Saddam Hussein and at the time of writing still are by that most schizophrenic of states Saudi Arabia. It is unlikely, however, that financial reward is a prime motive. Rather it is regarded as a bonus.

Saudi Arabia, both in the past and today, has been the major player in the development of fundamentalist Islam, which was the vehicle used by the Saudi ruling family in their rise to power. The Saudis are the leading proponents of Wahabi Islam and the Hanbali school of Islamic Jurisprudence, a system of thought which stresses an extremely literalist interpretation of the Qur'an, known as 'Hard Shari'a'. This includes amputation for petty theft, public executions, death sentences for insulting the prophet, the repression of women and severe punishment of women for sexual crimes, while often the male involved is unpunished.

A report by Amnesty International in July 2002 summarises the arguments cited by the Palestinians as reasons for targeting civilians. The Palestinians claim that:

> They are engaged in a war against an occupying power and that religion and international law permit the use of any means in resistance to occupation; that they are retaliating against Israel killing members of armed groups and Palestinians generally; that striking at civilians is the only way they can make an impact upon a powerful adversary; that Israelis generally or settlers in particular are not civilians. (*Without Distinction: Attacks on Civilians by Palestinian Armed Groups,* Amnesty International, July 2002)

Amnesty International, although no lover of Israel, concluded that the above stated reasons were not acceptable and could be considered as crimes against humanity. Nevertheless they took the opportunity to condemn Israel in a similar vein, accusing the Israelis, who have never sent a suicide bomber, of the infraction of human rights that should also be considered crimes against humanity – a totally ludicrous suggestion within the context of the report.

The Islamic view(s)

Some Islamic authorities support the suicide bombers as martyrs on the strength of the following *surahs*:

> Let those fight in the way of Allah who sell the life of this world for the other. Whoso fighteth in the way of Allah, be he slain or be he victorious, on him we shall bestow a vast reward. (*Sura* 4:74)

> Those who believe do battle for the cause of Allah; and those who disbelieve do battle for the cause of idols. So fight the minions of the devil. Lo! the devil's strategy is ever weak. (*Sura* 4:76)

> The punishment of those who wage war against Allah and His apostle and strive to make mischief in the land is only this, that they should be murdered or crucified or their hands and their feet should be cut off on opposite sides or they should be imprisoned; this shall be as a disgrace for them in this world, and in the hereafter they shall have a grievous chastisement. (*Sura* 5:33)

The real question of the differences between orthodoxy and orthopraxis was not highlighted; in the way this sort of view is presented, the Qur'an is only part of the picture. There are also differences between the views of commentators and those of jurists and still more differences between the sects. In addition to the Qur'an, the *hadith*, or sayings of the prophet, and the writings of the authorities play a prominent part in overall thought and consciousness. It is here that the more aggressive programmes may be found along with the writings originating from the schism between the Sunnites and the Shi'ites.

A recent poll conducted by the Palestinian Centre for Public Opinion found that 76 per cent of Palestinian respondents approved of suicide bombings that were targeted towards Israelis. Palestinian religious leaders have for some time been praising the virtues of suicide in the service of their cause, particularly in Friday broadcasts. Sheik Isma'il Aal Ghadwan, during one broadcast, commented upon the words of the Prophet to Jaber bin Abdallah who, even though he was sad after the battle of Uhud in which his father was killed, clearly marked out the position:

> Allah said to him: '. . . Do not consider those who have died for the sake of Allah as dead, but as alive, and as being provided for by their Lord.'
>
> This good news . . . has passed down to our people who still make great sacrifices, defending the honour of the Islamic nation. The sacrifice of convoys of martyrs [will continue] until Allah grants us victory very soon. The willingness for sacrifice and for death we see amongst those who were cast by Allah into a war with the Jews, should not come at all as a surprise.
>
> O believing brothers, we do not feel a loss . . . The martyr, if he meets Allah, is forgiven with the first drop of blood; he is saved from the torments of the grave; he sees his place in Paradise; he is saved from the Great Horror [of the day of judgement]; he is given 72 black-eyed women; he vouches for 70 of his family to be accepted to Paradise; he is crowned with the Crown of glory, whose precious stone is better than all of this world and what is in it . . . (Friday 17 August 2001, MEMRI Special Despatch No. 261, 23 August 2001)

The attacks have also won support in the wider Arab world (see Jeffrey Goldberg, 'The Martyr Strategy', *New Yorker,* 9 July 2001). Following the 9 August suicide bombing in Jerusalem, Fahmi Huweidi described his feeling of happiness in an Egyptian government sponsored daily newspaper:

> It would not be an exaggeration to say that the heroic and Fidaai [martyrdom] warriors are the only light in dark skies, they are the sole remaining sign of life in the Arab nation . . . If we can still lift our heads with pride, it is only because we still have as models those young men who chose to die so that our lives would have hope and meaning and so that our long night will see a dawn with a message of hope. (*Al-Ahram,* 14 August 2001)

In May Amru Nasif, in the Egyptian newspaper *Al-Usbu,* called for mass suicide attacks against Israelis, and volunteered himself for a suicide mission, hoping that he would reap a huge death toll of Israelis by his detonation. 'Mathematical calculations,' he declared, illustrated that

> Two hundred and fifty Palestinians have signed up for martyrdom operations, and it is not impossible to raise this number to a thousand throughout the Arab world. The average harvest of each act of martyrdom is ten dead and fifty wounded. Thus a thousand acts of martyrdom would leave the Zionists with at least ten thousand dead and fifty thousand wounded.

The suicide bomber and his role as martyr had become firmly established in the months leading up to 11 September, the trail being blazed by the Palestinians.

The Sheik of Al-Azhar, Muhammad Sayyed Tantawi, the highest religious authority in Egypt, ruled that Palestinian youth who bomb themselves among people who fight against them are considered martyrs (*Shuhada*). On the other hand, if they bomb themselves among babies, women and the elderly, they are not considered martyrs (Ruz Al-Yussuf [Egypt], 18 May 2001). A similar ruling was made by the Saudi Mufti.

The above luminaries were attacked almost at once by distinguished journalists and jurists. Dr Mustafa Ghalush, a lecturer at the Al-Azhar University, stated: 'He who incites and he who carries out are the same, according to Islam' (Al-Liwa Al-Islami [Egypt]), 14 June 2001, tr. MEMRI Inquiry & Analysis No. 65, 26 July 2001, henceforth MEMRI 65).

Dr Muhammad Kamal Al-Din Al-Imam, a lecturer on Islamic Law at the Alexandria Law Faculty, proposed that there was no such entity as an Israeli civilian, and furthermore attempted to qualify the reprehensible practice of using human shields (i.e. positioning missile launchers, mortars or pursued individuals in medical facilities, schools, etc. to gain international sympathy when the sites of necessity are attacked).

> The [Israeli] society as a whole are involved in attacks by the military force raised from various countries in order to occupy someone else's land. Muslim warriors by no means commit suicide. Each part in their bodies speaks [the language] of Martyrdom for the sake of Allah . . . religious authorities have allowed the killing of a Muslim, if the heretic enemy is using him as a shield and there is no other way of killing this heretic, but to kill the Muslim along

with him. It follows, therefore, that if it is permissible to kill a Muslim, it is surely permissible to kill civilian enemies. (Al-Liwa Al-Islami [Egypt], 14 June 2001, MEMRI 65)

The image of the *shahid* as martyr and classical noble warrior, rather than someone who kills and maims innocent non-combatants indiscriminately, was clearly expressed in the Egyptian press in support of the campaign: Had the Muslim knights possessed explosives at the time they would have used them . . . Therefore, what the Palestinian [Martyr] does to the Zionist enemy with his belt of explosives is the highest form of Martyrdom . . .' (Al-Haqiqa [Egypt], 12 May 2001, MEMRI 65).

In a similar vein the PA Mufti, Ikrima Sabri, also criticised the Saudi Mufti in a Friday sermon at the Al-Aqsa Mosque that was aired live by the PA radio, on the basis of early Islamic battle deeds (The Voice of Palestine Radio [PA], 25 May 2001).

Dr Mustafa Al-Shka', a member of the Al-Azhar Islamic (Egypt) Studies Centre, reminded readers: 'We were commanded to fight against the enemies using all means.' To encourage potential suicide bombers he stated:

My blood is required for the sake of Allah, but the form of its [sacrifice] was not determined. The important thing is that I kill as many enemies as possible and turn into a Martyr [*shahid*]. He who fights with a sword, kills one heretic; on the other hand, he who bombs himself kills many of the enemies of Allah, and therefore this is a higher level of Martyrdom. (Al-Liwa Al-Islami [Egypt], 14 June 2001, tr. MEMRI 65)

Dr Ali 'Aqleh 'Ursan, Head of the Syrian Arab Writers Union, declared:

. . . the march of liberation, that will take place only by the use of force, through Jihad, and through Martyrdom . . . It is the blood of Sayyed Al-Shamuti recalling the battles of Badr and Al-Qadisiya, where Muslim horsemen had battled large that writes history, and the black ink cannot soil the golden pages written in the blood of the Shahids, on their way to liberate Palestine, the Golan, and South Lebanon . . . (Al-Usb'u Al-Adabi [Syria], 9 June 2001, tr. MEMRI 66)

Apologists for Islam contend that in Islam several things are clear:

- Suicide is forbidden. 'O ye who believe! . . . [do not] kill yourselves, for truly Allah has been to you Most Merciful. If any do that in rancour and injustice, soon shall we cast him into the Fire . . .' (4:29–30).

The above speaks of what one might consider emotional, individual terms rather than deliberated, cynical terms.

- The taking of human life is allowed only by legal instrument (i.e. the death penalty for murder), but even then, forgiveness is better. 'Nor take life – which Allah has made sacred – except for just cause . . .' (17:33).

The problem here is the practice of mullahs and other Islamic officials issuing *fatwas,* which although in reality are supposed to be opinions, they are generally considered to be binding. Examples are the *fatwah* by Usamah bin Laden against Crusaders and Jews, and the infamous *fatwah* of Grand Ayatollah Khomeni that called for the murder of the author Salman Rushdie following the publication of *Satanic Verses.*

Revenge killing or killing in blood feuds were proscribed. The Islamic world was, and is to a large extent, tribal. 'After this, whoever exceeds the limits shall be in grave chastisement' (2:178–79). The above *surah* encourages a form of moderation, not a proscription against such acts.

- Harming innocent bystanders, even in times of war, was forbidden by the Prophet Muhammad (but not necessarily by his successors and interpreters). This includes women, children, non-combatant bystanders, and even trees and crops. Nothing is to be harmed unless the person or thing is actively engaged in an assault against Muslims. A brief overview of the early days of Islam shows this was not a generally observed practice.

What, however, remains unclear to Western leaders and what they fail to grasp is what is understood by the term Islam. In a similar way to other faith systems there are different forms of Islam, all with their own writings and traditions, e.g. Sunnite, Shiite, where the secondary interpretative document(s) have influence in everyday life. Whereas the

Islamic Conference of Foreign Ministers on Terrorism passed high-sounding resolutions, blaming Israel for the present situation, it is naïve in the extreme to think, or even suppose, that the meeting had any juris-diction over terrorist organisations or that they were prepared to take a proactive, or even, unless pushed too severely, a reactive response to the matter.

Dr Eyyad Seraj is a psychiatrist in the Gaza Strip. He considers that candidates for suicide bombings arise from all categories and view mar-tyrdom as the ultimate redemption. In a recent poll, according to Dr Serraj: 'In their minds, the only model of power and glory is the martyr . . . Palestinian society glorifies the martyr. They are elevated to the level of saints and even prophets. Out of the hopeless and the inhuman envir-onment they live in, there is the promise that they will have a better life in heaven.' Post-war Iraq saw suicide bombings turn into daily events and this destroyed any exit strategy planned by the Americans. It was patently obvious that forward planning had not considered that wholesale suicide bombing initiatives would provide an almost insoluble problem.

The advent of female suicide bombers

> Martyrdom is a central ethic of the al-Aqsa Intifada. It has created a balance of power between Palestinians and Israel and it will not be easily removed from the Palestinian political agenda. (Dr Meir Hadina, Tel Aviv University)

The notion of women becoming so-called martyrs is by no means a new concept. The Catholic Church boasts many martyred female saints and women terrorists fought with Italy's Red Brigades, Germany's Baader-Meinhof gang, and America's Weathermen. In more recent times there has emerged a new phenomenom: that of the female suicide bomber. They appeared in the Chechnyan assault on a Moscow theatre, where the black-clad, veiled female element was said to be colder and harsher than the males. Similarly in the November 2004 attack in Beslam, esti-mates put the death toll near a thousand people. The so-called Black Widows are generally thought to be revenge motivated. One could add to this number the actions by the Tamil Tigers, and factions in the post-Iraq War. It was, however, within the Islamic–Palestinian context that the phenomenom emerged and became refined. Sadly, as in other acts of terrorism, where the Middle East has set the trend, others follow or aspire to, as exampled in two recent Indian films, *Dil Se* (From the Heart) and *The Terrorist*, both of which feature female suicide bombers in the leading roles.

The involvement of Palestinian women in terrorist activity, either directly or indirectly, in planning or facilitation, is not a new phenomenom. The idea of a female as a suicide bomber, although generally considered a recent innovation, is thought to have started as early as 1987 when Atef Eleyan, a senior female Palestinian Islamic Jihad activist, planned to perpetrate a suicide attack using a car bomb in Jerusalem. Atef was captured and jailed (in Israel) for ten years, subsequently being released on completion of her sentence in 1997.

Islamic terrorist organisations, and initially the Palestinians, seized upon the opportunity to exploit the advantages of using females as suicide bombers, especially inside Israeli cities where they 'Westernise' their appearance by adopting Western hairstyles and short skirts (often brought with them) as they approach their targets. When crossing border checkpoints, the very notion of any kind of search of women initially was considered inappropriate by both sides. At present the searching of women is undertaken by female members of the IDF out of public view.

The recruiting grounds for potential female candidates range from the northern West Bank universities to towns and villages. The sponsors invest considerable time and effort in convincing women that this kind of activity does not contradict the Islamic principles nor 'the daily duties of the Muslim woman', as well as promising rewards both for themselves and their families in the hereafter.

Wafa Idris, a 27-year-old divorced Palestinian woman from the Al-Am'ari refugee camp near Ramallah, had the distinction of becoming the first female Palestinian suicide bomber of the period on 27 January 2002, killing one Israeli civilian and wounding approximately 140 others. The military wing of Fatah, the Al-Aqsa Brigades, took responsibility for the attack three days later. While the Western press were bemused by the incident, the Arabic press were swift to eulogise her and rejoice in what they perceived as a precedent for female suicidal activities. The first news-sheet to express the notion clearly and quickly was the London-based *Al-Quds Al-Arabi*, which proclaimed: This is the first time a young woman strapped a belt of explosives and bits of metal around her waist and blew herself up on Jaffa Road in the heart of the occupied city. Thus, she joins the convoys of the martyrs and sets a precedent [for women] to take pride in the history of the Arab and Islamic woman' (*Al-Quds Al-Arabi* [London], 28 January 2002). The Iraqi press trumpeted that Saddam Hussein had ordered a statue of her to be erected.

On Friday 29 March 2002 Aayat al-Akhras, (18), became the third and thus far the youngest female suicide bomber, detonating herself in the Supersol supermarket in the Kyriat Hayovel area of west Jerusalem, killing a security guard and a Jewish girl of her own age named Rachel Levy. The incident came within 48 hours of a suicide bombing in the seaside town of Netanya that left 22 dead and more than 100 wounded. The young woman's death was hailed as an act of martyrdom by the Al-Aqsa Martyrs' Brigade, linked to Yasser Arafat's Fatah movement. A representative of the a-AMB in Bethlehem claimed: 'We have 200 young women from the Bethlehem area alone, ready to sacrifice themselves for the homeland' (*The Guardian* [London], 30 March 2002).

On 12 April 2002, Andaleeb Takafka (20) from Bethlehem detonated herself at a Jerusalem bus stop, killing six Israelis and injuring a further 104 people. Hiba Daraghmeh (19) self-detonated outside the Amakim shopping mall in Afula in northern Israel after being stopped by security guards. The Al-Aqsa Martyrs' Brigades and the Palestinian Islamic Jihad both took responsibility for the attack. The attack was followed a few months later by another female, this time the PIJ claiming responsibility for the attack.

On 4 October 2003, the sixth female suicide attack took place at the Maxim restaurant in Haifa sponsored by Islamic Jihad. The detonation was undertaken by a single woman, Hanadi Tyssar Jaradat (29), a trainee lawyer from Silat Al Hartiya in Jenin, the sister of Fadi Jaradat, an Islamic Jihad militant who was killed, along with a cousin, Salah Jaradat, in June 2003 during an IDF operation to arrest them on suspicion of planning a terror attack inside Israel. Jaradat's attack was the second Islamic jihad by a woman. The explosion of 15 kg of explosive laced with ballbearings killed 19 civilians, among whom were five Israeli Arabs who were working in the restaurant, including a security guard employed to deter suicide bombers. The motivation behind the Haifa attack is thought to have been partially as revenge for the death of her relatives. Her 'living *shahid*' video testimony offered little insight: 'By the will of God I decided to be the sixth martyr who makes her body full with splinters in order to enter every Zionist heart who occupied our country. We are not the only ones who will taste death from their occupation. As they sow so will they reap.' It is common knowledge that at the funerals of militants, both Hamas and the Islamic Jihad use the event and the mourners' booths as recruiting stations, exploiting the raw emotions of the time. Secondly, as an educated woman, there may well have been a personal desire to be equal to men in a non-socially mobile society (see below). Thirdly, the question of why at her age in a traditional Islamic society she was unmarried may have caused her to be vulnerable to suggestion.

The truth behind the action, sadly, is far from any of the above suggestions. According to Hillel Newman, Israeli Ambassador to New England:

> According to numerous reports, Al-Reyashi had committed adultery and was given the terrible choice to die at the hands of her family or attain an 'honorable' death by becoming a suicide bomber. Her lover, a member of Hamas, gave her the explosives and instructions for conducting the deadly mission, and her husband drove her to the Erez crossing to commit the heinous act. (*Boston Globe*, 14 June 2004)

Following the carnage a few days later in the Gaza Strip, a pocket-sized card was handed out at the girls' school celebrating Hanadi as the 'bride of the Haifa martyrdom operation'. This resulted in a flurry of response to recruiting.

On Wednesday 14 January 2004, a young Palestinian mother of a three year-old and a one year old, Reem al-Reyashi (22), feigning a limp and requesting medical help, self-detonated herself at the entrance to a security inspection centre for Palestinian workers, killing four Israeli security personnel and wounding seven people. She told the soldiers that she had recently had an operation on her leg and a metal pin had been implanted that would register on the detector. She was allowed to pass, and when the alarm sounded, the soldiers told her to wait while they called an army woman to search her. Seizing the moment she detonated her bomb, estimated at about 10 pounds and packed with ballbearings and screws to make it more lethal (Greg Myre, *New York Times*, 15 January 2004). In

her living *shahid* video released after her death, dressed in combat
fatigues, with an automatic rifle in her hands and a rocket-propelled
grenade launcher on the desk in front of her, she declared:

> God gave me the ability to be a mother of two children who I love so . . . But
> my wish to meet God in paradise is greater, so I decided to be a martyr for
> the sake of my people. I am convinced God will help and take care of my chil-
> dren . . . it was always my wish to turn my body into deadly shrapnel against
> the Zionists and to knock on the doors of heaven with the skulls of Zionists.

Leila Khaled, the veteran Palestinian terrorist and leader of the Black
September airline hijacking gang, presently promoting 'Women's
Rights', pronounced:

> We are under attack . . . the Palestinians are ready to sacrifice themselves for
> the national struggle for the respect of their [Palestinians'] just rights . . . In
> these conditions, there is not a distance between life and death. Our existence
> is transformed into torment . . . women are involved in the [Palestinian] mili-
> tary organisation. (Interview in *Corriere Della Sera*)

Khaled's enthusiasm for females to become suicide bombers is shared in
a number of circles. Wafa Idris's mother, Wasfiyeh, concurs with Khaled
and described her daughter as a martyr and a 'daughter of Palestine' with
the implication that to deserve the epithet one had to be prepared to
become a *shahid*.

Islamic social and religious tensions

In December 2002, in an interview granted to the London-based newspaper *al-Quds al-Arabi* on 29 December 2002, Dr Mohammed Sayyed
Tantawi, the al-Azhar Sheikh (Egypt), who is the senior religious authority of Sunni Islam, pronounced himself on the issue of women's suicide
acts, authorising such acts when they are performed within the framework of the Palestinian struggle. The sheikh, who until then had
reservations about women carrying out suicide bombings, emphasised
that suicide attacks carried out by members of the Palestinian 'resistance'
are acts of sacrifice intended for the sanctification of Allah, whether per-

formed by men or women. The sheik further allowed women who engage in 'suicide activities' (*amaliyyat istish'hadiyyah*) to make concessions on their traditional attire (e.g. the compulsory veil), if such are needed to warrant the success of the suicide bombing. 'Furthermore, there is no difference between male and female when [it concerns] defending religion, homeland, self-respect, dignity and property; no difference whatsoever.'

The late Hamas spiritual leader Sheikh Ahmad Yassin at first had his reservations. Whether they were real or for political reasons remains unknown:

> The Palestinian woman has an important role in society and in supporting the fighters [he explained]. In our Palestinian society, there is a flow of women towards Jihad and martyrdom, exactly like the young men. But the woman has uniqueness. Islam sets some restrictions for her, and if she goes out to wage Jihad and fight, she must be accompanied by a male chaperone.

A few days later, Sheikh Yassin amended his position, saying that a woman going out to wage jihad must be accompanied by a male chaperone only 'if she is to be gone for a day and a night. If her absence is shorter, she does not need a chaperone' (*Al-Sharq Al-Awsat* [London], 31 January 2002 and 2 February 2002). Put simply, if she is going on a suicide mission she is not going to have the opportunity for an overnight stay.

Isma'il Abu Shanab, a Hamas leader in Gaza, said: 'Jihad against the enemy is an obligation that applies not only to men but also to women. Islam has never differentiated between men and women on the battlefield' (Middle East News Online, 28 January 2002). Sheikh Hassan Yussef Yassin, a Hamas leader in the West Bank, added:

> We do not act according to the opinion of the street or of society. We are men of principle . . . [and act] according to what our religion dictates. A Muslim woman is permitted to wage Jihad and struggle against the occupation. The Prophet [Muhammad] would draw lots among the women who wanted to go out to wage Jihad with him. The Prophet always emphasized the woman's right to wage Jihad. (*Al-Sha'ab* [Egypt], 1 February 2002)

Sheikh Ali Abu Al-Hassan, Chairman of the Religious Ruling Committee at Egypt's Al-Azhar University, stated that suicide attacks by women were permitted, even though at this time Sheikh Tantawi, who heads Al-Azhar University, had ruled against attacks on civilians. Al-Hassan declared:

> The martyrdom operation carried out among the Israelis by the young Palestinian woman is an act of Jihad permissible according to the Shari'a, and on this there is no disagreement . . . If the enemy has conquered and plundered even a single inch of Muslim land, Jihad becomes a personal duty of man, woman, slave, and master. [In such a case], the woman wages [Jihad] without her husband's permission, the slave without his master's permission, and the debtor without his creditor's permission.

Al-Hassan based his reasoning on well-known acts of female jihad during the raids led by the Prophet Muhammad:

> The Prophet's aunt came down from the women's citadel, and fought a man from among the infidels who had climbed up the citadel. She killed him, but took care to protect Islamic morality by refraining from stripping and disarming him. She told the poet Hassan bin Thabet: 'You go to him and strip him.' Likewise, Asmaa, the daughter of Yazid, participated in one of the battles against the Byzantines, and killed men. (*Afaq Arabiya* [Egypt], 30 January 2002, as cited in *Al-Quds Al-Arabi* [London], 31 January 2002)

Dr Samiya Sa'ad Al-Din, reflecting on the matter in the Egyptian government mouthpiece, *Al-Akhbar*, exclaims:

> Palestinian women have torn the gender classification out of their birth certificates, declaring that sacrifice for the Palestinian homeland would not be for men alone; on the contrary, all Palestinian women will write the history of the liberation with their blood, and will become time bombs in the face of the Israeli enemy. They will not settle for being mothers of martyrs! (*Al-Akhbar* [Egypt], 1 February 2002)

In May 2004 Israel prevented two young women recruited by the terror group Tanzim from executing attacks to 'clear their names'. The first woman, Tehani Zaki Ali Halil, was persuaded to carry out a suicide attack in Tel Aviv after being accused of infidelity. The other, a 19-year-old girl named Ramah Abed el-Majid Hasan Habaib, was recruited after accusations of premarital sexual relations (*Boston Globe*, 14 June 2004). Even worse are reports of abuse and manipulation of young women as part of the recruiting process. Young women, often who have been raped – sometimes by men in their own families, rather than face an ignominious death at the hands of their own families or religious zealots, prefer to take the 'martyr's way' to raise themselves from the shamed to the elite.

The recruitment by abuse has caught the attention of several feminist writers.

> Israeli and Palestinian feminists have worked together in rape crisis centres to repair the torn hymens of Palestinian rape victims. This is a life-saving procedure, since sexual abuse is perceived as a form of the woman having prostituted. There is no empathy, no post-traumatic stress disorder, no redemption, no revenge against the rapist, no legal prosecution of him. Instead for the woman or girl there is secrecy or death. In becoming suicide bombers, women trade in the lowly status of the raped woman for the higher status of a martyr. (Andrea Dworkin)

In conclusion, there appear to be three main strands underpinning the use of female suicide bombers. First, coercion. Secondly, empowerment for women in a male-dominated society. Thirdly, revenge either in the individual or a corporate sense. All three of these suggestions have the same element of cynical manipulation by the recruiters and the dispatchers of the *shahada* (who interestingly enough are not recorded as personally taking the way of the martyr).

Major sources

Bar-Tal, Daniel, 'Israeli–Palestinian Conflict: a Cognitive Analysis', *International Journal of Intercultural Relations*, V, 14, 1990.

Cline, Ray S. and Alexander, Yonah, *Terrorism as State-Sponsored Covert Warfare* (Hero Books, Virginia, 1986).

Coates, Anthony, *The Ethics of War* (Manchester University Press, 1997).

Dershowitz, Alan, *Why Terrorism Works* (Yale University Press, Newhaven, 2002).

Doran, Michael Scott, 'Palestine-as-Symbol', *Foreign Affairs*, January–February 2003.

Firestone, Reuven, 'Islam Hijacked', *The Jewish Journal of Greater Los Angeles*, 28 September 2001.

Firestone, Reuven, *Jihad: The Origin of Holy War in Islam* (Oxford University Press, 1999).

Firestone, Reuven, 'Conceptions of Holy War in Biblical and Qur'anic Tradition', *Journ. Rel. Ethics*, 24:1 (1996).

Hasan, Ahmad, 'The Qur'an: The Primary Source of Fiqh', *Islamic Studies*, 1999, 38(4).

Hill, Charles, 'The Herculean Task: the Myth and Reality of Arab Terrorism', in Talbott, Strobe and Chanda Nayan, *The Age of Terror: America and the World after September 11th* (Yale Centre for the Study of Globalisation and Perseus Press, Oxford, 2002).

Johnson, James Turner, *The Holy War Idea in Western and Islamic Traditions* (Pennsylvania State University Press, 1997).

MEMRI: various translations from the Arab press.

SECTION V

The final section considers the biblical theme of the restoration of all things which drew the contributors together. David Noakes illustrates his deep understanding of the prophetic corpus in the eponymous essay. Some of the content will be very new to readers, but a close reading will bring its own reward. He considers elements of the restoration of both the Land and the people, and the categories of those involved in the restoration. The final essay considers the destiny of the Jewish people and, therefore, *ipso facto* the role and destiny of the nations in the end times. Elements included are the biblical basis for the return of the Jewish people to their ancient homeland and the results of the return to various parties.

THE RESTORATION OF ALL THINGS

David Noakes

At the time of writing, it is a matter of weeks since a survey of the recent disturbing increase of anti-semitic attacks against Jewish people and property in Britain revealed that 80 per cent of those attacks were motivated principally by hatred related to the presence of the Jewish state in the Land of Israel. Such hatred is today largely fuelled by the grossly distorted media coverage of the continual conflict in that small country between Israelis and Palestinians.

Behind this human hatred, however, lie more profound and significant causes. What for centuries has been known as antisemitism is now presented in a new guise:that of anti-Zionism. The former is generally held, outwardly at least, to be unacceptable in our day as being racist and, therefore, politically incorrect, but paradoxically the latter is regarded as acceptable. In essence however they are identical, inspired from the same hidden source.

In November 1975, the General Assembly of the United Nations passed a resolution which declared that 'Zionism is a form of racism and racial discrimination'. Yet Zionism is in essence no more than the expression of the longing in the hearts of the Jewish people, after 19 centuries of exile and persecution, to return to the ancestral homeland of their forefathers and to enjoy peace and security in the Land which God has given by everlasting covenant to Abraham, Isaac and Jacob and their descendants (Gen 12–17).

Zionism, understood through the true perspective of the revelation of Scripture, is no modern phenomenon, but has its origins in the heart of the God of Israel Himself, and is clearly stated many times in His

271

word. Herein lies the key to understanding the true nature of anti-Zionism; it is rooted not in the political, social or even religious views of men, but in the age-abiding conflict between the God of Israel and His rebellious adversary, Satan, whose desire is to contest the word and will of God at every point – and never more than in matters concerning God's own covenant Land and people of Israel, and His chosen city Jerusalem.

The driving force behind anti-Zionism is therefore not human and political, but lies in an unrelenting demonic hatred which seeks to manipulate the minds of men and control the affairs of the nations. The supreme irony of the UN resolution already mentioned is that it was Zionism, an entirely biblical concept, which led to the creation of the modern State of Israel by an act of the United Nations Assembly, the same body which some 28 years later was effectively challenging the right of existence of that nation-state which it had established.

Christian Zionism

Zionism is today perceived as being essentially evil. Christian Zionism is viewed as unacceptable in much of the professing church, being regarded simply as an expression of a fundamentalist right-wing religio-political position. However, Christian Zionism is founded squarely upon the revelation of Scripture, as many have recognised in the centuries since the days of the great Puritan writers. During more than four centuries, men of God who have believed the clear revelation found in the prophetic writings of Scripture have been convinced that the unequivocal predictions of the word of God must be fulfilled in the return of the descendants of Jacob to the Land given by God's everlasting covenant to the Hebrew patriarchs and their descendants.

After many centuries of antisemitic attitudes and behaviour on the part of the church in Britain, the translation of the Bible into English and a genuine spiritual awakening brought about a remarkable change of heart. The Puritan movement of the sixteenth and seventeenth centuries gave rise to a strong desire for reformation of the church accompanied by doctrinal purity, both of which arose from a renewed understanding of the inspiration and authority of the word of God and a more thorough acquaintance with its contents. The result for many was an entirely new revelation of God's everlasting love and His continuing purpose for the nation and Land of Israel; and with this revelation, the realisation that the fortunes of the Land and the people are inextricably intertwined and that it is essential in God's purposes that the two be reunited.

In Britain, Christian Zionism is no new phenomenon. As early as 1589 this renewed understanding cost Francis Kett his life, when he was burned as a heretic. In 1621 Sir Henry Finch caused a great stir with his book *The Restoration of the Jews*, which had a somewhat utopian view of a restored Land of Israel which would function as a perfect theocracy. During the period of the English Civil War and the Commonwealth between 1640 and 1660, there was a strong belief in a restored Jewish state which would lead to the imminent return of Messiah and the establishment of His millennial kingdom. Such outstanding men as Cromwell, Pepys and Spinoza held this belief, based upon their understanding of the prophetic Scriptures, and Cromwell was inspired to readmit the Jews to England for the first time since their expulsion in 1290 by Edward I.

During the same period, the great theme of Jewish restoration to the Land of Israel inspired writings by men such as John Milton and Johann Comenius, while in the following century the truth of God's word was upheld by Wesley and Whitefield, and in the nineteenth century the concept of a restored Jewish state was openly recognised and upheld by outstanding men of their day such as Palmerston, Shaftesbury and Disraeli, Darwin, the well-known authors George Eliot and Robert Browning and the Scottish churchmen Andrew Bonar and Murray McCheyne.

From the time of the Napoleonic Wars, men of God who understood both the Scriptures and the signs of the times in which they were living, began to see and predict that Britain would become an instrument in the hand of God in His prophetic purposes of restoring the Jews to their ancestral homeland of Israel. Christian statesmen and preachers alike accepted the revelation of Scripture on the matter and declared the truths of it from their platforms and pulpits.

Rejection of the testimony of Scripture

Replacement theology, however, lacks this understanding, denying the revelation of Scripture which accounts entirely for the phenomenon which we are seeing in our own day, that of a nation being restored to her roots. Never in recorded history has any other nation dispersed into exile retained a sense of national identity through 20 centuries and returned to its original Land and language; yet this has happened before our eyes in our own generation. To those who deny that this is a work of God, the same reply is appropriate as that which Jesus gave in His response to the unbelieving Sadducees:'You are in error because you do not know the Scriptures or the power of God' (Mt. 22:29).

'Why do the nations rage, and the people plot a vain thing?' cries the psalmist in Psalm 2:1 (NKJV). 'The kings of the earth set themselves, and the rulers take counsel together, against the Lord and against His Anointed, saying, "Let us break their bonds in pieces and cast away their cords from us,"' he continues in verses 2–3.

This is precisely what we see in our own day:increasing worldwide rebellion against God and against the authority of Jesus His Messiah. Everywhere the authority of the word of God in Scripture and the divinity of Jesus are being called into question, not least within the professing church; but the same psalm provides God's response: 'He who sits in the heavens shall laugh; the Lord shall hold them in derision. Then He shall speak to them in His wrath, and distress them in His deep displeasure: "Yet I have set My King on My holy hill of Zion"' (Ps 2:4–6, NKJV).

These words are full of significance for our understanding. Through the prophetic writings, God has revealed the reason why today the most disputed area of land in the world is that of Israel, and the most disputed city that of Jerusalem, with the Temple Mount at its heart. The Land is God's chosen Land, declared to be His inheritance together with the descendants of Jacob (Joel 3:2); Mount Zion, the city of Jerusalem, is the chosen city of the great King (Ps 48:1–3); and in Psalm 132:13–14, God makes an unequivocal statement:'For the Lord has chosen Zion, He has desired it for His dwelling place: "This is My resting place forever; here I will dwell, for I have desired it"' (NKJV).

It is a bold professing believer who would dispute with the word of God which contains statements such as these: Zion, at the heart of the city of Jerusalem in the historic Land of Israel, is God's chosen dwelling place upon this present earth, and the place where the Messiah will return and establish His throne to rule the nations with a rod of iron and restore divine order to the rebellious nations. The time is coming when

Zion will be the seat of His authority, when the government will truly be 'upon His shoulder' (Is 2:1–4; Mic 4:1–5; Is 9:6).

God's promised restoration of Israel

In our own day, we are privileged to see the beginnings of a work which God predicted long ago. In many places, the Hebrew prophets have foretold that the Day of the Lord would come; a day which would culminate in God's restoration of the fortunes of the two houses of Israel and Judah (e.g. Jer 30:3; 50:4, 20, 33; 51:5) and the reuniting of those two divided kingdoms into the one house of Jacob, the messianic kingdom of Israel living in her ancient Land and ruled by her returned Messiah (Ezek 37:15–27).

From the time of the fall of Jerusalem in 586 BCE and the exile into captivity of Zedekiah, the last king of the southern kingdom of Judah, until the establishment of the modern State of Israel in 1948, national sovereignty and autonomy were lost to the Jewish people. During that time they were subjected continually to Gentile rule. As the prophet Hosea predicted: 'The Israelites will live for many days without king or prince, without sacrifice or sacred stones, without ephod or idol' (Hos 3:4). There would, as has now been the case for more than 2,500 years, be no kingdom or Temple; yet Hosea immediately adds: 'Afterwards the Israelites will return and seek the Lord their God and David their king. They will come trembling to the Lord and to his blessings in the last days' (v. 5).

In the midst of the sufferings of exile and of the subsequent subjugation of the returned remnant under the successive rule of the great Gentile empires foreseen by the prophet Daniel, the descendants of Judah clung to the hope of eventual restoration which their God had given through the prophetic writings. Thus it was that the burning question on the lips of the disciples of Jesus to the crucified and risen Messiah before His ascension was: 'Lord, are you at this time going to restore the kingdom to Israel?' (Acts 1:6).

The urgent desire of their hearts was for that national restoration which God had promised so many centuries earlier. However, they were obliged to be content with the enigmatic response which Jesus gave: 'It is not for you to know the times or dates the Father has set by his own authority' (implying that the word of God would undoubtedly be fulfilled, but at the proper time, which had not yet come).

On the Day of Pentecost, the day when the giving of the Law was celebrated, the Holy Spirit came, as Jesus had promised, to 'put [God's] law in their minds and write it on their hearts' (Jer 31:33). Subsequently we find Peter, emboldened by the Spirit of God, addressing a crowd in the Temple in a most remarkable way (Acts 3:11–26), which so enraged the religious establishment that Peter and John were jailed and brought before the authorities (Acts 4:1–22).

Peter's address confronted the nation of that time: 'Men of Israel . . .' (3:12). As he had done on the Day of Pentecost (Acts 2:22–36), he stated unhesitatingly the sin of the disowning of the Messiah by His own people, together with the fact of His resurrection (vv. 13–15).

Having acknowledged that the rejection of Jesus had been done in a state of ignorance on their part, Peter then proceeded to unfold to his hearers the revelation that it had nevertheless also been God's way of fulfilling the prophetic writings concerning the redemptive suffering of His Messiah; and to present to them the person of Jesus as the fulfilment of the Abrahamic covenant and the source of blessing to the nation if they would repent (vv. 17–26).

Tragically, as history bears witness, despite those who did repent and become followers of The Way, the nation as a whole continued in unbelief, and the terrible events of judgement followed in CE 70 as Jesus had predicted, while the birthright of Jacob's descendants in the salvation accomplished through Messiah's sacrificial death was made available to the Gentiles (Rom 11:11–12, 25; Eph 2:11–22).

Nevertheless, the ultimate purpose in the heart of God to fulfil the promised restoration of His covenant representative nation of Israel was not to be thwarted. It was restated by Peter on that same day: 'Repent, then, and turn to God, so that your sins may be wiped out, that times of refreshing may come from the Lord, and that he may send the Messiah, who has been appointed for you – even Jesus' (Acts 3:19–20). We should take note that when Peter used those words 'appointed for you', he was addressing not Gentiles but 'men of Israel'. Jesus was, and remains, first and foremost the Messiah of Israel; the gospel is 'first to the Jew, then to the Gentile'. His predicted return will be to Jerusalem, when at last His own people are ready to raise the cry, 'Blessed is he who comes in the name of the Lord'

(Ps 118:26; Mt 23:39). On that day the national repentance and turning to God for which Peter called (Acts 3:19) will take place and national sin will be blotted out in a 'fountain of cleansing' opened in Jerusalem (Zech 13:1) as a result of the outpouring by the Lord of a spirit of grace and supplication (Zech 12:10). Then at last the 'times of refreshing' (Acts 3:19) will come, when God sends His Messiah for the second time.

It is of the utmost importance that we should be aware of the context in which these events take place, for otherwise we shall fail to understand the significance of the times in which we are now living, and our interpretation of the eschatological writings of Scripture concerning the end of this age will consequently be flawed; they will be like the spokes of a wheel that has no central hub into which they could fit. When considering these eschatological predictions, it is only possible to obtain a clear and accurate picture if they are taken in the context of the whole prophetic revelation of Scripture, which states clearly that the return of Messiah will be first to His own chosen Land of Israel and city of Jerusalem, in order to save His covenant people from total destruction by Gentile armies (Is 63:1–6; Zech 12:9; 14:3ff.) and to reveal Himself, for who He is, to a repentant people.

His feet will stand upon the Mount of Olives (Zech 14:4). He

'will return to Zion and dwell in Jerusalem. Then Jerusalem will be called the City of Truth, and the mountain of the Lord Almighty will be called the Holy Mountain . . . 'I will save my people from the countries of the east and the west. I will bring them back to live in Jerusalem; they will be my people, and I will be faithful and righteous to them as their God.' . . . 'As you have been an object of cursing among the nations, O Judah and Israel, so will I save you, and you will be a blessing' (Zech 8:3, 7–8, 13).

Creation – the restoration of all things

In the context of prophetic statements such as these, let us now return to Peter's address to the 'men of Israel' and in particular to the statement of Acts 3:21 concerning Jesus 'whom heaven must receive until the period of restoration of all things about which God spoke by the mouth of His holy prophets from ancient time' (NASB). Jesus will return when that prophesied time of the restoration of all things comes. Who will accomplish this work of restoration? He will. Nowhere in Scripture is it suggested that any human person, group or nation can perform this task. It is He who will return to restore divine authority and order on the earth, ruling the nations with a rod of iron (Ps 2:9; Rev 19:15), ruling with His mighty sceptre extended from Zion (Ps 110:2). It is He alone who can judge with righteousness and cause the wolf to live with the lamb and the leopard with the goat (Is 11:1–9). Then, when He returns, will come the times of restoration, when 'the earth will be full of the knowledge of the Lord' (Is 11:9).

What is to be restored?

What is to be restored in that glorious day, that 'unique day . . . known to the Lord' when 'The Lord will be king over the whole earth. On that day there will be one Lord, and his name the only name' (Zech 14:7, 9)? What are the 'things about which God spoke by the mouth of his holy prophets from ancient times'? Is the church to be in some way restored, as some have suggested? Nowhere is that to be found in the prophetic writings. Rather, the Bride is to be completed, and presented to Jesus her Bridegroom 'as a radiant church, without stain or wrinkle or any other blemish, but holy and blameless' (Eph 5:27).

What, then, has God undertaken to restore, as revealed through the prophets? The Greek word Luke employs in Acts 3:21 is *apokatastasis*. This noun is found only in this one place in the Scriptures, and is derived from the verb *apokathistemi*, itself used on only three occasions, one of which is in Acts 1:6, which has the meaning of restoring something to its former state.

The fallen creation

Taking first the most all-embracing aspect of this meaning, this prophesied restoration of all things embraces the entire fallen creation, which is 'groaning as in the pains of childbirth right up to the present time' (Rom 8:22). Paul speaks of 'the glory that will be revealed in us' while at present 'the creation waits in eager expectation for the sons of God to be revealed . . . in hope that the creation itself will be liberated from its bondage to decay and brought into the glorious freedom of the children of God' (Rom 8:18–21).

The entire fallen creation is thus revealed as being at present in anguish as a result of the Fall, awaiting the restoration that will be initiated when Messiah returns, bringing His redeemed saints with Him. Through the atoning work of Messiah, God was not only reconciling the world of men to Himself (2 Cor 5:18–21), but 'was pleased . . . through him to reconcile to himself all things, whether things on earth or things in heaven, by making peace through his blood, shed on the cross' (Col 1:19–20).

This atonement is complete and all-embracing; when Messiah comes again He will establish reconciliation and order where there has been pain, disharmony, hostility and chaos, and Jew and Gentile will find in place of hostility and suspicion the joy of total reconciliation and of becoming at last truly 'one new man' in Messiah (Eph 2:15–16).

As Isaiah has foretold, the enmity of predators and prey in the animal kingdom will disappear (Is 11:6–9). 'They will neither harm nor destroy on all my holy mountain' (v. 9) declares the prophet. His declaration is repeated in Isaiah 65:25 at the culmination of a passage (vv. 17–25) that looks to the immediate restoration of Jerusalem and the nation of Israel, but even beyond (v. 17) to the ultimate creation by God of the new heavens and new earth, later revealed more fully to John in Revelation 21–22.

This crucially important aspect of the restoration of all things apart, however, the prophets' principal revelation has to do entirely with matters relating to the Land and nation of Israel.

The Land and nation of Israel

The Land is to be restored to the people and the exiled people to the Land. The Hebrew prophets foresaw with awful clarity that disobedience would bring exile and dispersion, but also that God would subsequently restore His people to their own Land. Moses foresaw the horrors of God's judgement in awful detail in Deuteronomy 28:15–68, including ultimate dispersion among the nations (vv. 64–68). It was not a matter of 'if' but of 'when' (Deut 30:1); yet in the same breath Moses also predicts ultimate reconciliation with God and restoration to the Land: 'Then the Lord your God will restore your fortunes and have compassion on you and gather you again from all the nations where he scattered you . . . and bring you back. He will bring you to the land that belonged to your fathers, and you will take possession of it' (vv. 3–5).

Many similar passages could be quoted, but the most outstanding and comprehensive prophetic revelation is to be found in Ezekiel 36, where first in verses 8–12 God speaks to the barren and desolate Land of Israel:

> But you, O mountains of Israel, will produce branches and fruit for my people Israel, for they will soon come home. I am concerned for you and will look on you with favour; you will be ploughed and sown, and I will multiply the number of people upon you, even the whole house of Israel. The towns will be inhabited and the ruins rebuilt. I will increase the number of men and animals upon you, and they will be fruitful and become numerous. I will settle people on you as in the past and will make you prosper more than before. Then you will know that I am the Lord. I will cause people, my people Israel, to walk upon you. They will possess you, and you will be their inheritance; you will never again deprive them of their children.

The nation's relationship with her God

In verse 16 of the same chapter (36), Ezekiel is then led to prophesy concerning the exiled people. Just as the Land of Israel does not prosper when its people are absent, so the people do not thrive when separated from the Land, for both together form God's declared inheritance (Joel 3:2). Thus in this remarkable passage (36:16–38), Ezekiel speaks the word of God to the whole house of Israel in exile. It is for His own sake, declares God, that He will restore an unholy and unbelieving nation to their homeland; and there He will restore them to Himself:

> I will show the holiness of my great name, which has been profaned among the nations, the name you have profaned among them. Then the nations will know that I am the Lord, declares the Sovereign Lord, when I show myself holy through you before their eyes. For I will take you out of the nations; I will gather you from all the countries and bring you back into your own land. I will sprinkle clean water on you, and you will be clean; I will cleanse you from all your impurities and from all your idols. I will give you a new heart and put a new spirit in you; I will remove from you your heart of stone and give you a heart of flesh. And I will put my Spirit in you and move you to follow my decrees and be careful to keep my laws. You will live in the land I gave your forefathers; you will be my people, and I will be your God (NIV) . . . Thus says the Lord God, 'On the day that I cleanse you from all your iniquities, I will cause the cities to be inhabited, and the waste places will be rebuilt. And

the desolate land will be cultivated instead of being a desolation in the sight of everyone who passed by. And they will say, 'This desolate land has become like the Garden of Eden; and the waste, desolate, and ruined cities are fortified and inhabited.' Then the nations that are left round about you will know that I, the Lord, have rebuilt the ruined places and planted that which was desolate; I, the Lord, have spoken and will do it. (vv. 33–36 NASB)

This is a work of restoration which God has declared unequivocally, both here and in numerous other places in the prophetic Scriptures, that he will surely accomplish (e.g. Is 11:11–12; 43:5–7; 49:8–23; Jer 32:37–41; Hos 2:16–23; Amos 9:13–15; Zech 8:3–8).

The Davidic kingdom

The kingdom is to be restored to Israel, declares the word of God. Although Jesus declined to reveal to the disciples the timing of the Father in the matter, the fact of this restoration is stated unhesitatingly in the prophetic Scriptures: '"In that day I will restore David's fallen tent [i.e. the house, or dynasty, of David]. I will repair its broken places, restore its ruins, and build it as it used to be, so that they may possess the remnant of Edom and all the nations that bear my name," declares the Lord, who will do these things' (Amos 9:11–12).

The God of Israel never breaks covenant, but keeps His word down to the last detail. The covenant made with David has never been abrogated: 'Your house and your kingdom shall endure for ever before me; your throne shall be established for ever' (2 Sam 7:16). Just as David was king of Israel, so his successor the Messiah, born into his own house, will take His throne literally as King of Israel and the word of God will be fulfilled: 'Sing with joy for Jacob; shout for the greatest of the nations' (Jer 31:7), for her King will also be King of the whole earth (Zech 14:9).

In Jeremiah's great passage concerning God's restoration of Israel in chapters 32–33, God first reaffirms His intention to bring back both Judah and Israel from exile and 'rebuild them as they were before' (33:7). He follows a further messianic prophecy (vv. 14–16) by moving straight into the following emphatic passage:

For this is what the Lord says: 'David will never fail to have a man to sit on the throne of the house of Israel, nor will the priests, who are Levites, ever fail to have a man to stand before me continually to offer burnt offerings, to burn grain offerings and to present sacrifices.' The word of the Lord came to Jeremiah: 'This is what the Lord says: "If you can break my covenant with the day and my covenant with the night, so that day and night no longer come at their appointed time, then my covenant with David my servant – and my covenant with the Levites who are priests ministering before me – can be broken and David will no longer have a descendant to reign on his throne. I will make the descendants of David my servant and the Levites who minister before me as countless as the stars of the sky and as measureless as the sand on the seashore."' The word of the Lord came to Jeremiah: 'Have you not noticed that these people are saying, "The Lord has rejected the two king-doms he chose"? So they despise my people and no longer regard them as a nation. This is what the Lord says: "If I have not established my covenant with day and night and the fixed laws of heaven and earth, then I will reject the descendants of Jacob and David my servant and will not choose one of his sons to rule over the descendants of Abraham, Isaac and Jacob. For I will restore their fortunes and have compassion on them"' (vv. 17–26)

From the previously quoted passage from Jeremiah 33, two further significant, but often overlooked, aspects of God's promised restoration of all things stand out with clarity.

The unity of Israel and Judah

The first is the assurance that both the southern kingdom (Judah) and the northern kingdom (Israel) will be restored to their inheritance in the Land. The sceptre of rulership which belongs to Judah will be restored to union with the birthright to the Land which belongs to Joseph (Ephraim or Israel). In the declared purposes of God, the descendants of all the tribes are to be reunited to form again the entire house of Jacob in the Land of their forefathers.

This prophetic prediction begs certain questions that cannot be considered here, but the weight of scriptural evidence is overwhelming. Here in Jeremiah 33, the prophetic statement is that God 'will bring Judah and Israel back from captivity' (v. 7); that He 'will fulfil the gracious promise I made to the house of Israel and to the house of Judah' (v. 14); and again in verse 24, 'Have you not noticed that the Lord has rejected the two kingdoms he chose?' Hosea also makes the firm declaration:

Yet the Israelites will be like the sand on the seashore, which cannot be measured or counted. In the place where it was said to them, 'You are not my
people', they will be called 'sons of the living God'. The people of Judah and
the people of Israel will be reunited, and they will appoint one leader and will
come up out of the land, for great will be the day of Jezreel.' (Hos 1:10–11)

Isaiah 11:12–14 predicts the regathering of the exiles of both Israel and
Judah, and declares that the age-old jealousy of Ephraim towards Judah
(who retained Jerusalem and therefore the Temple), and the hostility of
Judah towards Ephraim, will end, so that united they will overcome
their traditional enemies of Philistia, Edom and Moab. The broken
brotherhood between Judah and Israel (Zech 11:14) will be permanently
restored; God will 'bend Judah as I bend my bow and fill it with
Ephraim' (Zech 9:13).

This prophetic revelation of the restoration of the whole house of
Jacob through the regathering of both members of the divided kingdom
of Solomon, Judah and Israel, finds full expression in the key passage of
Ezekiel 37:15–27:

The word of the Lord came to me: 'Son of man, take a stick of wood and
write on it, "Belonging to Judah and the Israelites associated with him." Then
take another stick of wood, and write on it, "Ephraim's stick, belonging to
Joseph and all the house of Israel associated with him." Join them together
into one stick so that they will become one in your hand. When your coun-
trymen ask you, "Won't you tell us what you mean by this?" say to them,
"This is what the Sovereign Lord says: I am going to take the stick of Joseph
– which is in Ephraim's hand – and of the Israelite tribes associated with him,
and join it to Judah's stick, making them a single stick of wood, and they will
become one in my hand." Hold before their eyes the sticks you have written
on and say to them, "This is what the Sovereign Lord says: I will take the
Israelites out of the nations where they have gone. I will gather them from all
around and bring them back into their own land . . ."'

THE JEWISH PEOPLE IN THE END TIMES

Fred Wright

One could paraphrase Koheleth's weary dictum (Ecc 12:12b): 'Of the making of eschatological schemes there are many, and much study of them bring weariness to the soul'. The problem with many eschatological schemes is that their point of explication starts anywhere other than the biblical, prophetical scheme, which begins, continues and ends with the destiny of the Jewish people and the Gentiles who are grafted in through the blood of Messiah, Yeshua (Rom 11:11f.). It may be helpful at the outset to provide an epitome of the prophetic expectation of Israel. The prophetic voice arose in times of great stress and trouble, and the overarching message was that although Israel would be exiled for her sins and the Land laid desolate, there would be a day when the Lord would reach out to His people and return them to their ancient homeland where they would have a divine appointment with Him on the mountains of Israel (Ezek 34:11–13, 16). In the last days Israel will be delivered once and for all from her enemies, the Jewish people would fulfil their divine commission to be a light to the world, the Gentiles would come to the Lord and the kingdom of God would be a reality in the sensible world. It is, therefore, essential that a main strand of any authentic, biblically based eschatological scheme must consider the role of the Jewish people, and therefore *ipso facto* the Land of Israel, as they are inexorably linked.

Four profanations

The breaking of the covenant by the Jewish people led to a series of profanations, or things that do not illustrate the holiness of the Lord: the defilement of the Land, the defilement of the worship, the defilement of the people and most critically the defilement of the Lord's holy name (Ezek 36:16f.). The profanations led to exile in fulfilment of Leviticus 26:14–15, 33; Deuteronomy 4:27; 28:64a; 32:26, and must be reversed, and the subjects sanctified as part of the restoration of the covenant.

An outstanding prophecy is found in Zephaniah, where the Lord speaks in dramatic terms of rescuing the Land and gathering the people:

'At that time I will deal with all who oppressed you; I will rescue the lame and gather those who have been scattered. I will give them praise and honour in every land where they were put to shame. At that time I will gather you; at that time I will bring you home. I will give you honour and praise among all the peoples of the earth when I restore your fortunes before your very eyes,' says the Lord. (Zeph 3:19–20; cf. Amos 9:11f.)

The move will be contested by the nations (Ps 2; 83; Zech 12:2), as this is a signal of the realisation of the end times (Is 11:11–12). The Lord will respond and call the nations to account (Joel 3:1–2, 12–18). The biblical pattern of the return of the people to the Land and the return of the Lord consists of the following elements:

1. The rescue of the Land.
2. The regathering of the people.
3. The fruitfulness of the Land.
4. The raging of the nations.
5. The cleansing of the people, the worship and the Land.
6. The return of the Lord to the Land.

We need not be detained by points 1 and 3, which are at least partially fulfilled, although point 1 will re-emerge as an aspect of point 4. Points 2, 4 and 5 are given a more extended treatment, as point 2 is inexorably linked with point 4, while point 5 has received little attention. Point 6 will become apparent as the discussion progresses. Briefly, the rescue of the Land began with the Zionist movements such as Hovevi Zion, Bilu and so on, culminating in the Zionist Congress in the late nineteenth century. The Zionist aspirations found success in the Balfour Declaration, the San Remo Conference and fulfilment in the establishment of the State of Israel in 1948. The early agricultural *chalutzim* (pioneers) established the first settlement at Petah Tikvah and began to develop techniques that would indeed make the desert bloom like a rose (as a trip from the north to the south in Israel amply illustrates).

From the fall of the former Soviet Union and its satellites in 1989 there has been a steady movement of Jewish people to their ancient homeland (*aliyah*) (at the time of writing exceeding 1 million persons). A significant number of those returning have been sponsored or aided by Christian ministries such as Ebenezer, which have assisted around 110,000 Jewish people, mostly from the FSU, to return to their ancient homeland. The question that occasionally arises is on the lines of: 'Is this a fulfilment of biblical prophecies, misplaced romanticism or an attempt to hasten God's own programme?' Those holding an opinion such as the last usually feel that if this is the case, then the consequences could be dire.

The above opinion may be held by both Christians and Jews, including some Messianic Jewish Christians. In the case of some Messianic Jewish Christians it may be the excuse for not wanting to make *aliyah*, and for not supporting Israel for a variety of reasons, including Jewish self-loathing, or a desire to assimilate and leave Jewishness behind.

While all practising and some non-practising Jewish people understand that there will be a return to Israel at some point in history, some object to the present-day return and even to the State of Israel. The basis of the objection is found in the Jewish objections to the messiahship of Jesus; namely, the Messiah was expected to:

- gather in the exiles;
- rebuild the Temple;
- institute the reign of peace.

The objection is overcome by the proposal suggested in *Father Forgive Us*: 'The Church is the ongoing ministry of Yeshua in the power of the Ruach Ha kodesh (Holy Spirit) until he returns to fulfil the Kingdom.' The tasks of the church, therefore, are to:

- facilitate aliyah;
- build up the temple of the Holy Spirit in the life of each believer;
- work towards reconciliation and Just Peacemaking.

A second strand to the above objection to *aliyah*, concerns the notion of restoring the Jewish people to the Land, only for them to be destroyed in a third Holocaust (the Crusades are considered to be the first). The answer to this is simple. God has promised that when He restores the Land they will dwell in safety and not be plucked from the Land (Amos 9:15; Is 60:18–22); this of course does not preclude having to fight for the Land as evidenced in the first Exodus.

The *aliyah* is the greatest prophetic sign of the modern times and the greatest expression of God's grace and mercy to the Jewish people, the church and even those who have no faith whatsoever (Is 11:11–12). A major reason that certain people hold the negative viewpoint is due to their personal or group eschatology. For those holding the dispensationalist view, the very issue of Israel and the Jewish people is capable of making their eschatology fall like a house of cards.

Dispensationalist theories

The turn of the eighteenth century was a time of great upheaval and insecurity in the wake of the American and French revolutions. In these times a series of prophetic movements arose, all with eschatological elements. Among these were the Millerites, later to be known as the Seventh Day Adventists. By far the dominant and most influential was the teaching of the dispensationalists. The dispensationalists view history as seven specific periods of time (dispensations), in which God dispenses His authority over creation in distinct ways and there is a dichotomy between Israel and the church. According to Cyrus Schofield, a dispensation is a period of time during which man is tested in respect to his obedience to some specific revelation of the will of God. In this scheme men are tested by the revelation; judgement follows upon the failure of men within the referents of the revelation.

The dispensations are:

- *The dispensation of innocence,* which covered the period from the creation to the Fall (sometimes referred to as the Edenic dispensation).

- *The dispensation of conscience,* covering the period from the Fall to the Flood (sometimes referred to as the Antediluvian dispensation).
- *The dispensation of human government,* covering the period from the Flood to the events of the Tower of Babel (sometimes referred to as the Noahic dispensation).
- *The dispensation of promise,* covering the period from the call of Avram to the giving of the Law (sometimes referred to as the Abrahamic dispensation).
- *The dispensation of Law,* covering the period from the giving of the Law until Christ. The key element is the tearing of the veil in the Temple signifying the end of the Law (sometimes referred to as the Mosaic dispensation).
- *The dispensation of grace,* commencing with the birth of Jesus and concluding when the church is taken up into heaven (1 Thess 4:13–18; 1 Cor 15:51–54). This is the first return (sometimes referred to as a secret rapture, as it is known only to believers).
- *The dispensation of future things* (sometimes referred to as the dispensation of the kingdom). The final revolt and the Second Coming complete the picture.

To those holding such belief it is implicit that one is living in the last (or next-to-last) dispensation before the end of the world and/or the beginning of God's kingdom on earth. Dispensationalism was developed in the mid-nineteenth century by John Nelson Darby, and found its most popular expression in the Schofield Reference Bible. Although the ideas are generally attributed to either Darby or the Irvingite Catholic Apostolic Church, as F. F. Bruce commented the ideas were: 'in the air previously'. Following is a brief history of the development.

Morgan Edwards

Morgan Edwards was a Baptist minister in Pennsylvania in the mid to late 1700s. As part of his theological training course in Bristol he wrote a speculative essay on a literal interpretation of the millennium. He separated the 'rapture' from the Second Coming by at least three-and-a-half years. The essay, published in 1788, is considered to be the first time that the 'rapture', if that is the proper term to use at this stage, was presented as a separate coming of the Lord. Although his work is considered by pre-tribulationists as foundational, it appears that Edwards himself was content with the prevailing historicist view and presented his work as hypothetical, and it remained the only example of such thinking in his written works. The book entitled *Two Academical Exercises on Subjects Bearing the Following Titles, Millennium, Last Novelties* is not a polished eschatological dissertation and thesis, but the speculative essays of a student, and needs to be approached as such. He does not cite, or rely on, the work of other authors to support the 'rapture' concept and appeals to the early fathers only in order to affirm the notion of a literal millennium. As the title suggests, he regarded the work as 'novel' and the superscription on the front page reads, 'May we know what this new doctrine, whereof thou speakest, is? For thou bringest certain strange things to our ears: We would know, therefore, what these things mean (Acts 17:19–20).' The present writer finds it interesting that dispensationalists who are attempting to place Morgan Edwards in the driving seat of establishing their views do not accept his contentions in the second essay, which deals with the events following the rapture, including the new heaven and new earth and the new Jerusalem; that the lake of fire is on the moon and all of the other planets in our solar system are inhabited; that the two witnesses of Revelation are Elijah and the apostle John (as opposed to Enoch).

Emmanuel Lacunza

Like his predecessor, Francisco Ribera, Emmanuel Lacunza was a (Chilean) Jesuit priest who sought refuge in Italy following the expulsion of the Order from the lands ruled by the king of Spain. His book, *The Coming of Messiah in Glory and Majesty*, was completed in 1790 and first published posthumously in Spanish in 1812 under the assumed name of Rabbi Juan Jehosophat Ben Ezra, supposedly a Jew who had accepted Christ. Building upon Ribera's work, he taught the novel notion that Jesus returns not once, but twice, and at the first stage of His return He 'raptures' His church so they can escape the reign of the 'future Antichrist'. His work also posited the salvation of the Jewish people and restoration to their ancient homeland. His work was received with suspicion and immediately found a place on the list of books proscribed by the Catholic Church.

Edward Irving and the neo-Pentecostals

Edward Irving (1792–1834) was a colourful and often controversial minister of the Church of Scotland. Irving was born in Annan in the south-west of Scotland in 1792, and gained his licence to the ministry of the Church of Scotland in 1815. In 1819 he became well known as the assistant of the famous Dr Chalmers in Glasgow. In 1822 he accepted the position of Pastor of the Caledonian Chapel in Hatton Garden, London. He soon gained popular support, and shortly a larger church was built to house the congregation in Regent Square (1827). In the year 1825, in an address to the Continental Society entitled 'Babylon and Infidelity Foredoomed', he proclaimed that the church, rather than being on the threshold of expansion and blessing, was about to enter a time of complexities and judgements as a prelude to the return and reign of the Lord. After the address and its subsequent publication, he acknowledged the influence of Hatley Frere, a premillennialist and speculative promoter of prophetic understanding of the end times.

In 1826 Irving encountered the work of Manuel Lacunza above, *The Coming of Messiah in Glory and Majesty*. According to Lacunza, with the exception of the letters to the churches, the book of Revelation describes imminent apocalyptic events. Lacunza's speculative work had a profound effect on Irving, who promptly began to study Spanish in order to produce an English translation. He completed his task and added a 203-page preface (published by L. B. Seeley & Sons in 1827, with the elaborate title *The Coming of Messiah in Glory and Majesty, by Juan Josafat Ben-Ezra a converted Jew*, Translated from the Spanish), with a Preliminary Discourse in which he gave an overview of his own prophetic understandings of the end times.

After having his licence revoked in 1830 on the charge that he held to the sinfulness of Christ's humanity, Irving founded his own church, the Catholic Apostolic Church, on 7 November 1832. Shortly afterwards he ordained twelve apostles and expounded a detailed teaching on the gifts of the Holy Spirit. The manifestations of speaking in tongues and healing featured regularly. His congregation became a rallying point for millennial expectations, in no small part due to him giving his theology an immediacy concerning the Second Coming of the Lord.

John Nelson Darby (1800–82)

John Nelson Darby was an Anglican priest (1825) and scholar who left the Anglican ministry to join the newly formed group known as the Brethren. The Brethren movement began with a series of meetings held in Dublin during 1825 when a small group, dissatisfied with the spiritual condition of the Protestant church in Ireland, met for prayer and fellowship. In 1827, Darby entered the fellowship and shortly after, the movement began to develop in the mainland, particularly in Plymouth, with Darby as the leading representative. Meetings developed a new form that became known as a Bible Reading. The Reading was presented in the form of an address on a topic, word or concept through a series of otherwise disconnected passages, and the speaker would briefly comment on the passages. Contextual considerations were abandoned in favour of a thematic approach. In common with most nineteenth century theologians John Nelson Darby believed that the Law of Moses had passed away at the cross.

It is considered by some that the secret rapture of the church prior to the tribulation, which has become an essential part of dispensationalist eschatology theory, developed from the Powerscourt Prophetic Conference held near Dublin in 1831. At the 1833 Powerscourt Conference, Darby presented his view of the church as a parenthesis in the prophetic fulfilment between the sixty-ninth and seventieth weeks of Daniel. From 1838 onward Darby made several visits to Switzerland and it is considered that he used these times to gather his thoughts upon the matters. In 1840, in a series of eleven lectures delivered in Lausanne, he gave the first systematic exposition of his thought.

Samuel P. Tregelles, a noted biblical scholar remembered for his contribution to the study of the history of the Greek text of the New Testament, rejected Darby's new interpretation as the 'height of speculative nonsense'. Tregelles records that he considers that Darby first got the notion of the secret rapture from an utterance in the name of the Holy Spirit in Edward Irving's church (*The Hope of Christ's Second Coming*, 1864). Darby left about 40 volumes of writings, and some 1,500 assemblies across the world claimed him as their founder.

The doctrine of the separation of Israel and the church arose from Darby's attempt to justify his theological position within the Bible.

Considering 2 Timothy 2:15, 'rightly dividing the word of truth' (KJV), as the key element in developing a biblical hermeneutic, he and others began to divide and apportion biblical texts to support their speculations. Once the die was cast, scriptures came to be considered to be only applicable to certain categories of people, namely Jew, Gentile (non-Jewish, non-Christian) and Christian. Schofield taught that the Lord's Prayer was a Jewish prayer and therefore ought not to be used by Christians. A glaring example of Schofield's ideas and their misapplication is found in the Schofield Reference Bible's superscription of Isaiah 40, where the passage is headed 'God Comforts His Church'(!) Under the scheme, much of the New Testament and most of the Old Testament was considered unsuitable for contemporary usage.

Charles C. Ryrie, along with others of the same stripe, considered that most of the Old Testament was irrelevant as it was Law-based, and the Law was abolished for Christians. The Ten Commandments were also considered an irrelevancy as they fall into this category. Dispensationalism, with its selectivity and categorisations, may reasonably be considered to be reflective of cultural relativism. The doctrine of the separation of the church and Israel is, at its heart, deeply antisemitic and provides a fertile seedbed for replacement theology. In common with many doctrinal positions in any denomination, the average pew-dweller is unaware of the theological nuances, or for that matter anything other than a superficial understanding of them. The dispensationalist view by its nature cannot admit the modern State of Israel as a prophetic fulfilment, and also cannot actively support Jewish evangelism due to its eschatological scheme. The average churchgoer would not understand this, as it will not have been explained, or even alluded to.

The rise of the Pentecostalists in the 1950s and 1960s saw the doctrine modernised, or refined, by writers such as Ryrie, Hoyt, Walvoord, McClain and Dwight Pentecost, whose works became known as revised dispensationalism. The trend continued and in the 1990s further refinements were added by Saucy, Blaising and Bock. Revised dispensationalism, which became known as progressive dispensationalism, has found a niche with those who while wishing to maintain a historical–historicist view, are also aware of progression.

One thing that is certain, however, is that the return of the Jewish people to their ancient homeland should be an essential ingredient of most eschatological schemes that await a physical return of the Lord. In the following, some of the scriptures will be quoted at length due to the assumed contentious nature of the subject matter.

The Bible states that God granted the Land of Israel to the Jewish people as an eternal covenant (Gen 12:6–7; 15:18; 17:3; 28:3–4; 48:3–4; Ps 105:6–9). As a precursor to the end-time events, the Jewish people will be regathered to their ancient homeland. The gathering will be of a greater magnitude than the first exodus from Egypt (Jer 23:7–8), traditionally comprising some 2 million people. Historically this cannot have happened following the return from the Babylonian exile as the biblical record (Ezra and Nehemiah) relates that only the southern tribes of Judah and Benjamin returned, along with some priests and Levites. The ten northern tribes did not return, remaining scattered throughout the lands of their conquerors. However, there were a few representatives of the northern tribes who survived the sword along with some of the very old and the disabled who remained in the Land. Hannah the prophetess in Luke's Gospel is referred to as being of the tribe of Asher (Lk 2:36).

The number of returnees following the exile is variously numbered from as low as 15,000 to a high figure of 55,000 (Neh 7:8(f.); Ez. 8:1(f.). The figure is a tiny number in comparison with the first exodus, although the jury is still out on the exact number. The figures are important as the prophecies indicate that a second exodus will far outnumber the figure of the first exodus to the extent that people will no longer discuss the first (Jer 16) due to the magnitude of the second.

The end-time return will include not only the remnant that returned from the Babylonian exile and were subsequently scattered by the Romans; it will be a return of the whole remnant remaining of the tribes of Israel. 'At that time,' declares the Lord, 'I will be God of all of the clans of Israel and they will be my people' (Jer 31:1; cf. Ezek 36:10; 37:15–22).

God's unfolding plans and purposes for the Jewish people are nowhere more clearly stated than in the prophetic corpus, and essentially that of the major prophets. Following is a selection of the prophetic scriptures concerning the return of the people to the Land, beginning with the words of Moses, regarded by the Jewish people as Israel's greatest prophet:

So it shall be that when all these things (misfortunes) have come to you, the blessings and curses which I have set before you and you call them to mind in all the nations where the Lord your God has banished you, and you return to the Lord your God and obey Him with all of your heart and soul according to all that I commanded you today, you and your sons, then the Lord your God will restore you from captivity and have compassion on you and I will gather you again from all the peoples where the Lord your God has scattered you. If your outcasts are at the end of the earth, from there the Lord your God will gather you and from there He will bring you back. (Deut 30:1–4, Jewish Bible)

Even before the events that were to wrench the Jewish people from their Land and lead them into exile, the prophets in the midst of their warnings of impending doom always brought a word of comfort and restoration:

The Lord will have compassion on Jacob; once again he will choose Israel, and will settle them in their own land. Aliens will join them and unite with the house of Jacob. Nations [Gentiles] will take them and bring them to their own place. And the house of Israel will possess the nations as menservants and maidservants in the Lord's land. They will make captives of their captors and rule over their oppressors. (Is 14:1–2)

It should be understood that the expressions of servitude above are in relation to the Lord. It never has been, never is and never will be that one people group is elevated above another in terms of relationship and acceptance. All people are equal before the Lord in this life – in status, but not in function. The function of the Jewish people is to be God's representatives. Therefore it is hardly likely that they would impose servitude, as their greatest gift from the Lord was relationship.

In that day the Lord will thresh from the flowing Euphrates to the Wadi of Egypt, and you, O Israelites, will be gathered up one by one. And in that day a great trumpet will sound. Those who were perishing in Assyria and those who were exiled in Egypt will come and worship the Lord on the holy mountain in Jerusalem. (Is 27:12–13; see also Is 35:8–10; 43:1–2, 5–6, 8–13; 60:4, 8–9)

'However, the days are coming,' declares the Lord, 'when men will no longer say, "As surely as the Lord lives, who brought the Israelites up out of Egypt," but they will say, "As surely as the Lord lives, who brought the Israelites up out of the land of the north and out of all the countries where he had banished them" For I will restore them to the land I gave to their forefathers.' (Jer 16:14)

'I myself will gather the remnant of My flock out of all the countries where I have driven them and they shall dwell in their own land. But I will gather the remnant of My flock out of all countries where I have driven them, and bring them back to the folds; and they shall be fruitful and increase. I will set up shepherds over them who will feed them; and they shall fear no more, nor be dismayed, nor shall they be lacking,' says the Lord. 'Behold the days are coming,' says the Lord, 'that I will raise up to David a branch of righteousness; a king shall reign and prosper and execute judgement and righteousness in the earth. In His days Judah will be saved, and Israel will dwell safely; now this is His name by which He will be called: The Lord our Righteousness. Therefore, behold, the days are coming,' says the Lord, 'that they shall no longer say, "As surely as the Lord lives who brought up the children of Israel from the land of Egypt" but "As the Lord lives who brought up and led the descendants of the house of Israel from the North country and from all the nations where I have driven them and they shall dwell in their own land."' (Jer 23:3–8, Jewish Bible)

The Messiah is returning as *the Lord our Righteousness*, who will institute a reign of justice and righteousness upon the earth at the time of the regathering. When Yeshua came the first time, He came as the *Suffering Servant* of Isaiah 53. The second advent of Messiah is inexorably linked with the re-gathering. It is at this time that the people of Israel will look upon 'the one they have pierced' (Zech 12:10).

The return from the Babylonian exile could not possibly begin to fulfil this scripture either in scope or magnitude. At the most, the total of those who returned then was probably in the region of 50–60,000 people, although some estimates put it as low as 10–20,000. The returnees were members only of the southern tribes of Benjamin and Judah, along with a number of priests and Levites.

For thus says the Lord: 'Sing with gladness for Jacob, and shout among the chief of the nations; proclaim, give praise, and say, "O Lord, save Your people, the remnant of Israel!" Behold, I will bring them from the north country, and gather them from the ends of the earth, among them the blind and the lame, the woman with child and the one who labors with child, together; a great throng shall return there. They shall come with weeping, and with supplications I will lead them. I will cause them to walk by the rivers of waters, in a straight way in which they shall not stumble; for I am a Father to Israel, and Ephraim is My firstborn. Hear the word of the Lord, O nations, and declare it in the isles afar off, and say, "He who scattered Israel will gather him, and keep him as a shepherd does his flock." For the Lord has redeemed Jacob, and ransomed him from the hand of one stronger than he . . .' (Jer 31:7–11, NKJV)

The above passage saw an illustration of its truth during Operation Solomon in May 1991 when 15,000 Ethiopian Jews were airlifted back to Israel, and the flights contained the blind, the lame and expectant mothers. Eleven babies were born during the 24-hour-long operation.

'Behold, I will gather them out of all countries where I have driven them in My anger, in My fury, and in great wrath; I will bring them back to this place, and I will cause them to dwell safely. They shall be My people, and I will be their God; then I will give them one heart and one way, that they may fear Me forever, for the good of them and their children after them. And I will make an everlasting covenant with them, that I will not turn away from doing them good; but I will put My fear in their hearts so that they will not depart from Me. Yes, I will rejoice over them to do them good, and I will assuredly plant them in this land, with all My heart and with all My soul.' For thus says the Lord: 'Just as I have brought all this great calamity on this people, so I will bring on them all the good that I have promised them . . .' (Jer 32:37–42, NKJV)

This passage speaks of singleness of heart and action by the Lord and of the people coming with the fear of the Lord which is the beginning of wisdom (Ps 111:10; Prov 9:10) and leads to life (Prov 19:23). It is in this manner that the people will cease to be defiled. It is also implicit that the covenant will be re-established.

The defiled Land must be cleansed in order for clean worship to be established. An element of the return will be a removal of all the elements of defilement.

Therefore say, 'Thus says the Lord God: "Although I have cast them far off among the Gentiles, and although I have scattered them among the countries, yet I shall be a little sanctuary for them in the countries where they have gone."' Therefore say, 'Thus says the Lord God: "I will gather you from the peoples, assemble you from the countries where you have been scattered, and I will give you the land of Israel."' And they will go there, and they will take away all its detestable things and all its abominations from there. Then I will give them one heart, and I will put a new spirit within them, and take the stony heart out of their flesh, and give them a heart of flesh. (Ezek 11:17–19, NKJV)

The theme of restoration and a commentary upon the matter appear later at Ezekiel 36:16.

I will accept you as a sweet aroma when I bring you out from the peoples and gather you out of the countries where you have been scattered; and I will be hallowed in you before the Gentiles. Then you shall know that I am the Lord, when I bring you into the land of Israel, into the country for which I raised My hand in an oath to give to your father(s). (Ezek 20:41–42, NKJV)

The above passage is of special relevance. The Lord raising His hand in an oath has forensic quality:

When God made his promise to Abraham, since there was no-one greater for him to swear by, he swore by himself, saying, 'I will surely bless you and give you many descendants.' (Heb 6:13–14)

The following are further examples in relation to the raising of the divine hand in relationship to the grant of land: Genesis 24:7; 26:3; 50:24; Exodus 6:8; 13:5, 11; 32:13; 33:1; Numbers 11:12; 14:16; 32:11; Deuteronomy 1:8, 35; 6:10, 18, 23; 7:13; 8:1; 9:5; 10:11; 11:9, 21; 19:8; 26:3, 15; 31:20–21, 23; 34:4; Joshua 1:6; 5:6; 21:43; Judges 2:1; 1 Chronicles 16:15–18; Nehemiah 9:5; Psalm 105:8–11; Jeremiah 11:5; 32:22; Ezekiel 20:6; 28, 42; 47:14.

For this is what the Sovereign Lord says: I myself will search for my sheep and look after them. As a shepherd looks after his scattered flock when he is with them, so will I look after my sheep. I will rescue them from all the places where they were scattered on a day of clouds and darkness. I will bring them out from the nations and gather them from the countries, and I will bring them into their own land. I will pasture them on the mountains of Israel, in the ravines and in all the settlements in the land. I will tend them in a good pasture, and the mountain heights of Israel will be their grazing land. There they will lie down in good grazing land, and there they will feed in a rich pasture on the mountains of Israel. I myself will tend my sheep and make them lie down, declares the Sovereign Lord. I will search for the lost and bring back the strays. I will bind up the injured and strengthen the weak, but the sleek and the strong I will destroy. I will shepherd the flock with justice. (Ezek 34:11–16)

The summons

The return of the people is exampled by two summonses: one to the Jewish people and one that involves all mankind.

In that day the Lord will reach out his hand a second time to reclaim the remnant that is left of his people from Assyria, from Lower Egypt, from Upper Egypt, from Cush, from Elam, from Babylonia, from Hamath and from the islands of the sea. (Is 11:11)

The 'islands of the sea' would not only be places like Cyprus and Crete, but also the bigger islands, some of which were unknown; Australia and the Americas could well be considered within this category.

The restoration will be one of the final acts of history. The people will not be dispossessed of the Land again as they were formerly. This time they will remain (Amos 9:15; Ezek 34:28; Is 60:15–16; 49:22–23; Mic 4:4; Zech 8:20–23; 14:16).

In the middle passages of Isaiah we find great exhortations which help us to understand that the salvation of Israel is inexorably linked to the return of the people and the acceptance of their Messiah (Zech 12:10f.; Jer 23:3–6; 31:9, 10, 33; Ezek. 34:23–24; 36:24–28; 37:23–27).

'Hear, you deaf; look, you blind, and see! Who is blind but my servant, and deaf like the messenger I send? Who is blind like the one committed to me, blind like the servant of the Lord? You have seen many things, but have paid no attention; your ears are open, but you hear nothing.' It pleased the Lord for the sake of his righteousness to make his law great and glorious. But this is a people plundered and looted, all of them trapped in pits or hidden away in prisons. They have become plunder, with no-one to rescue them; they have been made loot, with no-one to say, 'Send them back!' (Is 42:18–22)

Within the historical context the Jewish people have been despised, rejected, looted and plundered, and slaughtered without cause. There has been no one to stand for them. A simple overview of history illustrates that the Jews have been persecuted in all of the nations where they have been domiciled during the dispersion. In the last days the Lord redeems the situation by calling the Gentiles to assist in the carrying home of the Jewish people. Isaiah 49:22 offers the most succinct picture. The reference to a banner refers to the ancient practice of lifting a standard as a call to assembly: 'See, I will beckon to the Gentiles, I will lift up my banner to the peoples; they will bring your sons in their arms and carry your daughters on their shoulders.' *It is the calling and the privilege of the Gentile nations to be a vehicle to help the Jewish people return to their ancient homeland to keep their appointment with the Lord* (cf. Is 14:1–2).

The fivefold dynamic of the return

Ezekiel 36:16f. is known as (the) *Kiddush Ha Shem*. On 16 occasions the Lord says 'I will'. On each occasion it speaks of a benefit of the return of the Jewish people to their ancient homeland. The benefits are enjoyed by God, the Jewish people, the church and those who are 'far away'. In addition there is the promise of the redemption of the created order. He will:

- show the holiness of His great name (v. 23);
- take them out of the nations (v. 24);
- gather them from all of the countries and bring them back into their Land (v. 24);
- cleanse them from their impurities and idols (v. 25);
- sprinkle clean water on them and they will be clean (sanctify them) (v. 25);
- give them a new heart and put a new spirit in them (salvation) (v. 26);
- remove their heart of stone and give them a heart of flesh (repentance) (v. 26);
- put His Spirit in them and move them to follow His decrees (v. 27);

- be their God and they will be His people (v. 28);
- save them from their uncleanness (v. 29);
- call for the grain and make it plentiful (restore the fertility of the Land) (v. 29);
- increase the fruit of the trees and the crops of the field (v. 30);
- resettle their towns and the ruins will be rebuilt (v. 33);
- do the above (v. 36);
- yield to the plea of the house of Israel;
- increase their number (v. 37).

God

The passage clearly states that God's holy name is profaned among the nations while the Jewish people are in the exile (vv. 20–23). God, out of concern for the holiness of His name (v. 22), is going to bring about the return. It is important to note that when God refers to His name, He is not referring to a label for purposes of identification. In the Scriptures names carry the qualities of the person, hence the practice of changing names. A vivid example is in the book of Ruth where following the death of her sons Naomi says to Ruth (1:20–21): 'Do not call me Naomi [comfort]; call me Mara [bitter].' God is effectively saying He is concerned for His reputation and His character. By the return of the Jewish people to the Land in fulfilment of God's words to the prophets, the primary benefit is accorded to Him whose name is shown to be holy. The first petition of the Lord's Prayer can be seen as a reference to this passage.

The Jewish people

The Jewish people benefit in several ways, but mostly by salvation becoming immanent upon the remnant when they keep their appointment with the Lord on the mountains of Israel (Ezek 34). They will be washed clean with water (v. 25), given a heart of flesh in place of a heart of stone (v. 26) and filled with the Holy Spirit (v. 27). The Lord will be their God and they will be His people (v. 28), they will be settled in their ancient towns, and the cities will be rebuilt (v. 33); the desolate land will be cultivated (v. 34). The fulfilment of verses 33–34 can be seen in wonderful reality by anyone who has visited the Land of Israel.

The church

The church benefits by the inclusion of the Jewish people, who bring with them the richness of their heritage and biblical and linguistic history. Paul expresses this clearly in the Epistle to the Romans: 'If their transgression means riches for the world, and their loss means riches for the Gentiles, how much greater riches will their fulness bring' (Rom 11:12); 'If their rejection is the reconciliation of the world, what will their acceptance be but life from the dead?' (Rom 11:15). The former passage may be compared with a monochrome picture being transformed into colour. In the second passage it has traditionally been considered that the reference to life from death refers to the spiritual deadness of the Jewish people. It may be worth considering that the passage may have a secondary application to the church, which has suffered the consequences of its own antisemitism in practising a faith that has centred more on death than life. The notion is strengthened by Paul's insistence that he is speaking to the Gentiles (v. 13). Some of the greatest moves forward in the study of the New Testament have come about through the interest post-1948 of Jewish scholars who have produced some remarkable works, not least because they have not only had the linguistic skills but also a better first-century understanding of the New Testament cultural, religious and philosophical background – riches indeed!

Those who do not recognise the Lord

Isaiah 11:11 speaks of the end times where the Lord raises a banner to the nations. In the Scriptures, as with ancient military history, banners are rallying points, points to run to in order to gain protection, symbols of belonging, or signs of royal rule or residence. The banner in this instance is the Lord returning the people from the four corners of the earth. The event is closely linked to the return of the Messiah as mentioned above. The return will be of such magnitude that all the world, and particularly those who do not know the Lord, will pay attention and be given an opportunity to respond before it is too late. The Lord in His grace and mercy uses the return of the people as the last great sign prior to His return.

The physical land

This will once again become verdant. When the British took up the Mandate, there were so few trees in Israel that they could be counted. Today the Jerusalem forest alone has 6 million trees (Is 27:1f.; 41:17–20). A trip to the supermarket will illustrate the truth and fulfilment of the prophecy. Shelves are filled with fruit and vegetables produced in parts of Israel that within living memory were wastelands.

Where are we now?

Although the Jewish people have been returning at a steady rate since the fall of Communism, the current return is not the full-blown end-time event. The last days and the fortunes of the Jewish people are well described in Isaiah 27:1f.: 'In the days to come Jacob will take root, Israel will bud and blossom and fill all the world with fruit' (v. 6). The fulfilment of that can be seen by a visit to any supermarket, where the shelves are filled with Israeli agricultural produce. Isaiah continues in verse 8 to explain that by warfare and exile the Lord has contended with His people, but they have not been destroyed; this was part of His atoning plan for them. On this glorious day their sin will be removed (v. 9; cf. Rom 11:27) when the deliverer comes from Zion. This will be the day of the threshing of those who have opposed the Lord, His representative people and Land. Those perishing in Assyria and exiled in Egypt will be gathered up.

It has been suggested that there is little in the New Testament to support the Old Testament prophecies concerning the Land and the covenants. Rather than this pointing to the notion being a new or foreign concept it implies the opposite. The Old Testament was well known to the hearers of the preaching of Jesus and the apostles as something fundamental to their own faith. The first petition of the Lord's Prayer (Mt 5) is in reality a plea for the restoration of the whole house of Israel as illustrated in Ezekiel 36:16f. Acts 1:6–8 certainly implies that there will be a time in the future when the kingdom will be fully restored to Israel; there is no reason to spiritualise this passage. Peter, in his speech recorded in Acts 3:17–21, emphasises that Jesus remains in heaven until certain things foretold by the prophets take place and 'all things' are restored. Logically this must include the restoration of Israel's statehood.

The raging of the nations

In the last days the Lord will judge the nations as they rage against God's plans. There will be two major wars. The first one will in all probability be the initiator of the second.

Psalm 83 gives a composite historical picture of the situation: "'Come,' they say, 'let us destroy them as a nation, that the name of Israel be remembered no more'" (v. 4). This gives a picture of intended ethnocide. Psalm 2 likewise gives a picture of the nations raging as they plot against the Lord's choice. Jerusalem will become a cup of reeling to the nations (Zech 12:2), an event that started in the 1920s and escalated, particularly from the ending in 1967 of the Holy City being trampled underfoot by the Gentiles (Lk 21:24), and is still escalating. The first effective war appears to be the conflict referred to as the Battle of the Valley of Jehoshaphat, more generally known as the Gog and Magog War. First the prophecy of Joel concerning the event: In those days and at that time, when I restore the fortunes of Judah and Jerusalem . . .' (Joel 3:1). The expression 'restore the fortunes of Judah and Jerusalem' refers to the time of the Messiah when the restoration of the people to the Land and the restoration of worship are established. The current return of the Jewish people, although a trickle rather than a full exodus, is the precursor which may well provide the trigger that increases raging by the nations and reaction against the Jewish people in the diaspora, causing a large-scale flight to Israel.

> I will gather all nations and bring them down to the Valley of Jehoshaphat. There I will enter into judgment against them concerning my inheritance, my people Israel, for they scattered my people among the nations and divided up my land. (Joel 3:2)

The above passage is consistent with the prophecy of Isaiah:

> But you, O Israel, my servant, Jacob, whom I have chosen, you descendants of Abraham my friend, I took you from the ends of the earth, from its far-thest corners I called you. I said, 'You are my servant'; I have chosen you and have not rejected you. So do not fear, for I am with you; do not be dismayed, for I am your God. I will strengthen you and help you; I will uphold you with

my righteous right hand. All who rage against you will surely be ashamed and disgraced; those who oppose you will be as nothing and perish. (Is 41:8–11)

It is considered that a potential focal point for the nations set to destroy Israel is Damascus (Syria), from whence they plot and move to destroy Israel (Ps 2; 83). The prophet Isaiah declares:

An oracle concerning Damascus: 'See, Damascus will no longer be a city but will become a heap of ruins. The cities of Aroer will be deserted and left to flocks, which will lie down, with no-one to make them afraid. The fortified city will disappear from Ephraim, and royal power from Damascus; the remnant of Aram will be like the glory of the Israelites,' declares the Lord Almighty.

'In that day the glory of Jacob will fade; the fat of his body will waste away. It will be as when a reaper gathers the standing corn and harvests the corn with his arm – as when a man gleans ears of corn in the Valley of Rephaim. Yet some gleanings will remain, as when an olive tree is beaten, leaving two or three olives on the topmost branches, four or five on the fruitful boughs,' declares the Lord, the God of Israel.

In that day men will look to their Maker and turn their eyes to the Holy One of Israel. They will not look to the altars, the work of their hands, and they will have no regard for the Asherah poles and the incense altars their fingers have made. In that day their strong cities, which they left because of the Israelites, will be like places abandoned to thickets and undergrowth. And all will be desolation.

You have forgotten God your Saviour; you have not remembered the Rock, your fortress. Therefore, though you set out the finest plants and plant imported vines, though on the day you set them out, you make them grow, and on the morning when you plant them, you bring them to bud, yet the harvest will be as nothing in the day of disease and incurable pain.

Oh, the raging of many nations – they rage like the raging sea! Oh, the uproar of the peoples – they roar like the roaring of great waters! Although the peoples roar like the roar of surging waters, when he rebukes them *they flee far away, driven before the wind like chaff on the hills, like tumble-weed before a gale.* In the evening, sudden terror! Before the morning, they are gone! This is the portion of those who loot us, the lot of those who plunder us. (Is 17)

Notice the reference to the imprecatory elements of Psalm 83, where the psalmist calls for such a judgement. Referring to the raging nations the Lord clearly states their destiny.

> In future years you will invade a land that has recovered from war, whose people were gathered from many nations to the mountains of Israel, which had long been desolate. They had been brought out from the nations, and now all of them live in safety . . . You will say, 'I will invade a land of unwalled villages; I will attack a peaceful and unsuspecting people – all of them living without walls and without gates and bars . . .' (Is 38:8, 11)

The nations that have raged against Israel will be brought to the place of judgement for the way they have viewed the role of Israel and the Jewish people and sought to destroy them. It is important here to restate that the Jewish people are God's representative. Attempts to remove them or separate them from the Land are acts *not simply against the Jewish people, but acts against God*. As His name is profaned when the people are absent from the Land, those who try to remove them are to be judged accordingly.

> The survivors from all the nations that have attacked Jerusalem will go up year after year to worship the King, the Lord Almighty, and to celebrate the Feast of Tabernacles. If any of the peoples of the earth do not go up to Jerusalem to worship the King, the Lord Almighty, they will have no rain. If the Egyptian people do not go up and take part, they will have no rain. The Lord will bring on them the plague he inflicts on the nations that do not go up to celebrate the Feast of Tabernacles. This will be the punishment of Egypt and the punishment of all the nations that do not go up to celebrate the Feast of Tabernacles. On that day HOLY TO THE LORD will be inscribed on the bells of the horses, and the cooking pots in the Lord's house will be like the sacred bowls in front of the altar. Every pot in Jerusalem and Judah will be holy to the Lord Almighty, and all who come to sacrifice will take some of the pots and cook in them. And on that day there will no longer be a Canaanite in the house of the Lord Almighty. (Zech 14:16–21)

The cleansing

The Scriptures mention three kinds of cleansing; namely by fire, water and blood. Cleansing, or purifying, is generally a physical outpouring of the Lord's judgement. Essential to this topic is that the subject of holiness usually misses a most important point when under discussion – the holiness of the Lord, Himself. It is patently obvious that the Lord, because of His holiness, cannot return to anything that is defiled – land, people or worshipping community. In a sense this is what the prophet speaks about concerning the return of the Messiah to the Mount of Olives in a threefold action of cleansing. After the passage in Zechariah 13, which relates to the cleansing or refining of the people following this cleansing, we find a remarkable passage concerning the return of the Lord and the cleansing of the Land:

> On that day his feet will stand on the Mount of Olives, east of Jerusalem, and the Mount of Olives will be split in two from east to west, forming a great valley, with half of the mountain moving north and half moving south. (Zech 14:4).

As the Mount of Olives is a Muslim graveyard, it is biblically defiled. Therefore the Lord could not, because of His own holiness, stand upon it. As part of the cleansing and redemption, continuous light will shine upon it and living waters will flow out from Jerusalem, flowing east and west.

A beautiful picture of the cleansing of the people is found in the prophecies of Ezekiel (Ezek 36:16), where he speaks of those returning to the Land being washed clean with water. Later he gives a vivid picture of the destruction of the enemies of Israel:

> 'And I will call for a sword against him on all my mountains,' says the Lord. 'Every man's sword will be against his brother. And with pestilence and with blood I shall enter into judgment with him; and I shall rain upon him and his troops and the many peoples that are with him, *a torrential rain, with hailstones, fire and brimstone*. And I shall magnify Myself and I shall sanctify Myself [show Myself to be Holy] and make Myself known in the sight of many nations.' (Ezek 38:21–23, Jewish Bible)

As the account progresses the prophet details the burial of the aggressors and twice speaks of a period where Israel is searching for the bodies of all those who have been destroyed in order to cleanse the Land. Whereas the passages in one sense speak of a cleaning-up operation of corpses, they underlie the issue that the Land must be cleansed of defilement. The fiery judgement and cleansing are further vividly illustrated:

> 'This shall be the plague with which the Lord will strike all the people who fought against Jerusalem: their flesh shall dissolve while they stand on their

feet, their eyes shall dissolve in their sockets, and their tongues shall dissolve in their mouths.' (Zech 14:12, NKJV)

Behold, the day is coming, burning like an oven, and all the proud, yes, all who do wickedly will be stubble. And the day which is coming shall burn them up. (Mal 4:1, NKJV)

The notion is taken up in the New Testament by Peter:

The day of the Lord will come as a thief in the night, in which the heavens will pass away with a great noise, and the elements will melt with fervent heat; both the earth and the works that are in it will be burned up. (2 Pet 3:10, NKJV)

The refining, or cleansing, will affect the worshipping community as the Lord restores the fallen tabernacle of David, considered by some to represent the purest time of worship in Israel's history (Amos 9; cf. Acts 15).

The end-time wars come about as a result of the final rebellion against God led by the anti-Messiah and his cohorts. The ensuing judgement upon the nations results in a cleansing of the Land and people, freeing them to worship within a clean setting.

It is beyond the scope of this essay to examine doctrines of the anti-Messiah beyond the following considerations, where the character is considered to be Jewish and an embodiment of Jewish evil. As the title of the figure is generally Antichrist, rather than anti-Messiah, this term will be used for convenience.

The Antichrist

And from heaven the same Christ will return in judgment, when wickedness will then be at its greatest in the world and when the Antichrist, having corrupted true religion, will fill up all things with superstition and impiety and will cruelly lay waste the Church with bloodshed and flames (Dan ch. 11). But Christ will come again to claim his own, and by his coming to destroy the Antichrist . . . (Second Helvetic Confession 1566)

The subject of Antichrist holds a deep fascination for many. A trawl through the Internet reveals numerous sites dedicated to the subject, offering the identity of the character. Once one has discarded Tony Blair, George Bush (both Snr and Jnr), Prince Charles, Prince William, the Pope and a variety of prominent churchmen of all denominations, one is left wondering how it all started! Many Christians are somewhat surprised to discover that the term 'Antichrist' does not appear in the book of Revelation, and is found in only two of the Johannine epistles (1 John 2:18; 2:22; 4:3 and one reference at 2 John 7). Allusions and parallels do appear in Revelation, along with the Pauline corpus (especially 2 Thessalonians 2:2) and the Gospels for the supposed figure. Paul's character of 2 Thessalonians 2:2 is possibly drawn from Daniel:

> A king will arise, insolent and skilled in intrigue. And his power will be mighty, but not by his own power, and he will destroy to an extraordinary degree and prosper and perform his will; he will destroy mighty men and the people of the saints. And through his shrewdness he will cause deceit to succeed by his influence; he will magnify himself in his heart, and he will destroy many while they are at ease. He will even oppose the Prince of Princes [i.e. act as Antichrist], but he will be broken without human agency. And the vision of the evenings and mornings is true. But keep the vision secret, for it pertains to many days in the future. (Dan 8:23–26; cf. 9:26)

Identifying the Antichrist

The Antichrist is generally viewed as Satan (incarnate) or his agent. To understand the notion, one first needs to consider his role as an angel in heaven prior to his casting out as a consequence of his rebellion. The legend is drawn from Isaiah and Ezekiel, but finds its developed notion in 1 Enoch (c. 25 BCE), which draws on Middle East combat mythology and cosmic conflict. The scheme finds its clearest expression in Revelation 12–13, where the theme of 1 Enoch is taken up:

> The great dragon was hurled down, that ancient serpent, called the Devil, or Satan, who leads the whole world astray. He was hurled down to the earth, and his angels with him. (Rev 12:9)

The Johannine epistles

There is an immediate tension with the use of the term in the Johannine epistles (1 Jn 2:18; 2:22; 4:3; 2 Jn 7). The subjects who are the referents in both instances are Christians holding a different, or contradictory, doctrine of Christ, especially one disputing the incarnation (docetism). In neither case does it refer to Satan, or spiritual powers. Where the term *Antichristos* appears at 1 John 2:22, 1 John 4:3 and 2 John 7 in the Greek text, it is placed without the definite article (the). The inclusion of the definite article appears more as an editorial nod to the concept of the term referring to an individual. Paradoxically in English translations the term does not take the upper case (capital letter) when used with the definite article. It is evident that Antichrist is a spirit, present at the time of writing the documents, causing dissention within the early church. In the Johannine epistles, the term does not refer to an individual. The above understanding was taught by the early church as evidenced in Polycarp's epistle to the Philippians, where he echoes John: 'For everyone who does not confess that Jesus Christ has come in the flesh is an Antichrist . . . and is of the devil' (Polycarp, *To the Philippians*, 7.1).

Paul

It is considered by some evangelicals that John may have drawn his character from the earlier Pauline writings, especially 2 Thessalonians 2:1–12. The notions of the Antichrist and the man of lawlessness whose appearance is a herald of the last days became converged as the churches of Asia Minor came under persecution. It is considered that Paul drew his character from the themes of the man of wickedness in the Psalms and a developed Second Temple characterisation of an eschatological precursor to the end times who represented the embodiment of wickedness. It may be that he had in mind 'the man of the lie' who appears at 4Q166 (4QpHos [superscript] a) a *'pesher'* on Hosea (2:8–14). The verse refers to the relation of God, the husband, to Israel, the unfaithful wife. The unfaithful ones have been led astray by the man of lies.

The literature of the early medieval period (seventh to eleventh centuries) illustrates that the idea of a real, sensible individual as the Antichrist had by this time become a mainstay of Christian theology. Various manuscripts and glosses carried lurid pictures, and variegated strands of thought emerged, the popular level being more influenced by the Sybilline oracles and notions of the last emperor, who would defeat the forces of the Antichrist and reign in co-dominium with the returned

Lord. The Antichrist was often depicted as being Jewish, or as having a Jewish mother who was impregnated by Satan (i.e. John Chrysostom).

A further notion that arose as early as the second to third centuries CE was that the Antichrist would arise from the tribe of Dan. The idea arose from the omission of Dan in the tribes listed in Revelation 7 at the sealing of the 144,000. The tribes of Joseph and Manasseh are listed, while Ephraim and Dan are omitted. The notion was strengthened in that Dan's tribal sign was an eagle, which soon became associated with the imperial Roman eagle. The division of the tribe of Joseph is the key to the matter. If Manasseh is included, Ephraim should also be included. If Joseph is included, then both Ephraim and Manasseh should be omitted. There are three suggestions that can be easily discounted and a fourth that offers a probable solution:

1. *Editorial*. The tribe was deliberately omitted by either the writer or a redactor because of their connection with idolatry (Judg 18:30) and the setting up of the golden calf under Jeroboam (1 Kings 12–28; 2 Kings 17:6; 2 Chron 11:14–15; 18:18) as a rival shrine to Jerusalem.

2. *Scriptural*. Irenaeus appealing to Jeremiah 8:16 ('from Dan we shall hear the sound of swift horses') – a view also supported by Hypolitus.

3. *Pseudepigraphic ascription*. The Testament of Dan is claimed to describe Dan as the son of Satan (Testament of the Twelve Patriarchs VII: 5). The text does not support the contention, as when the reference is made, it is speaking of a time of rebellion before restoration, not of genealogy.

4. *Scribal error*. A misreading of Man(asseh) for Dan.

The notion of Jewish people being the birthing group of the Antichrist was a contributory factor to some of the most virulent elements of anti-semitism in the Western tradition.

Other suggestions offered as to the nationality of the Antichrist include:

- *Babylonian*. Due to the representation of Babylon as the home of evil, Babylon was preferred by some early writers, including Jerome, who contended: 'Antichrist will be born near Babylon. He will win the support of many with gifts and money. He will sell himself to the devil and thereafter will have no guardian angel or conscience.'

- *Syrian.* Some have speculated that he will come out of Syria in the footsteps of his prophetic ante-type Antiochus Epiphanes (215–164 BCE).
- *Grecian.* As Antiochus and the Seleucids were of Greek origin, Greece has found favour in some eyes.
- *Italian.* In Daniel 9:26 the Antichrist is referred to as 'the prince who is to come', and he is identified as being from the people who will destroy the city and the sanctuary. The Romans fulfilled the prophecy in 70 CE and thus the conclusion that he will be Roman (Italian).
- *Western European.* It was fashionable in the 1970s, when the EC numbered fewer than ten nations, to anticipate the Antichrist emerging as the tenth nation appeared. Happily this view no longer has credence.
- *Non-specific Gentile.* On the grounds of Revelation 13 where the end-time figure is presented as rising out of the sea, 'the sea' is considered by some to represent the Gentile nations as opposed to 'the land', which represents Israel. The notice in Daniel (11:37), that he 'will exalt himself above every god and will say unheard of things against the God of Gods' is considered to imply that he is not of the house of Israel, who are monotheistic. The argument is weak, as when the figure appears he could easily arise among pagan or post Judeo-Christian nations.
- *Jewish.* This is because the writings are from a Jewish genre and are concerned with the Messiah and an anti-Messiah. Whereas it is true that it is not implicit that the Jewish people will receive the Antichrist as their Messiah, it implies that they will accept him as a great political leader and be deceived along with everyone else. Taken the notion of the figure, it would be unlikely to be any other than either a Jewish messiah-type figure (Dan 9:27) or one of a number of persecuting Roman emperors or their type. An early expression of such thought is by Lactantius: 'Nero will again reappear on earth as a messenger and forerunner of the Evil One who is coming for the devastation of the earth and the overturning of the human race *redivivus*.' The passage on which Paul obviously bases the figure of the

man of lawlessness is clearly presented as one who is suspending the sacrifices of the rebuilt Temple and offering defiling sacrifices. As is well known, the prophecy reached fulfilment on more than one occasion, first under Antiochus IV Epiphanes, who sacrificed a pig over the holy books, and secondly the rededication of the Temple site by the Romans to Olympian Zeus, with the attendant sacrifices. The popular American preacher Jerry Falwell caused a furore when he proclaimed that the Antichrist would be Jewish and probably was alive at the present time.

It seems clear that Antichrist is a spirit that is capable of manifesting in a number of ways, notably as the driving force of antisemitism. It appears that this spirit will manifest powerfully and uniquely in an individual at a certain point within the historical process. Whether this individual is ethnically Jewish or not is irrelevant, in the sense that he is the fruit of hostility to Jewish people in the rest of the world.

LOVE NEVER FAILS

Twenty-five Christian ministries in the United Kingdom share a particular interest in Israel. These are ministries which support various projects in Israel, teach about Israel, are helping the Jewish people to return to their Promised Land, or prayer ministries that pray for Israel and for the Palestinian people. Representatives of these ministries have come together under the name *Love Never Fails* to work and pray together to promote issues concerning Israel, working mainly in the church. Out of their meetings this present collection of essays was born.

At the Christian Feast of Tabernacles in Jerusalem in 1997, Sister Pista from the Evangelical Sisterhood of Mary, Darmstadt, challenged the participants to consider the need for the church to repent of its 2,000-year history of antisemitism before the new millennium. This challenge was picked up in the United Kingdom and a small group of leaders from around a dozen Christian ministries joined together under the name *Love Never Fails* to express a heart of repentance within the church.

Over the next two years, a number of services of repentance were held in various places around the UK, particularly in places where there had been specific acts of antisemitism. These included, for example, cities where Jews had been slaughtered or where the civic leaders had paid extra money to the king to have Jews excluded from living within their city walls. These times of repentance culminated in a service in the Palace of Westminster in November 1999. A solemn declaration containing thousands of signatures was presented to the Deputy Lieutenant for Greater London, expressing sorrow for the church's antisemitism, and conveyed to Her Majesty the Queen.

Then in 2001, the move of repentance returned to Jerusalem, at a major conference organised by the Sisters of Mary. A contingent from *Love Never Fails* took part in the conference under the title 'Changing the Future by Confronting the Past'. True repentance is only shown by deeds, and not just by words, so we sought ways in which we could express our change of heart towards Israel and the Jewish people.

The original ministries have now been joined by others. Each year we produce a newspaper called *Why Israel?*, which is distributed free through ministry mailing lists and at exhibitions and conventions. We have also taken space at some Christian resources exhibitions to have a stand, also called *Why Israel?*, to challenge those attending to consider this important issue. In early 2004 we also published a booklet, *Are We on the Edge of Judgement?*, based on a talk that the late Derek Prince gave in Jerusalem shortly before he died.

Besides speaking to the church, our aim is to express the love of the Father's heart for His covenant people, Israel. When the Jewish community held a Solidarity with Israel rally in Trafalgar Square, London, in 2002 *Love Never Fails* was able to mobilise several thousand Christians from around the country to attend the rally and express Christian support for Israel. This was the first occasion at which such solidarity had been publicly expressed from the Christian community, and it produced a groundswell of thankfulness and interest from many Jewish people.

Behind this response there were three major concerns in the Jewish community about the growth of Christian interest. First, that such friendship conceals a hidden agenda of proselytisation. Second, that Christians' support for Israel is motivated by zeal to work out our own prophetic agenda. Third, that the Christians would prove fair-weather friends and desert Israel if the pressure of antisemitism returned.

Critics may look for evidence in this book to support such fears. The growth of the messianic movement is described here as part of the history of modern Israel. Readers will note that from 1917 to 1967 it hardly grew at all. In the 40 years since then its multiplication from 150 to around 10,000 members has been indigenous growth rather than the work of overseas missions. As Gentile Christians we make no secret of our belief that Jesus is the promised Messiah, but our friendship with the Jewish people is not conditional upon their acceptance of this belief. We also believe that Jesus will return as the Jewish Messiah and Saviour of the world, but our support for Israel is not simply as an instrument for that purpose. It is based on recognition of God's covenant love for his people, their need of a safe place to work through the application of their faith in the modern world, their right of self-determination in their ancient homeland, and the belief that their return is in fulfilment of the Scriptures. There are testing times ahead for Israel in working through the moral and security issues of co-existence in their neighbourhood, but we believe the Jewish people have a unique calling and a great future in the purposes of God.

For Christians this demands an attitude of humility that has been lacking through the centuries. We stand with the Jewish people in opposing the demonisation of Jews which has disgraced the church in Europe, and spread more recently in the Arab world. Today, antisemitism frequently presents as anti-Israelism and while Israeli government policies must be open to legitimate criticism, as policies of any state, when this becomes an attack on the very legitimacy of the state itself, it must be resisted and denounced as unacceptable.

Attitudes and words need to be expressed in action. There is much scope for ministries of compassion to the needy among both Jewish and Arab communities in Israel. Friendship at a local level can be expressed in helping at the synagogue in this country or in political involvement when truth is misrepresented in the media and actions are judged out of context. Reconciliation requires the building of bridges and much prayer. In all these areas *Love Never Fails*.

Geoffrey Smith,
Chairman, Love Never Fails

A project of CFI Charitable Trust, Registered Charity no. 1101899, co-supported by: Bridges for Peace, Centre for Biblical and Hebraic Studies, Chesed International Ministries, Christian Friends of Israel, Church's Ministry among the Jewish People, Christian Israel Public Action Campaign, David Noakes, Ebenezer Emergency Fund, Evangelical Sisters of Mary, Exobus, Focus on Israel, Hatikvah Film Trust, Hephzibah Fellowship (Cambridge), International Christian Chamber of Commerce, International Christian Embassy Jerusalem, Joseph Storehouse Trust, Land & Life Ltd, Lydia Fellowship International, Messianic (Christian) Educational Trust, Paul Heyman International Ministries, Prayer for Israel, Shofar Foundation International, Prayer Warriors International, Revelation TV, Streams in the Desert, Third Name Link.